LOVE IS FREE. GUAC IS EXTRA.

# LOVE IS FREE. GUAC IS EXTRA.

## HOW VULNERABILITY, EMPOWERMENT, AND CURIOSITY BUILT AN UNSTOPPABLE TEAM

### MONTY MORAN

LIONCREST
PUBLISHING

LOVE IS FREE. GUAC IS EXTRA.

*How Vulnerability, Empowerment, and Curiosity Built an Unstoppable Team*

ISBN   978-1-5445-1595-3  *Hardcover*
        978-1-5445-1597-7  *Paperback*
        978-1-5445-1594-6  *Ebook*
        978-1-5445-1596-0  *Audiobook*

TO THOSE WHO MAKE OTHERS BETTER.

# CONTENTS

# ACKNOWLEDGMENTS

I HAVE SUCH DEEP GRATITUDE FOR THE MANY PEOPLE who have enriched my life in so many ways, and I give thanks to them all. But perhaps those who most powerfully inspired the creation of this book were the hundreds of thousands of crew members, managers, and leaders at my law firm and at Chipotle who believed in my new vision for leadership, and formed the backbone of a culture like I've never seen before or since. I want to thank each and every one of them for their faith, their passion, their love, and their many emails, letters, and texts, which continue to grace my inbox today. I feel such love for all of them!

I thank my family for their endless love, countless lessons, and undying support: my parents, Rennie and David, my brother David, my children, Matthew, Michael, and Sara, my wife, Jenny, and finally, Chelsea, my cocker spaniel who sat patiently on my feet (or lap) while I wrote.

I thank my many friends (in no particular order) who encouraged me to write this book or read early versions and gave their support: Tim Spong, David Chrisman, David Gottieb, Bill

Seward, Chris Johnson, Christopher Welch, Quentin Owens, Kyle Deaton, Ariuna Namsrai, Gugii Munh-Orgil, Mark Crumpacker, Stephanie Spong, Jim Gash, Patrick Mutombo, Janet Kerr, Mark Campbell, Nate Griffin, David "Pup" Longwill, Rob Beckham, Jeffrey Kindler, Brady Miller, Stephanie Copeland, Jessica Jones, Gregg Sullivan, Donna Ludwig, Betsy Hobson, Mats Lederhausen, Kenneth Starr, Kimbal Musk, and Corky Messner.

I thank all of my many teachers in life, but particularly Edith Wartburg, June Howard, Marjorie Sauer, and Sheila Riley, each of whom cared enough to lead me, at a young and impressionable age, to be a better version of myself.

And finally, I'd like to thank my publisher, Scribe Media, its CEO, JT McCormick, publishing manager, Emily Anderson, and in particular, my editor, Hal Clifford. We all have Hal to thank for his tough discipline, which made this book shorter, and better. Hal told me there were four books in the materials I originally gave him, and in time, I learned that he actually meant this in a nice way!

# FOREWORD

I AM EXCITED ABOUT THE JOURNEY YOU'RE ABOUT TO embark upon with my good friend, Monty. This book is less of a textbook written by a leadership professor and more of a conversation with a transformational leader. I'm confident you'll learn much more about leading—and loving—from this easy-to-read and easy-to-apply memoir than you would from reading a whole stack of leadership textbooks. While Monty rose to the level of international prominence and became a Wall Street darling in the context of the fast-casual restaurant industry, this book's principles and teachings apply to every industry and sector. You'll become a better leader—and a better person—simply by reading this book.

It's full of hilarious and touching stories, thoughtful nuggets of wisdom, and loads of enduring truth. It's always about the truth with Monty, and it has been since I first met him thirty years ago at Pepperdine University School of Law. We were in Professor Bob Brain's first-year Torts class in Room E. Monty sat in the front row wearing a tank top and a huge smile. From the beginning of our friendship, Monty has reminded me of my dad—never met a stranger and always interested in talking about the other person. That's one of the reasons why I've always liked him. In fact, that's probably why I flew out for his own father's funeral many years later, as I knew Monty loved his father as much as I love mine.

That first semester of law school, Monty confidently and voluntarily engaged in class discussions while most of us sat in trepidation, hoping not to be called upon. He was, by far, the most curious person in the class. Some show-offs tried to answer every question asked. While Monty certainly had as many *answers* as the rest of us, he had more *questions* than anyone. And while some arrogantly asked questions in a misguided effort to prove how smart they were, Monty always asked with sincere humility—genuinely curious to learn more. In contrast, I was one of the quieter kids in the class who sat several rows back. I knew enough to know how much I didn't know, but I lacked the confidence and vulnerability Monty demonstrated daily.

I studied harder than anyone. Final exams were brutal, but I felt like I'd put forth my best effort and thought I'd probably done well enough to keep my scholarship. Monty, on the other hand, was absolutely convinced he'd failed out. So much so that he talked his way into a meeting with Dean Ron Phillips and sought to withdraw from law school, reasoning that if he withdrew before the start of the second semester, he'd receive a full refund of that semester's tuition. Fortunately, Dean Phillips was able to convince Monty to stay, explaining that because the exams were graded on a curve, perfection wasn't required to receive a passing grade.

Not only did Monty pass his exams, he was in the top 10 percent of the class. Thereafter, his unquenchable curiosity teamed up with his unrelenting dedication to excellence to catapult him into the top few people by graduation time. Good thing I got an early head start, or I wouldn't have been able to hold off his late charge in our friendly class rank competition.

Our quest for competition continued beyond law school. Monty and I both love poker, particularly Texas hold 'em. The complex strategy, personal psychology, and social interactivity combine to provide an adrenaline rush akin to skydiving. A few months after Monty transitioned from leading a prestigious law firm to leading Chipotle, I flew out to Denver to visit corporate headquarters and met a few of his team. A few years later, Monty invited me to the annual ski trip and poker tournament he hosted for a number of his friends. I'm not much of a skier, but I leapt at the chance to join the tournament.

While I won the tournament (and over a thousand bucks), what I remember most about that weekend was staying up half the night after the tournament talking with Monty about the leadership philosophy he'd developed at his law firm that he was implementing to great effect at Chipotle. It was all about inspiring and empowering those around you, and I'm eager for you to spend the next few hours reading this book and learning what I learned that night.

By that time, I'd also left the full-time practice of law to become a Torts professor at Pepperdine and was teaching in the same classroom where I'd first met Monty. I was so taken by what Monty shared with me that I wanted my students to hear the same thing. Monty readily agreed to come. The students may have initially showed up for the Chipotle burritos we served, but they were transfixed the entire lunch hour and left with so much more than full stomachs. Monty was so good that we invited him back to keynote a conference on entrepreneurship a few months later.

Since then, I've invited Monty back to Pepperdine every few

years so each new generation of students could learn from him. He was the first speaker at a new leadership lecture series we created, he was named Distinguished Alumnus of the Year in 2008, and he gave the keynote commencement address at the law school and business school graduation ceremony. He also served as host to Pepperdine's annual law dinner in 2018, which marked the twenty-fifth anniversary of our graduation from law school.

In his role as president and co-CEO of Chipotle, Monty traveled the world. One such trip brought him to Rwanda with Bono (yes, that Bono). That trip led to a conversation between us about my ongoing work in neighboring Uganda to assist the judiciary in providing access to justice to those imprisoned in this East African nation. During that conversation, I let Monty know that I'd just finished writing a book about how my life and that of a Ugandan teenager had not only been transformed by our meeting in a rural juvenile prison, but that my representation of him in Ugandan court had led to major changes in the criminal justice system there. Without hesitation, Monty offered to read the book while it was under consideration by publishers.

A few weeks later, Monty called and let me know that he'd cried throughout *Divine Collision*. Not only did he offer to endorse the book, but he made me promise to take him with me on a future trip to Ugandan prisons so he could join in this work. He confessed, however, that it might be a while before the pace of his work at Chipotle would slow enough for him to take ten days away.

But that day came, and I greeted Monty as he landed with a small team of American lawyers at the Entebbe Airport in Uganda. Despite the multi-leg, punishing journey, Monty was beaming as he stepped out into the humid midnight air and gave me the same big hug he always gives me when I see him. Six months earlier, Monty had decided to retire from Chipotle after an incredible and transformative twelve-year run at the helm. This had cleared the way for him to join our annual prison project, during which a group of lawyers and Pepperdine law students partner with a team of Ugandan lawyers and law students for intense work inside several rural Ugandan prisons.

I watched amazed as Monty quickly befriended the Ugandan lawyers, law students, and prisoners. His infectious laugh, his quick mastery of Ugandan criminal law, and his intense interest in the personal stories of the Ugandan prisoners served as a compelling example for the Pepperdine students on how to lead and how to love. When negotiating a plea agreement on behalf of the prisoners with the Ugandan prosecutors, I often have to admonish other American lawyers to observe local customs by speaking softly and sitting with—rather than standing over—the Ugandan prosecutors. None of this was necessary with Monty. I often saw him sitting next to, rather than across from, the prosecutors as they smiled and shared personal stories with each other. Where negotiations are the norm for lawyers seeking fair sentences for prisoners, with Monty, there were never any negotiations. Instead, Monty explained to the prosecutors that he knew they were fair and wanted justice more than anyone. He walked them through the individual cases and explained that their desire for justice would be fulfilled only by the terms that he was offering. They always agreed!

At one of the prisons, Monty pulled me aside and asked me a surprising question. "How much is 15,000 shillings, Jimmy?" he asked.

"About five bucks."

"That's it? OK. I need to borrow 15,000 shillings."

"OK, what for?"

"The prosecutor says that if I give him this money, then my client can go free."

I stared at Monty in disbelief. "Are you serious? The prosecutor is soliciting a bribe? And you want to pay it?"

"No. The prisoner is accused of stealing a bushel of bananas and the charges will be dropped if he pays the owner the value of the bananas."

"I understand," I explained, "but our role is to assist the Ugandans in implementing the new criminal justice procedures they have launched. We are not here to buy freedom for individual prisoners."

While he understood, Monty was having none of it. "OK, Jim. Can I borrow 15,000 from *you*? I will then *loan* the prisoner the money so he can pay his debt and go home. Maybe he'll pay me back someday..." he mused with a grin.

I handed Monty the money. There was no talking him out of it. This prisoner, who was now Monty's friend after spending an hour with him, had been in prison for six months, away from his wife, kids, and life. The bond of love had already formed so strong that there was no way Monty was going to let his new friend stay in prison a day longer.

That evening, I had my own surprise for Monty. I'd arranged for the rustic safari lodge where we were staying to secure a cake to help us celebrate Monty's official retirement from Chipotle, which took effect that very day. I gave a little speech and invited Monty to say a few words. Fighting back tears, he explained how he didn't expect to be spending his last official day with Chipotle at a remote village in Africa, but that there was nowhere else he would've rather been. We all cried a few tears that evening.

A couple of years later, the president of Pepperdine retired, and the search began for Pepperdine's next leader. Several months into the process, I was notified that I was one of the finalists. Shortly before my day-long interview, I spent a couple of hours on the phone with Monty. That was the best pep talk I've ever been given. I wanted the job, of course, but it felt like he wanted the job for me even more than I wanted the job for myself.

"Listen to me, Jimmy," he said, slowing his cadence to signal the importance of what he was about to say. "Your job on earth is to figure out how you can impact the most people for good with the talents and passion God has given you. You've been doing that in Uganda for the last decade. But there is no better opportunity for you to have the biggest impact on the most people in the world than by leading Pepperdine. Just think of the leverage you'd have to expand the good you're doing around the globe. You'll be empowering a generation of students to spread love around the world. You were made for this, OK? So, your job next week during the interview is to leave them believing that they'd be crazy not to hire you."

Nine months later, as I looked out across the audience of 2,000 at my inauguration as Pepperdine's eighth president, my eyes locked on another pair of tearful eyes. Monty simply smiled and nodded at me from the front row.

In a nutshell, that's Monty. You'll see that in the pages that follow. At its core, his message is that leaders need to empower those around them by loving and inspiring them to achieve their potential, so they can empower those around them to do the same.

I'm not sure what's next for Monty. That is, of course, entirely up to him. He's been pursued by some of the biggest and most profitable corporations in the world. None has sufficiently captured his interest. I'm not the only friend of his who's encouraged him to use what God has given him to lead this country by seeking elective office. Our country is badly in need of leaders like Monty. I have no doubt that you'll agree after reading the pages that follow.

JIM GASH

PRESIDENT, PEPPERDINE UNIVERSITY

# CHAPTER 1

# KARINA

WHEN I WALKED INTO THE CHIPOTLE RESTAURANT ON Upper Street in Islington, a suburb of London, England, I immediately sensed that something was missing.

The air felt heavy and serious. I felt the freshness and light of my optimism drain, as though I'd entered a child's room right after they'd been punished. My feelings were quickly validated when I glimpsed the stressed faces, nervous smiles, and worried eyes of the crew members, who stood behind the gleamingly clean counters and prep surfaces.

The place looked perfect: delicious-looking food and a capable crew. Clean, organized, crisp, and respectful, like the footlocker of a perfectly trained soldier. The feeling in the air made clear to me that it hadn't come to be that way through the passionate work of empowered souls. There was no chance of that. Instead, it came to be this way through strong management, through discipline and austerity, through command and control. And while I undoubtedly appreciated the cleanliness and order of the place, this was not the Chipotle culture we had worked so hard to build. It was not a culture of empowerment.

Chipotle's head of European operations had invited me specifically to this restaurant in order to celebrate the work of the manager, Karina, with the hope that I would grant her the most coveted title in the company: Restaurateur.

Karina was a woman of Eastern European descent, smart and energetic, with a look of extreme competence and great determination. She looked like a winner, someone anyone would quickly wish to hire—disciplined, articulate, and proud. She carried herself with authority and purpose. She took her job extremely seriously. As a recent immigrant to England, it was literally her top priority to succeed in this job. She was completely committed to being an excellent general manager (GM) in this Chipotle restaurant. So why was I not satisfied?

Karina was a good manager, but she was not a leader. This meant that she fell short of what I was looking for to fill the elite position of Chipotle Restaurateur. This was 2013, and my eighth year leading Chipotle, and for all eight years, I'd been working tirelessly to build a special culture based on helping people reach their highest potential through becoming excellent leaders. For years, I'd been preaching that there was an enormous difference between a manager and a leader.

Management is about getting someone to consistently work hard to effectively produce a result that you want from them. It is what most companies are looking for. When they find it, they are immensely satisfied, and they reward their "good managers" with raises, promotions, and broad responsibility. As Chipotle's president and co-CEO, I had my sights set on something much more ambitious: I wanted a culture of thousands of leaders. It would be difficult to achieve. I knew that, but I was certain such a culture would set us up for extraordinary success and be immensely fulfilling. I truly believed I could help change the world by helping thousands of people develop a kind of "enlightened style" of leadership.

## WHAT LEADERSHIP IS

I have my own definition of leadership.

> Leadership is the act of empowering one or more people to achieve a purpose, which is both desired by the leader, and which allows those being led to realize and enjoy their full potential.

Put simply, where management is about getting people to do something for you, leadership is about getting people to do something for themselves. These methods of running an organization or business are not equal, even if both have the power to produce an outcome. Leadership is far superior.

While I spoke to Karina for over an hour, I didn't say a word to her about restaurant standards, other than to tell her that hers were terrific. I didn't talk about anything that she should do differently in her food preparation, organization, or customer service. Instead, I asked about her history, her triumphs, and failures. I asked about her family, and how she'd come to England. I asked her about her team members, how she had come to know them, and what they were like. I listened carefully and took the time to get to know her quite deeply. I acknowledged her discipline and hard work. As I complimented her obvious commitment to her restaurant, I saw tears well up in the corner of her eyes—the kind of tears that sometimes come to us when we feel the relief of being seen, valued, and understood. When we know someone cares for us and is not judging us. When we've been working hard to hide our fears, anxieties, and emotions, and suddenly realize that it's safe to let down our guard.

She explained how hard she was working, taking no time off, and how badly she wanted to succeed. She explained how ashamed she was that her team didn't seem to understand her. She then looked up at me, and as she wiped her eyes and nose with the tissue I handed her, she said, "I'm so sorry...I'm not sure why I'm crying...It's stupid...It's just...I've been working so hard...I don't know...I'm really not sure why I'm crying. I hope my team doesn't see me like this!"

"Aha!" I said. "But this vulnerability you are showing me is exactly what your team needs to see! Stop hiding it from them! It's the key to connecting with them and becoming a powerful leader," I explained, leaning far forward in my chair as if the excitement in my posture might convince her how right I was.

Karina, holding her tissue apologetically over her nose, slowly looked up, and with her curious eyes suddenly full of clarity and light, she asked, "Really?"

I continued speaking quickly and excitedly. As I went on, I could see relief coming over her. I could see she was taking it all in. I could see the gears turning in her mind. She was understanding every word I said, and her eyes began to dance around excitedly. I was overwhelmed with the desire to set her free, to watch her thrive. She knew this. She could tell that I was speaking from my heart because now there were tears in my eyes! Tears stemming from my own feelings of vulnerability, and my recollection of times in my past when I beat myself up for not feeling that I was doing my best. I desperately wanted to spare Karina from the pain of self-doubt and insecurity that had plagued me throughout my young life. She could read in my tears and the excitement in my voice that I completely understood her, and that I wanted to help her. I continued to let my vulnerability and compassion pour through me, as I wanted so badly to set free the beautiful and incredible leader I could see behind her proud eyes.

"To empower your team, they need to feel a connection to you." I continued. "And to establish that connection, they need to see who you really are! They need to see the beautiful Karina deep inside! The one who wants to be seen, understood, loved, and cared for! They need to see that you're a human being!"

Karina laughed knowingly as she wiped her tears, which now flowed stronger, but were now the tears of relief, joy, and excitement, not sadness.

"They need to see your beautiful heart!" I continued, as I smiled and laughed with her. "They need to know that you are afraid of failing, that you need them, that you trust them, that you care about them, that you're committed to them. It's exactly this effort to hide your beautiful, vulnerable self from them that's causing them to feel distant from you, resist your leadership, and be afraid of you. You look so strong, as though you need no one but yourself! Why wouldn't they feel unwanted, unneeded, and unimportant?" I gave her no time to answer this rhetorical question, and I continued.

"Your primary weakness is your effort to appear so damn strong! Real strength comes from being the most genuine version of yourself: from being open, honest, and truthful. You need to go talk to them, tell them that you need them, that you don't have all the answers, and that you cannot do this without them. This will allow you to connect with them and empower them." Then I slowed my speech down, and in a quiet voice, intending to emphasize that these forthcoming words were so powerful they had to be said quietly, almost secretly, I gave her the wonderful punch line. "Once they're empowered, they will carry you on their shoulders. You will have become their leader."

Karina's eyes widened. She got it. She instantly understood that in her desperate attempt to hide her weaknesses from her team, she had cut them off from her heart. She had kept them at a distance and prevented a connection. Once Karina opened up to them, and exposed her vulnerability, magic happened.

Two weeks later, I visited the restaurant again. It was completely transformed. It was a place of love, smiles, laughs, lightness, and friendship. It was a warm and welcoming home. People were confident, proud, and had an obvious sense of belonging. They looked with admiration and warmth at the once stoic and seemingly cold Karina. With relative ease and joy, they continued to run a wonderful restaurant with delicious food and friendly and warm customer service. It was a Restaurateur restaurant. It did not need to be "managed" anymore.

When I promoted Karina to the elite Restaurateur position on the spot, the whole team erupted in tears of joy. You'd have thought they were all promoted. And they were, in that each of them was a critical part of a special team. They hugged each other, lifting each other off the ground. They yelled and screamed. This promotion acknowledged that they were an excellent and empowered team. They were a team of all top performers, empowered to achieve high standards—my definition of a Chipotle Restaurateur.

There is a lot to the art of leadership; it is not simple, but nuanced. It cannot simply be had through hard work, willpower, or a desire to succeed. It is more about human connections, vulnerability, and love.

This is why I say that leadership is the highest calling.

Celebrating with Karina's team right after her promotion to Restaurateur, Upper Street, London, England, in 2013.

## WE CAN ALL BE LEADERS

We were blessed with tremendous success during my twenty-two years as a CEO, both at my law firm, Messner & Reeves, LLC, and at Chipotle Mexican Grill. During these years and ever since, I've often been asked how I came to be the way I am. Where did I learn to lead people? Where did my ideas come from? How did I figure out how to build the kind of corporate cultures that led to exceptional business results? I've generally answered that I wasn't sure. But since my retirement, the questions keep coming, and I've had more time to consider how I might give a better answer. This book is my effort to answer some of those questions and discuss my philosophy of leadership.

Earning success in my career as a leader has required hard work, discipline, sacrifice, and difficult choices. I've spent thousands of hours getting to know myself and the people I work with. I've pored through vast amounts of information to unlock answers to the many questions that spin in my head every hour of every day. I've drawn upon all the lessons of my lifetime, and I've confronted personal limitations, fears, and anxieties. I've challenged myself daily to be a more empathetic, caring, courageous, loving, and introspective person, so I can be worthy and capable of helping others. I've asked millions of questions, listened to answers, and learned to communicate clearly, concisely, consistently, and effectively.

In writing this book, I have reflected extensively on the formative years that sculpted my thoughts and initial direction, and I will share some of these stories with you. I've also reflected on my philosophy about truth, love, and God, which inform how I think about the fascinating topic of leadership. You might not expect to encounter these subjects in a book about business and leadership. I consider them essential.

During my time as a leader, I've wrestled with insecurities, fear, pain, and heartbreak. What made me most effective as a leader was not my ability to ignore or brush aside these challenges. It was my willingness to embrace them as an essential part of what made me human. One's capacity to be fully human is perhaps the greatest prerequisite to being an effective leader, and to having a more authentic and meaningful existence. But the value of leadership is not limited to CEOs and executives. Each of us is called upon to lead—in our families, among our friends, or with our colleagues. I hope that what I've written will help you become more effective in sharing your heart and ideas with the people in your life. I firmly believe that the greatest legacy any of us can leave is to have made others in some way better. This is what makes us more fulfilled at work and, more importantly, in life.

We can all be leaders. Each of us, regardless of our unique

experience and background, have the same fundamental desire to be seen, known, understood, valued, and loved. A true leader understands this and uses this knowledge to more deeply and powerfully connect with the people around them—at work and at home.

No matter what our upbringing was, whether we ate from a silver spoon or were in extreme poverty, our surroundings offer us an incredible multitude of lessons and wisdom every single day, if we are present, open, and curious enough to accept them. This is the gift of our life—our unique human experience on earth. I have found that people tend to be confronted by the exact lessons most relevant to the advancement and growth of their souls. Whatever lessons life presents are likely to be what you most need to learn. It pleases me to think that maybe, in some small way, your decision to pick up this book will prove helpful on your path to becoming the most genuine and powerfully positive version of yourself while making deep connections with the people and world around you. My hope is that the words that follow might help us discover some things together, myself while writing, you while reading, that will enrich us both, and bring more quality to our time and effort in this life.

While it is my overarching hope that you will greatly learn and benefit from what I've written, I also very much hope that you enjoy reading this book. I've lived an eventful and exciting life so far, and I'm delighted to be able to share some of it with you—to teach, to inspire, and to entertain. Good leadership, while difficult, also happens to be amazingly rewarding, exciting, and fun.

Before I dive into my history and the more prescriptive lessons, I am going to step back and describe some philosophical underpinnings of my philosophy of leadership. I know, that sounds boring. But I don't think you'll find it to be.

# CHAPTER 2

# LOVE, VULNERABILITY, AND TRUTH

LET ME START WITH A BRIEF DESCRIPTION OF MY CHIPO-
tle background, to give you an initial understanding of what I
did. I began with Chipotle as its general counsel (Chipotle's top
lawyer) in 1996, when we had only eight restaurants. I was not
a Chipotle employee at that time. Instead, I was the CEO (aka
managing partner) of a law firm called Messner & Reeves, LLC,
and from that position, I handled Chipotle's legal needs, while
also serving hundreds of other clients. After almost a decade in
that position, I left my law firm to become president and co-CEO
of Chipotle for twelve years, from March 5, 2005, until my official
retirement date of June 9, 2017.

My first two years as an employee of Chipotle were spent

as president and COO, after which the board promoted me to co-chief executive officer. During my many years working with Chipotle, we experienced amazing growth. We grew from eight restaurants, all in Denver, to well over 2,000 restaurants throughout the United States, as well as Canada and Europe. We went from a few hundred employees to a team 70,000 strong. Our stock price went from less than a dollar a share as a private company, to over $750 per share as a publicly-traded company, and our market capitalization went from several million to over $23 billion. Our customer count grew to over 1.5 million customers a day. We were a golden child of Wall Street and were credited with creating a whole new category of dining called fast casual. By any definition, we enjoyed amazing success, and Chipotle remains a powerful figure in the restaurant world today.

During this time, I was part of an amazing team of tens of thousands of dedicated individuals. As president and then co-CEO, I was honored to be the one primarily responsible to set the course for Chipotle's direction and commensurate success. I learned to succeed in this role through a lifetime of asking questions, connecting with people, and paying attention—but also from running on trails, playing poker, and mopping floors. To best explain what happened at Chipotle, I have to tell you a much wider story that involves a look back at some of my personal history.

## THE INTERTWINED STRANDS OF LEADERSHIP

My approach to leadership is not mechanical—it's more about intuition and vulnerability. Sure, there are lots of specific things to do, but they arise from a foundation that a lot of people in business would consider unconventional.

You will find many concepts in this book that are not new: some are thousands of years old. What you might find new is the context in which I present them. What I am trying to do is give you all the wisdom that I can summon (in an abbreviated format), plus the benefit of my unique upbringing, minimum-wage jobs, travels, career, and experiences from a life that is now over a half-century long. I've used the wisdom I've gleaned from these many experiences and insights to successfully lead large organizations. Please understand that some of the things I discuss (e.g., Buddhism, Christianity, and the concept of ego) are vastly complex subjects that I have drastically simplified to provide something more digestible in these pages. To provide you with the greatest benefit, I've included only the most useful aspects from a few of my experiences. Finally, the concepts I teach are not easily separated from one another—they support and reinforce each other. They are intertwined strands that form the strong rope of leadership.

I will ask you to bear with me while I talk about some "softer" concepts, like truth and love, which do not often find their place in a book about business or leadership. But in my view, leadership has so much to do with love that a discussion about the former cannot be complete without a discussion about the latter. And, since there cannot be love without vulnerability, it too must be discussed. This is very convenient because I really like talking about love and vulnerability!

Our most natural state as healthy human beings is to blossom, grow, learn, develop, and attain more wisdom. To constantly move towards a higher level of consciousness: towards becoming the best version of ourselves. That's what happens when we're in our natural, healthy state. We grow and blossom, just like plants do and animals do. When we don't grow and blossom, it is because some dysfunction is present.

One job we have as leaders is to see and recognize dysfunction and help people break free of its grip, so that they return to their natural state of developing, growing, and blossoming. Like removing a fish caught in a net, such that with a swish of its tail, it returns gleefully to its journey in the sea.

I believe that leadership is our highest calling, since leading entails helping others become the best version of themselves by giving as effectively as possible of ourselves. It is our job to ensure that those in our care are confident in their ability and encouraged by their circumstances, such that they can achieve an important vision. We do this by creating an environment that catalyzes their natural growth, development, and unfolding. This, in turn, unlocks their greatest wisdom, power, and energy, such that they reach their highest potential in furtherance of the vision we illustrate.

## WHY PEOPLE FOLLOW

The only source of a leader's power is that others choose to follow.

As leaders, we must not believe that we deserve the power bestowed upon us. Rather, our power arises only from others' choices to follow us, and only to the extent that we can harness their energy towards our mission. Put differently, we are at the mercy of those we lead, to the extent that they will follow us only if it appeals to them to be a part of creating the change we are asking for.

We must find in ourselves the wisdom and skill to merit the continued support of our teams. That wisdom, in large part, comes from being in touch with the people we seek to lead. To be in touch with them means to get to know them, trust them, challenge them, believe in them, and to commit to helping them be their very best. We need to have full access to our hearts and to offer it to them. We need to become more, not less, human. We need to be in touch with who we are, and share ourselves with them, such that we are worthy of their continued trust and confidence. We must be wise enough to know when we should lead them or allow them to lead us, because a great leader must at times be a good follower. We need to be aware that most of the time, the light is more effectively placed on one or more of our team members than ourselves.

Our humility as leaders should arise naturally, because leadership does not reside just in a person, but in a person's ability to tap into and be in touch with a force greater and more significant than any person. It resides in a beautiful and worthy vision. It resides in the intelligence of instinct, and in the wisdom taught by history. It resides in our ability to make complex matters simple, and our ability to see the obvious. To lead effectively, we need to reach further and further levels of humility, even as we may be regaled by titles and positions said to be of high rank, so that we don't lose sight of what propelled us into a position of leadership in the first place.

Exposing ourselves so deeply can cause a bit of anxiety. "Will people think I am weak? Am I good enough?" I have often worried that what I had to give wasn't enough and that people deserved more. It takes courage to share our authentic self with others. But this vulnerability allows us to establish a connection with people, which is necessary to lead effectively. We have to trust that we will survive sharing ourselves in this way. (We will, by the way. Actually, it will be incredibly invigorating.) When we feel our own authenticity flowing from our heart, those we lead will feel drawn to this, and they will trust us to take them to a better place.

## LOVE AND LEADERSHIP

I believe that the growth, development, and unfolding of our soul is the purpose of our life on earth. The magical power that most powerfully promotes our development is love, a universally present force that arises in our hearts when we are able to be fully present and quiet the distracting din of our mind and its many judgments.

This discussion of love is central to discussing leadership because leadership is about helping people grow and blossom toward becoming the best version of themselves. Leaders help others on their journey.

Love is what remains when one releases judgment. The absence of judgment allows true understanding, which gives rise to forgiveness, acceptance, compassion, and, thus, love. To love someone is to feel their truth, feel their essence—the reality of their being—beyond personality or ego. When you know a person's truth and are completely present such that you can feel their essential nature, a feeling of love naturally emerges.

The words "I love you" imply a closeness, a depth, an understanding, and a camaraderie of souls. By saying you love someone, you are saying, "I see you, know you, understand you, appreciate you, accept you, and I feel a kinship, a closeness to you arising from that association." There is an awareness that the two of you share a sacred connection—a familiarity and oneness with a universally available consciousness.

While love is magical and wonderful, it is not rare. Love is free! It is what is left over when one removes everything else. In my view, it is synonymous with truth, and God.

When I say "God," I am not referring to the God of any specific religion. Instead, when I use the word *God*, I am referring to a powerful force that is greater than us, that is beautiful, forgiving, and all-knowing—the purest embodiment of love and goodness.

It's very hard not to love someone whom you deeply understand. I love some strange and difficult people, many of whom are quite unpleasant outwardly. If you're willing and able to set aside your judgments in favor of curiosity and understanding for someone's situation and take time to know them deeply, then it is inevitable: a deep affection, love, will naturally arise. A connection born out of fellowship and understanding. Experiencing this may lead you to an awareness, even if fleeting, that we are all offspring of the same wondrous, mysterious universe. When we let our guard down and make room for curiosity and the desire to know and understand others, we start to feel a lot more love, even for people who are famously "difficult."

We are all in this together. We are not truly separate, even if we are from different countries. What creates the feeling of separateness is our fear—fear of someone misunderstanding us, not valuing us, judging us, or taking advantage of us. To prevent this, we erect barriers that prevent a connection. Especially in cities, where the overwhelming number of people makes it hard, even risky, to be completely open to a connection with everyone. However, it's this connection, when nurtured by compassion, understanding, and complete acceptance (which implies no judgment) that grows naturally into love. If our heart is open to it, we can find this connection with almost anyone, almost anywhere, as long as they, too, are open to it. Remembering this concept is critical to leadership because excellent leadership requires that we overcome our fear and establish this deep connection.

Nearly all of us share in common a desire to be seen, understood, and accepted for who we are. We want to feel we are somehow remarkable and special. The reality is, we are. Unfortunately, we often don't see this, because we believe that we are special only when we compare positively with others. This is ego-based thinking, and the ego has the mistaken view that our value lies in our separateness, when the exact opposite is true. What makes us special is what we have in common, that we are all part of a wonderful and infinite consciousness. There is room for all of us to be special (no one has to be un-special) since the universe does not grade on a curve!

The Christian way of looking at this is that God loves all of us, without regard for our good deeds, so long as we recognize Jesus Christ as our savior, ask for forgiveness of our sins, and accept God into our hearts. It is a beautiful concept, really. Christians say that we cannot earn God's love. Instead, it is a gift from God. It is an act of providence. It is free if we merely have faith and believe. It is the gift of Jesus, who died for our sins.

The Buddhists say that all suffering arises from desire. There is a term, *Dukkha*, which refers to the constant dissatisfaction of our existence caused by not having what we want, or having what we do not want, or being separated from what we want. The way to eliminate suffering is essentially through the elimination of ignorance, which is wisdom. Wisdom is achieved by coming to know things as they really are, which takes practice. The Buddhists have various methods by which to do this.

Like many Americans, I was exposed to the Christian outlook as a child since I went to a variety of Christian churches. I appreciate many things about Christianity, and I believe the truth of Jesus' words. But my understanding of truth, my philosophy, is informed by many learnings and experiences and isn't completely tied to any one religion. I see elements of truth appearing in the wisdom of Judaism, Hinduism, Islam, Buddhism, Zen, Christianity, and many other religions. What I have learned by reading about and speaking to religious people from all over the world is that the fundamental message underlying these "different" religions is quite similar. Namely, that there is something out there much greater than us, and it is beautiful, forgiving, and all-knowing, and the best way to live is to partake of it as fully as we can! Throughout this book, I sometimes refer to this as universal consciousness. But in my mind, I've come to believe that this universal consciousness is essentially synonymous with love. Or truth. Or God.

No matter how you choose to go about it, to look for the love I'm describing is a beautiful practice. Our failure to see it notwithstanding, it's all over the place. Closing the blinds doesn't mean the sun's not shining. If we can cultivate an openness, and calm our rejection of our current situation, we'll see and experience more and more of it, for the simple reason that it is everywhere.

So...what? Should we just love everyone? Well, sure! But it's not that simple. As often as not, one or both of any two people will erect barriers to complete openness, which inhibits the connection I'm talking about. Great leaders find a way to make this connection safe, such that a close connection and trust emerge.

I believe love is all around us. I believe love is infinite. I believe that love has no opposite, and that it is available for everyone and everything at all times. The fact that we do not always feel the warmth of love around us is a result of our own limitations, such as our limited senses, our dysfunction, our effort to build ourselves up as something greater than those around us, and our limited understanding of reality. If we call this reality the truth, then we could say that the truth exists independent of our ability to fully comprehend it. But if we could somehow fully understand the truth, we would see that the truth of the universe is good, is love, and is God.

When I say love has no opposite, I mean the existence of love needn't imply the simultaneous existence of a cosmically powerful evil force or being. Nor does it imply the existence of a physical place called "hell." If there is a hell, I believe hell is a psychological state wherein we are greatly separated from the truth—from love and from God. It is hell to be in that mental state, where our misunderstanding, dysfunction, or mindset limits us from participating as fully as possible in the warm glow of love. Heaven, by the same reasoning, describes not a physical location, but a complete unity with God, truth, and love. I believe this union is possible, and this state of consciousness could be called heaven, or many other familiar names, such as awakening, enlightenment, *moksha*, or self-realization. Ultimately, I believe it is our destiny to find this connection with universal consciousness, and that our life on earth is a part of this journey. But this journey is not linear. It has many twists and turns.

Leaders help others on their journey. Love is the mechanism that allows them to do that.


## VULNERABILITY AND LEADERSHIP

In our work toward growing into the best version of ourselves, there are many challenges. Our society, for one, tends to reward and idealize things that are impediments to our personal growth—society celebrates wealth, fame, and appearance more than it celebrates integrity, character, and virtue. Likewise, in our society, emotional vulnerability is often mistaken for weakness. Society has this backward. While we are taught that strong people are tough, don't cry, don't need others, and don't show their emotions, this is a fallacy. People exhibiting these characteristics are often scared stiff, and in their fear, erect barriers to prevent deep connections between themselves and the world. The truth is that our greatest strength lies in our vulnerability. This is because a vulnerable person allows their truth to exist without defense. They have real confidence because they derive their support from truth and are not propped up by falsehoods. After all, the truth does not need any defense. The truth is the truth, regardless of what anyone thinks it is. So, when we expose the truth about ourselves, then we can stop wasting our energy defending ourselves. We are who we are. We are in touch with the truth and can just be.

Truth is the most powerful thing there is (keep in mind that truth and love and God are largely synonymous to me). Nothing can diminish it. It is incorruptibly strong and irrefutable. Likewise, people who allow themselves to be seen for who they are (in other words, who are vulnerable) avoid expending energy maintaining a false sense of self, and become stronger. They embrace the truth of the present moment, see what is real, and open themselves up to a world of richness and real experiences, rather than spending energy protecting what is not real.

Analogously, ice, which is rigid, breaks. Water, which is malleable, doesn't break. If you throw a rock in water, the rock sinks through, and the water reforms just as it was. It needs nothing to protect it. Likewise, people who are truly strong "make friends" with the truth. They accept it and welcome it. They spend very little time defending themselves and become comfortable being challenged, questioned, or criticized. Of course, this does not mean that such people do not grow and change. Of course they do. Indeed, they grow and change much more effectively since they are strongly rooted in reality. By learning to be a witness to yourself, you can come to see that you are often defending yourself, at least internally. For example, if you are criticized, it may hurt your feelings. But the thing that is hurt is not "you," but a false construct of yourself that you have created and are defending. It is your ego that is hurt. Your real self can't be hurt by criticism.

It's true that what I am sharing won't offer much comfort to us, initially, when our feelings are hurt. I often experience hurt feelings myself, but I have found it a helpful practice to observe what it is that triggers these hurt feelings. What I always find is that what hurts is that I am defending a false image of myself that I am attached to and want to maintain. What actually hurts us is our rejection of some truth in favor of a fantasy or our desire to be something we are not. If we can learn to accept who we are now and forgive ourselves, then we can operate from a stronger place if we do seek to change ourselves. But we cannot effectively make change in ourselves or others if we are not first in touch with, and accepting of, the truth. By accepting the truth of our present experience as a daily practice, we stop wasting time and stop creating pain and suffering by rejecting reality, while developing a deeper awareness of ourselves and the world around us. From that awareness, we can tap into greater wisdom and begin to make choices from a position of strength. Bruce Tift, a psychotherapist from Boulder, Colorado, wrote a book called *Already Free*, which addresses this practice in wonderful detail. I am very grateful for the insight his work has given me.

Let's look at an example. We all want to feel that we are worthy of respect. Unfortunately, we often lack the wisdom or confidence to know that we are worthy of respect without regard to our appearance. So, since we do not trust that we are inherently worthy, but want that feeling, we may construct a false "self" and decide that we are worthy of respect because of our expensive necktie, wristwatch, handbag, clothes, or some temporary conditions like our outward appearance. We then commit to creating this false self-image and spend energy and money to prop it up and keep it alive. Then, one day, someone calls us a loser, and we find that it hurts our feelings. Certainly, being called a loser didn't make us a loser, and it didn't actually change us or diminish our worthiness. So why does it hurt? What was the power of the comment that it caused us pain?

The answer is that the comment destabilized our self-made, false image of worthiness that we had built up to make ourselves feel worthy of respect. Since our false image (which provided some fleeting, short-term comfort) has now been threatened, the original discomfort that we spent time working to eliminate with our work on our outward appearance is reignited. Our ego is activated, and we get unpleasant sensations that we had temporarily distracted ourselves from with our false, self-created image. If we could know the truth, which is that we are worthy of respect without regard to our fabricated, self-made image, and understand that our worthiness does not depend on anything at all, we would not be hurt.

What hurts is that the attack reignited our own feelings of inadequacy. We are hurt because the other person's comment has interrupted our fantasy that we are worthy of respect because we have expensive accessories, thereby leaving us exposed to the original, uncomfortable feeling that motivated us to create the fantasy in the first place. So, really, the hurt is a sensation caused by our own self-aggression. It is not really what the other person said. Blaming their comment is another way to distract ourselves from the real pain, which lies within ourselves. As long as we choose to find our comfort in false images that require defense, we are susceptible to these kinds of hurt feelings. These are our reactions to an assault on our fiction—an assault on what is not real and therefore needs to be defended. This is a very important concept because a leader who builds and relies on a false sense of worthiness will be quickly distracted, threatened, and will feel weakened (and therefore be less effective) when their authority, leadership, or one of their ideas is challenged. But a leader who builds no false sense of worthiness is not susceptible to such feelings of diminishment and can remain focused on the mission at hand.

With practice (and it may be a lifetime of practice), each of us can begin to learn that our worthiness does not depend on our wristwatch, necktie, handbag, or any other outward manifestation. We can surrender our falsehoods and trust that our authentic self is good! The more we can realize this, the less we need to engage in defensive behaviors, which are not effective anyway and make us unpleasant to be around. Cultivating vulnerability is a good way to engage in this practice. Declining to defend ourselves when we feel attacked offers a surprising level of relief. It is relaxing to choose not to defend ourselves. By doing so, we realize that the truth is what it is. We are who we are. No comment makes it more or less so.

Because becoming more vulnerable requires us to stop defending falsehoods and embrace the truth, becoming more vulnerable has a beautiful consequence. We bring out the best in ourselves and the people around us. This is an absolutely central skill for an effective leader since the most powerful tool any leader has is a team that is at its best. Being vulnerable creates a fresh and open culture that allows room for others to flourish. When we stop defending what is not real, others feel safe doing the same, and that allows their wisdom to shine since they too are disburdened and able to relax with the truth of their essential nature.

When we stop defending ourselves, others will find it unfair or less entertaining to try to diminish us. No one feels good about hitting someone who is not defending themself. Think about the saying, "Put up your dukes! Let's settle this!" Or the saying, "Don't stab me in the back!" Or the concept, "Pick on someone your own size!" The idea behind these familiar phrases is that it is not fair to attack those who cannot, or are not, defending themselves.

This is why support groups can offer a lot of comfort to people. In an Alcoholics Anonymous meeting, for example, a participant feels liberated because the group doesn't assume that the participant's alcohol problem makes them a bad person. They feel free to be themselves by virtue of not being judged. In other words, by being around people who won't criticize them for this particular problem, the participant may feel comfortable letting down their guard. They can stop defending themselves, which gives them an opportunity to find out what is real. Again, it is relaxing to stop defending. It allows room for personal growth.

When we think of strength, we tend to think of someone like the characters played by Clint Eastwood, Chris Hemsworth, or Daniel Craig—serious, stern, unflinching people who seem to need nothing from anyone. In reality, the most powerful people are the ones who are the most vulnerable. Those who do not defend a false self and who open their hearts and share of themselves. Jesus, Mother Teresa, Mahatma Gandhi, Martin Luther King, Buddha...all of them are examples of beings who allowed themselves to be vulnerable, and in their vulnerability, found the strength to move the world.

We, as humans, are inherently limited. Our brains are only so big. Our bodies are only so strong. Our ability to understand the whole truth of the universe is limited. These limitations affect us all. We may as well surrender to this fact and stop defending some fantasy that we can personally overcome these limitations. Such a surrender allows us to experience as fully as possible the truth of the universe: the truth that is God and is love. In other words, we can choose to be connected to something far greater than we are. We can partake of it. We can be a student who listens to all the wisdom of our world—a satellite dish taking in all that we can experience in our world and beyond. We can allow there to be a fluency between our hearts and something vastly more powerful. This fluency arises from vulnerability. If we allow this, then our personal limitations lose their importance. We become free. We are no longer cut off from greatness, but rather have rejoined it. This connection to greatness, the universe, God—whatever you choose to call it—and which comes from absolute vulnerability, is liberation.

Liberation is good. We should want it for ourselves and for others. It is a gift to teach and share this liberation, and that is another reason why leadership is so important. The most effective leaders are the ones who are most able to liberate those whom they lead, such that the team can become an empowered, powerful force of change and growth.

I've come to my understanding of love, God, truth, and vulnerability through a lifetime of experience. These understandings shaped my character from a young age, shaped how I led several growing and successful companies and had a lot to do with the success of those companies. There were no neat and tidy aha moments during which my understandings fell neatly into place. Instead, there was a journey during which I gathered bits and pieces of knowledge that slowly fit together into a worldview.

## GRATITUDE AND LEADERSHIP

Goals are an important part of being a leader, and they are given a lot of attention in the business world. But it is an equally important concept in one's development to enjoy the journey and learn all that it has to offer. Of course, this is closely related to being present. If you are living for the present moment, you will always be appreciating the journey.

The pressure to attain certain goals is, ironically, often a hindrance to one's ability to attain them. This is especially true when young people enter the workforce, hoping to get ahead and become somebody important. Often, this ambition is coupled with dissatisfaction with what they are doing now. "I can't wait until I get out of this dead-end job and get a real job." But this kind of attitude, this desire to "hurry up and get the lousy part of life out of the way," is seriously misguided. It will tend to prevent people from becoming their best selves, all while making life a lot less fun. The reality is, there are no dead-end jobs. There is no getting ahead. There are no lousy parts of life that should be met with impatience. Instead, each part of our experience holds extremely valuable lessons for our development and should be cherished. Ironically, those who cherish whatever job they have, without trying to get to the next one as soon as possible, will be much more likely to find themselves in positions of greater influence.

One advantage I had as a young person was that I felt grateful for each and every job I ever had. I'm not sure what led me to feel such gratitude. I probably inherited it from my mother, who was born in Germany during World War II and grew up with scarcity. She didn't take things for granted, wasted nothing, and always felt lucky for anything she had. But wherever it arose, my gratitude for every opportunity I was given led me to work hard, to have a positive attitude, and to try to reward every employer for their decision to hire me. As I've grown older, I've noticed that success is inextricably related to gratitude. People who are grateful tend to give more, get more, and enjoy a lot more fulfillment in their lives. But they also tend to find a way to enjoy their work, no matter what it is, which leads them to do a much better job, all while sporting a terrific attitude. These are the people employers feel lucky to have. These are the people employers promote to positions of greater influence and power. These are the people who tend to find the most success, all while enjoying the ride.

Gratitude is essential to becoming the best version of yourself, and thus to your ability to be a leader. Gratitude is a lubricant for positivity. It invites and encourages the power of positive thinking to permeate our soul. There are few things more conducive to a healthy disposition, as well as excellent relationships with others and the world around us, than gratitude.

When I talk about gratitude, I mean that we are thankful for things exactly as they are. That we give thanks for the lessons we are learning, the situations we find ourselves in, and the people who we are working with. We can literally learn to trust in the present moment and allow it fully, agreeing to accept it for what it is, and the lessons it provides us.

When you allow yourself gratitude, you become the fullest, most authentic version of yourself. You calm down. You relax. You become softer and more approachable. You become more attractive. Ultimately, cultivating gratitude helps you live a better life, and it certainly makes you a better leader.

Leaders who are grateful are trusted. People see them as unselfish, appreciative, and caring. They tend to be people others feel good about following. So, even when you are not feeling gratitude, express it. And when you are feeling it, express it again! You will find that expressing gratitude helps you to feel it, and feeling it is tremendously empowering, both to ourselves and to those around us.

I recently found a sentence in one of my old high school journals that read, "The reason I've always gotten what I wanted is that I've always wanted what I got." I think this statement is completely true. Looking back on the many early jobs I've had, few people would call them special. Yet I felt honored to have them, and always found meaning in my work, so I worked hard. If we cultivate gratitude, and practice being thankful for what we have, we will find ourselves more fulfilled, energetic, and with more opportunities to lead and help others. This attitude has been central to my life's journey, which is where I came to an ever-deepening understanding as to how to lead people.

Let me take you on a portion of that journey.

CHAPTER 3

# EARLY LESSONS

THERE WAS NO SINGLE STARTING POINT TO MY JOURNEY of leadership. Many different lessons combined to create a stream of character traits that have allowed me to do what I have done. Since I have to begin somewhere, I will start with the first job I got right after I graduated from college.

I finished school at the University of Colorado in 1988 and, after three months traveling throughout Europe with a backpack, rail pass, and a grand total of $400, I started to feel that I was falling behind and that I'd better get back to the States to make something of my life. (These sentiments were foolish, the result of immaturity and a less restrained ego, but all of that is a different story, perhaps for another time.) Upon my return, I moved to California, since a childhood friend of mine had landed a job in Los Angeles with Farmers Insurance, and suggested that perhaps I could do the same.

I got the job and became a property claims adjuster. My job was to meet with people who had suffered damage to their homes through fires, flood, or vandalism, evaluate their insurance claims, and decide an appropriate amount to pay them. I had to make sure our policyholders were taken care of without giving away the farm from the insurance company's point of view. The job was a ton of responsibility, and it still amazes me that they entrusted these often multimillion-dollar decisions to youngsters like me, just out of college. I had to read and understand the many insurance policies, interpret them, explain them to policyholders, and make tough decisions as to whether to accept or deny a claim. When denying a claim was necessary, the job required me to develop great diplomacy since the result of the denial could cause an insured to become very angry! Denials usually occurred when I suspected an insured was engaging in insurance fraud—the act of faking a loss to get your insurance company to pay money to you.

There were many telltale signs that a claim for a house fire, for example, was fishy. Examples included pets being removed from a house just before the fire (even criminals seldom burn their pets), photo albums removed, and valuable items swapped for cheap ones before the fire, and then burned beyond recognition. There were also telltale signs of arson, such as A-shaped smoke marks on the walls indicating the ignition of an incendiary fluid (normal fires make V-shaped marks). The fraud extended well past policyholders. I quickly learned that some of my fellow adjusters, and a number of contractors who did insurance repairs, were also on the take.

At times it became necessary to tactfully inform a policyholder that we would not pay for their claimed loss, since we'd concluded fraud was involved. This was never easy. Naturally, people protested these decisions, often threatening, "You'll hear from my lawyer." But the number of times I actually heard more from them or their lawyer were few, and for the most part, these criminals crawled away in shame and didn't resurface in my world. It always seemed that those who protested most fiercely and made the biggest scene were usually the ones most culpable. It reminds me of the famous line from Shakespeare's *Hamlet*: "The lady doth protest too much, methinks." Someone telling the truth usually sounds calm and confident, not enraged and unraveled. It was satisfying when the bad apples faded away, and I could calmly close their files, unpaid. But it was even more gratifying to be able to quickly and effectively help restore the lives of those who'd suffered a real loss and were in need. Through my thousands of interactions with people who'd bought insurance from Farmers, I was quickly learning that the most fulfilling thing in this world was helping others. And since my job put me in a position where I was able to help others on a daily basis, I just loved it. Any job that gives someone the opportunity to help others is a real gift, and I have been fortunate that most of my jobs have fit that description.

I spent most of my working hours in very troubled neighborhoods in LA; places where property damage was often caused by arson and vandalism. I learned a lot being in these neighborhoods. My coworkers gave me stern warnings to avoid these places. For some reason, I didn't believe them. But it did spark my curiosity. I would drive around, going to all the places that I'd been warned to avoid. Some areas were riddled with graffiti, broken windows, bent street signs, and rundown buildings. I had no fear. I was just curious. Who lived in the houses? Why? How bad was it? Were they scared? As my work carried me into more and more sketchy places, I had more opportunities to learn from the people who lived there.

The reality was that the vast majority of the people in these neighborhoods were good, caring, and law-abiding. They were ashamed and afraid of the gang activity and wanted it to stop. I met many who had sons or brothers who'd taken up with gangs, usually to feel a sense of protection and belonging, and their families were despondent about it. They'd do anything to help out, but there was often no easy answer. Moving away was financially difficult, and they had a community of friends and family who they wanted to stay with.

With only a few exceptions, I was never hassled. The reason was that I carried no negative assumptions or judgments about the people who lived in these neighborhoods: I was just very curious. I didn't believe they were bad, dangerous, or scary, so they weren't. I felt completely comfortable walking the bad neighborhoods, and I believe my comfort put others at ease. I remember once while working for Farmers Insurance and wearing a nerdy white, short-sleeved button-up and tie, I was looking up at houses, searching for a certain address. My focus on house numbers had me inadvertently looking right up at a bunch of big, tattooed guys on the front porch of a small house, drinking, smoking, and talking forcefully over their loud music. As I looked in their direction, one of them yelled, threateningly, "What're you lookin' at?!"

"I was trying to see the address behind you. Do you know where 1217 is?"

I'll never forget how quickly his aggression softened. He was suddenly friendly. "Yeah, man...it's just down the next block, right down there," he said, pointing down the street.

"Oh, great! Thank you!"

"No problem, man. Take it easy!" he answered. He was so nice, I was surprised he didn't offer a beer. But imagine if I had become defensive and used an aggressive tone in response. I'm confident the interaction would have gone much differently.

This sort of thing happened a lot, and it offered some critical life lessons. One lesson is that most people are inherently good.

What makes them act badly is almost always a defensive reaction designed to protect themselves. They become defensive when they're threatened, or when they're afraid they'll be attacked. For instance, if someone predicts that you are about to insult, harm, or judge them, they will often protect themselves by insulting you or attacking you first. "The best defense is a good offense." But if you can assert yourself as friendly or subordinate before they have an opportunity to feel threatened, then that will prevent defensiveness on their part, and they will not feel the need to become aggressive. Or, if they are already in a defensive place, you can neutralize the situation by quickly demonstrating that you are not a threat.

Asking for help puts you in a vulnerable, subordinate position. It lets others know that you need them, which causes them to feel empowered. When we are vulnerable and subordinate, it triggers the desire in others to be helpful, thereby diffusing any defensiveness on their part. This is a powerful way to ignite other people's creative minds and put them in the position of leading a problem-solving effort. It also makes you a more approachable person who will have deeper relationships, since it draws others toward you in a positive way. It helps keep others from becoming defensive, especially when you are dealing with potentially difficult situations or problems.

My dog, Chelsea, an English Cocker Spaniel with a red coat and friendly demeanor, has taught me a lot about being subordinate. She almost never gets in a fight on the trail, because when other dogs approach her, she rolls on her back, draws her paws in so that her claws are hidden, and completely exposes her soft underbelly and throat to the other dog. It immediately puts the other dog at ease, and there is no need for them to assert their dominance, or to be aggressive. Then, when all is safe, she gets up and begins to play. Minutes later, she is often chasing and leaping and barking at her usually much larger and stronger playmates. But it all begins with this nonthreatening approach.

This power of assuming a subordinate position or asking for help is quite remarkable because the instinct to be helpful to others needing help is powerful, almost impossible to resist. Try this sometime: when someone approaches you with aggression, respond by asking them for help. What you'll find is that their instinct to help you will quickly overshadow their aggressiveness, and lead to a more productive and positive interaction.

In Buddhism, there is a notion that the one who begs for food or money is doing a favor to the one from whom they beg, because they are allowing that person to give, and by so doing, to improve their karma. It is a universal truth that giving is more gratifying and fulfilling than receiving. One experiences this concept in a close friendship. Aren't your closest friends the ones you feel most comfortable asking for a favor? And aren't you eager to do a favor for them if you have the chance? It is almost ironic that we end up closest to the ones to whom we give the most, and from whom we accept the most. I had a friend who refused to ever ask others for help, as she felt she was imposing. But likewise, she was slow to do a favor for others as well. Unfortunately, by trying to be self-sufficient and never accepting help from anyone, she prevented the formation of real friendships. She became lonely.

Asking someone for help quickly makes them feel valued, needed, and wanted. It brings closeness and forms a bond between people. When people feel valued, needed, and wanted, they feel trusting and become vulnerable. Vulnerability is the mental state from which love can flow and good actions arise. Conversely, feeling defensive or threatened is the mental state from which most negative actions arise. So, by asking questions and allowing ourselves to be subordinate, we promote vulnerability. Vulnerability is the foundation of healthy, close, trusting relationships. And, as I discussed earlier, it is also a critical aspect of leadership.

## TRIAL BY FIRE: MY LEGAL EDUCATION

After two years working for Farmers Insurance and inspired by watching lawyers I worked with in my role as an adjuster, I decided to go to law school in 1990. I wanted to be a trial lawyer. Truthfully, I didn't really know there was any other kind! I chose Pepperdine University in Malibu, California, due to a combination of its beautiful, beachside location (I love to surf!) and reputation as a great law school. I found law school to be incredibly challenging, and I ended up excelling there. The three years leading up to my graduation taught me a great deal, and I was eager to put my new skills to work.

Monty's Pepperdine Law School Graduation, 1993. Father David Moran, brother David Moran Jr., Monty, and mother Rennie Moran.

I took a job with the LA firm Morris Polich & Purdy, where I was seen as a strong recruit and immediately invited to work on the most prestigious cases—big cases defending clients like jet-engine manufacturer, Pratt & Whitney, and the drug company, Pfizer Inc. But I learned that the job of a first-year lawyer on these huge cases involved doing work that didn't require much skill—mostly sorting through boxes, organizing, and logging documents. These were multiyear cases with tens of millions of dollars at stake. All the young associates wanted to work on these, except me. I quickly figured out that if I stayed on these cases, it'd be years until I'd get any real trial experience of my own. The big cases were going to be tried by a senior partner with a couple of junior partners in tow, and a senior associate carrying their briefcase. As a lowly first-year associate, I saw no room for me to get the experience I wanted.

I asked the senior partners if there were any smaller cases I could work on. My supervisor said there were some personal injury fraud cases but told me, "Those are crappy work!" But when he said that, I knew it meant they'd be my cases. I wouldn't just be doing grunt work on behalf of a partner; I'd be doing all the work myself. I told him I wanted them. And so began a couple of the busiest, most unsupervised years of my legal career. The cases were auto accidents and slip-and-falls, where it was suspected that the accident was staged in an effort to defraud the defendant out of money. The cases involved relatively small amounts of money, tremendously unethical plaintiffs, and the most unscrupulous, scariest, immoral plaintiff's attorneys in Los Angeles. (The plaintiff is the person bringing the lawsuit, and the defendant is the person being sued and needing to defend against it).

It was considered shit work by some lawyers, but the reality was that these cases had more to teach a young lawyer than any other kind. Moreover, the lawyers (like me) who did this work got little oversight, and received huge caseloads, so the education came quickly! I was in court nearly every day, took multiple depositions on most days, and had to learn to outsmart and outwork some of the slimiest lawyers Los Angeles had to offer. Suddenly I had a caseload with more mediations, arbitrations, trials, and depositions on the calendar than I knew what to do with. I was staying up late most nights preparing for hearings. Over the next few years, I took over 1,000 depositions, had countless oral arguments before judges, arbitrations, mediations, and jury trials, and more courtroom experience than any other young lawyer in the firm.

These cases usually involved car accidents where the accident investigator suspected that something wasn't right. It turns out that thousands of people had figured out that they could stage a car accident, or intentionally cause one, and sue the other driver to gain a profit. The simplest example would be a rear-ender accident where the plaintiff would drive in front of another car (and they'd select nice cars that were most likely insured) and slam on their brakes to cause the car behind them to impact the rear of their car. Since the car in back has the legal responsibility to stay far enough away to stop, it was usually the rear car's fault, and they would therefore be responsible to pay for all damages to the lead vehicle, as well as all personal injuries claimed by the occupants (and injuries were where the big money was).

There was a huge number of these fraudulent claims, and many lawyers were hired to try to negotiate smaller settlements. My job was to prove that the plaintiffs had engaged in intentional behavior, and either settle for a smaller amount or get their case dismissed.

## THE POWER OF QUESTIONS

One of the major tools I used to win these cases was the deposition—the taking of recorded testimony, under oath, from the people bringing the lawsuit. The goal of the deposition was pretty clear. It was to obtain admissions from the plaintiff that would enable me to prove in court that the plaintiff's claim was baseless or fraudulent and that my clients shouldn't have to pay.

Over the years, through taking countless depositions, I learned what people look like when they are being deceptive, and also the refreshing look of someone who is being truthful. I learned to use my tone and body language to reward someone telling the truth and discourage dishonesty. I learned techniques to extract the truth even from those who'd rather keep it from me. It was fascinating how people often seemed visibly relieved when the truth came out, even if it undermined their legal case.

Bringing out the truth began by building a relationship with the witness. You'd think that my role as the lawyer on the other side would prevent a bond between the plaintiffs and me, but it didn't. Most people are scared of having their deposition taken, and they'll take a friend anywhere they can find one, during this stressful time. I was glad to be that friend. I don't mean this only in a crafty way; I much prefer a positive relationship, even if it is with the opposition.

Once a relationship was built, I was quick to demonstrate my satisfaction when I heard truthful answers, and I'd make it clear that I believed them and admired their honesty. While I didn't punish deceptive answers, I would allow my face to communicate that I didn't believe them, by wearing a puzzled look on my face, which let them know I was probably going to ask a lot more questions and dig a lot harder into that particular subject. In time, witnesses began to reward me with more truth in order to avoid this deep digging on my part, which would take a lot of time and be exhausting and anxiety-provoking for them. They would start to give me more truth and less fiction, quite to the consternation of their lawyer. Through hours of this behavior, many people who had started out lying began to be more and more truthful. When they told the truth, their cases were usually soon dismissed. For the ones who didn't tell the truth, they stuck by their lies with such fervor and such vigor that the story that they told often became utterly ridiculous and even physically impossible. Then, many of those cases were dismissed as well.

I became fearless about asking questions. Since the job required it, I was given latitude to ask, without offense, questions that society would otherwise deem quite inappropriate. Just like an offensive lineman in football isn't seen as a monster for hitting hard during a football game, I was seen as fair for asking the most brazen questions. For instance, I got comfortable asking people if they were lying. I asked them if the pain from the accident had affected their sex life. I asked the tiniest details about their medical treatments and then asked why their recollection wasn't consistent with their medical records. I would ask on and on and on, until, eventually, I could see them tiring out. They'd become exhausted, sick and tired of lying, and at that moment of exhaustion, I was just warming up. I'd ask what shoes they were wearing at the time of the accident and what clothing they were wearing.

*"Where were you going? Why did you need to go there? Who was with you? Why did you bring them? Do they believe you were hurt in the accident? How do you know they believed you? Have you spoken to them about your injuries? If I ask them, will they remember your injuries? Were they hurt too? How do you know? Did you get out of the car after the accident? What was the weather like? How many other cars stopped? What kind of cars?"*

I'd ask every detail about every day they treated with any doctor. I'd ask about days they didn't get treatment, and why they didn't need help on those days.

As I went on and on, tirelessly asking every question under the sun, I would sometimes see defeat in their eyes. I'd literally see that they were fed up with this. That they did not care anymore. That they wished they'd never gotten involved in this sordid scheme. Then, I would ask them about that! I would say, "I can see you are tired of this, aren't you?" They'd say, "Yes!" Then I would say, "It's a lot of work to keep this whole story straight, isn't it?" But I would ask this question with genuine compassion for them. They could see that I was not being nasty or sarcastic, but totally genuine. I really understood them. They were so relieved and pleased that I understood them, that they'd really warm up to me. They'd forget I was the enemy.

I didn't hate these people or even look at them as criminals. I looked at them as people who had allowed bad judgment to get in the way of living a good life. I saw my job in the deposition not only to get the truth from them, but to help them see that bad judgment was not something that had to continue to be a part of their life in the future. I prided myself on having a better rapport with and knowledge of who these people were than their own attorneys did. That wasn't as hard as you might think, because their attorneys only cared about using these people to extract money from the defendants (of which 30-50 percent went to the attorney). But I had a higher calling. My goal was to really get to know these people, understand the truth of their situations, and help them understand that divulging that truth was going to be the best thing for them in the long run.

In a strange way, I took a legitimate interest in these people. I honestly believed that I could help them become better people while simultaneously winning for my client. The lofty optimism of my goals, compared to the greedy pessimism and cynicism of their lawyers, created a powerful context in which these people could see the error of their ways and come clean. I knew that everyone, even these litigants, deep in their hearts wanted to be seen for and accepted for who they really are, and by lying, they prevented themselves from really being seen. In other words, I found that even people who came in intending to lie really wanted, deep in their hearts, to be truthful. I considered it my job to help them get there.

The interviewing skills I learned taking depositions were immensely helpful in my work at Chipotle, both in developing the Restaurateur program I describe in chapter 8 and in conducting the one-on-one meetings that became foundational to Chipotle's success (you'll read about these in chapter 6 and beyond). But I didn't learn how to ask questions just by doing depositions. As you'll read throughout this book, curiosity and questioning have come to be a central theme in my development as a person, a lawyer, and a leader.

## THE POWER OF CONFIDENCE

One of my early cases was a defense case involving an auto accident. I felt pretty good about my case, but it was far from perfect, and I knew there was a real risk of losing at trial. But I also had a feeling that the plaintiff's lawyer, a very experienced trial lawyer in his mid-sixties named Ralph Wolfson, was counting on a settlement to avoid the expensive preparation he'd have to undertake to be ready for trial. The last formal proceeding that took place before trial was called a mandatory settlement conference. These conferences were the courts' last-ditch effort to bring a matter to resolution before wasting a lot of taxpayers' dollars on a long and complex trial. Judges pressured parties to settle these cases to clear off their dockets. I knew Wolfson would much rather make a quick buck than have to slog it out at trial, where victory was uncertain, so I expected he'd make his lowest demand for settlement. But I had already decided I was not settling this case. Not for any amount of money. I planned to go to trial to secure a complete victory for my client unless the plaintiff agreed to a complete dismissal.

The funny thing was, I'd never tried a single case at this point. I was a total rookie. Ralph Wolfson, on the other hand, had tried loads of cases. He'd been practicing longer than I'd been alive.

At our meeting, he played that card, and he played it in a big way. He said, "Monty, why don't you just give us $20,000, and let's settle this thing."

"Well, Ralph, I think I can win this one at trial, and so I intend to do that."

"Monty, do you know that I am personal friends with Judge Clark?" he said, referring to the trial judge who was presiding over our case. "We play tennis together every weekend. Our daughters were in high school together."

"I didn't know that. Do you think that Judge Clark is going to treat my client unfairly because you guys are friends?"

"Well, of course not," he said, frustrated by my very appropriate response. "It's just, I know a thing or two about this judge and about the way he tries cases!"

"I don't doubt that for a minute!" I said, almost gleefully.

"You know that your client is going to be pretty frustrated with you if you get hit by a big judgment on this one?"

"Yes, I am sure that they won't like that."

"Monty, do you know how many jury trials I've had in this town?"

"No."

"Seventy-two, Monty. I've had seventy-two jury trials."

"Wow," I said, sincerely impressed by the number.

"Monty, can I ask you a question?" He didn't expect or wait for an answer but instead continued. "How many jury trials have you had?"

"None," I said. "Never had one yet," I added, as if the "yet" made me seem a bit more prepared.

"So why are you so sure it's a good idea to risk losing this case against me at trial?" he asked, flummoxed and impatient.

"Well, the way I see it, if I lose to you, everyone back at my office expects that. They know it is my first, and their expectations are low. But what an honor to be able to try my first case against a lawyer with your reputation and experience," I said sincerely, with no sarcasm, "and if I win a case against the great Ralph Wolfson, imagine how awesome that will be! I'll be a hero in my office!"

His face, formerly wrought into a forced, wry sort of smile, literally dropped. He frowned, and the wind just fell out of his sails.

"Have it your way," he said. "Then we're going to trial."

But I knew that very second that we wouldn't.

When we went back in front of the judge, Wolfson made a show like he was eager to go to trial, but I knew it was an act. The way his face looked when I told him what an honor it would be to have my first trial against him said it all. My best offer was that I would not ask for any fees or costs if he dismissed the case by 5:00 p.m. that day. The judge was frustrated by my stubbornness, and Wolfson even more so. When we left the court, the judge instructed us to return for trial on a date the next week. But lo and behold, at 4:45 p.m. that afternoon, my fax machine lit up and off rolled a written agreement to dismiss the case in exchange for a full release of my right to seek any reimbursement of fees. A total victory. I felt on top of the world.

## LISTENING BEYOND WORDS

During these years as a young trial lawyer, I learned an awful lot. It is possible, by showing our genuine curiosity, to ask even very direct questions in a way that isn't offensive. We can learn to tell when someone is being truthful. We can improve our skills of listening not only to people's words, but to the much more reliable nonverbal communication that accompanies their words. Those nonverbal cues—cadence of speech, body language, intonation, hand gestures, eye movements, and the things that someone is not saying—are usually much more revealing than words. Often, words are more distracting than helpful. Knowing this can help us more effectively find out the truth in any situation and become a much better leader.

I have practiced this approach to communication throughout my life and developed a strong ability to avoid allowing a person's words to distract me from understanding what they really mean. You can develop this ability, too, as I describe in chapter 14, and you'll find it very rewarding.

I began observing and responding to nonverbal communication at an early age—we all do. My fifth-grade teacher, Mrs. Edith Wartburg, was a tall, strong, and severe woman in her late fifties, and could be very serious. I was a bit afraid of her, but I could feel that she had a reservoir of warmth deep inside, and I quickly loved her. I disrupted her class less than others (I was a rambunctious kid who was eager to try to elicit laughs from my classmates), because it was so obvious to me that she'd not take kindly to it. If I was out of line, she had only to cast a glance my way. Her glance had a magical power. When she'd look my way, her eyes communicated the following complicated message in an instant: "I'm looking because I heard something, but I'm confident that it must not have been you disrupting my class, Monty, because certainly you wouldn't do that, would you?" She looked out of the tops of her eyes, over silver bifocals, and her eyelids rose as if awaiting an answer to the question that only her eyes had asked. I'd quickly come to attention. She'd not said a word. She didn't have to. It was amazing. I learned from Mrs. Wartburg how powerfully someone can speak to you without saying a single thing.

People tend to do a decent job listening to words but often fail to understand what someone is really communicating. This is true because words convey only a fraction, and an often-unreliable fraction, of what is really being conveyed. For this reason, leaders need to develop the ability to listen well beyond the words. We need to avoid becoming so distracted by words that we fail to develop the most accurate understanding. We need to develop an understanding of the meaning of someone's tone, body language, intonation, cadence of speech, and level of excitement in addition to their words.

While words are usually at least partly misleading, the various forms of communication that accompany words tend to be much more reliable, difficult to fake, and trustworthy. If you focus on and interpret these other forms of communication correctly, you will be able to see much deeper inside someone, understand them better, know them better, and lead them better. So, we should not accept that the words someone says are true unless the many other nonverbal cues support such a conclusion.

When taking countless depositions at Morris Polich & Purdy, I would start by making the witness comfortable with unimportant questions and establishing a baseline. In other words, I would see how they responded when they were relaxed. Then I would compare this behavior with their behavior while they answered the questions that were relevant to their legal claim. From this, I learned to spot how people sound and behave differently when they are being deceptive. For instance, people tend to be less relaxed when they are being deceptive. Their bodies become stiffer, and their voices may seem more deliberate and definite. They may blush, cover their mouth, point a lot, look more intently in your eyes, avoid blinking, and sit more forward in their seat. I also learned to use *my* tone and body language to reward someone telling the truth, and to use the same skills to discourage dishonesty. I learned techniques to extract the truth even from those who'd rather keep it from me.

Nowadays, one of my hobbies is playing poker. I love the game, and I've read loads of books about it. One thing you quickly learn in poker is that the poker players who are bold and gutsy always seem to be the winners. Of course, you can't be foolish. But, as they say, fortune favors the bold.

This concept is equally true, maybe even more so, for trial lawyers. This is true because where most poker players are pretty gutsy, most litigators are not gutsy at all. They are filled with bravado and act like big shots when trial is only a distant threat. But when trial starts to look close, when it is looming large, you'll see them try all sorts of tricks to avoid it. Lowering their settlement offers. Threatening you with how awesome they are in court. Telling you they're friends with the judge. Letting you know that they are super ready for trial, and that they are going to win. But the vast majority of them are bluffing. If you look for the signs of their fear, you learn to see them. When you do, you'll see that they'll do almost anything to avoid a trial. Their clients are afraid. Everyone is. I was afraid too, and that's why I made up my mind early that I was going to go to trial. End of story. With that determination alone, I would have won many cases. But with that determination coupled with extensive preparation and the high confidence that came with that preparation, I chalked up a strong record. When I did go to trial, it went well because I was ready and I was confident. The judge could see I believed in my case, and so could the jury. It was so much fun. I loved the practice of law and the gamesmanship that went with it. It was a challenging and interesting time of life for me. Trial work was stressful and scary, but in overcoming my fear, I gained a lot of confidence.

Skillfully observing nonverbal communication proved immensely important to my success as a trial lawyer and later as a leader at Chipotle. In the cases that actually went to a jury trial, I would carefully observe the jurors and the judge and look for clues as to whether they were tracking with me and agreeing, or whether they were doubting what I was saying. For instance, if they were gently nodding their heads in agreement with me, with a pleasant look and raised or neutral eyebrows, that was some indication that I was winning my case. But if they held their head very steady and had a furrowed brow, I'd better quickly alter my approach to make sure I was as effective as possible in my advocacy.

In my leadership of Chipotle, I used these skills in every aspect of my work. I had one-on-one conversations with crew members in restaurants, interviews with new candidates, and discussions with my colleagues in the corporate office. Even when people are shy about sharing something with you, you'll be surprised how easy it is to tell what's on their mind if you really pay attention. And if you share with them what you perceive they're thinking, you gain credibility with them. They'll say things to you like, "How did you know I was thinking that?" and then they'll be more inclined to open up to you, since they figure you already understand them. I used these techniques to develop trusting and deep relationships very quickly with thousands of different people. This helped me understand what our employee base was thinking, which gave me an enormous advantage in leading the whole company.

## A TOUGH LESSON FROM MY FATHER

I first learned effective communication while navigating my relationship with my father. My dad was a wickedly smart cell biologist. He graduated from Princeton University, received his PhD from Brown, and then did his post-doctoral work at Harvard. This pedigree might've made him a snob, but he was far from it. The truth is he wanted to be an American Indian and dreamed of living in a teepee, flying his falcons (he was an avid falconer), and living off the land. Some of this likely stemmed from his disdain for his New York City upbringing.

Dad was really funny. He was so bright and used his huge vocabulary to great effect in making us laugh. He seemed to have unbelievable knowledge about almost everything, and I loved asking him questions. He was quiet and needed a lot of time alone, and my desire to pick his brain exhausted him. I could often feel his desire to be left alone and for me to stop peppering him with questions. It made me feel pretty insecure. While Dad was warm to us and loved us, I could not help but feel that I was a bit in the way.

Despite his great sense of humor, I was aware that I annoyed my dad a bit. I talked too much for his liking and too loudly. I asked many questions when he was concentrating on something else. I interrupted. I walked too loudly on the floor. I was not the quiet, gentle person that he was. He didn't do well with conflict or being challenged. If I disagreed with him, his neck would stiffen up, his voice would become serious, and I felt disliked. Sometimes, when I'd ask him questions, he'd say, "You're cross-examining me like a goddamn lawyer!" (He hated lawyers.) But I was intensely curious and wanted badly to get answers from him, so I had to master the art of asking him questions in a way that he wouldn't find offensive. I learned to ask him as a curious monk seeking wisdom from his guru. My tone was of complete respect, my demeanor one of reverence. When I got this right, I could tell immediately. His neck would relax, he'd feel honored and respected, his tone would soften, and he would gladly answer my many questions. I liked the soft tone. It made me feel loved.

Mastering this art of extracting information and positive attention from my father led me to become an expert at reading body language. I'd analyze his mood before approaching him, and I learned to distinguish between when he was receptive and when he didn't want interruption. I learned what he was communicating through his posture, tone of voice, cadence of speech, body movements, and other nonverbal cues. If I got it wrong, it was painful, so I got good at it quickly. I learned to obey my read of his mood to avoid being emotionally hurt. I think this caused me to be attracted to trial work. Being a trial lawyer would allow me permission to be inquisitive, without it being a bad thing. Also, I'd developed the skills for it, so why not?

The downside of these interactions with my father was that I felt a need to constantly earn his love, attention, and affection. I still suffer with difficulties believing I am worthwhile or valuable unless I earn it through the approval and appreciation of others. The trouble with this is that I often sacrifice my own needs and desires in order to earn the approval of others. This tendency would both help and hinder me as a future leader.

# CHAPTER 4

# MESSNER & REEVES, LLC

MY FIRST PROFESSIONAL OPPORTUNITY TO FLEX MY LEADER-ship muscle and learn through actually leading a team of my peers began when I returned to Colorado from California in the fall of 1996. Newly married and wanting to start a family, my wife, Kathy, and I both agreed that Colorado would be a great place to raise our kids. I was a young lawyer who had enjoyed considerable success and growth at my first job as an attorney at Morris Polich & Purdy. I was feeling confident and excited, but also apprehensive about the major changes that awaited me. Immediately after arriving back in Boulder, I began sending out resumes to and interviewing with Denver and Boulder law firms.

I received several offers but was most intrigued by Messner & Reeves, LLC, an eight-lawyer firm. I had been making $100,000 at my LA firm and knew that I would be making less in the smaller

Denver/Boulder market. The partners of the firm invited me to dinner to make me an offer.

We had a fun dinner at a nice restaurant in Denver. Corky Messner, a heavyset former US Army Ranger from West Point Military Academy, was clearly the man in charge, but brought with him his two co-founders: a six foot four, 260-pound, loud and boisterous litigator named David Pavek, and a quiet, smart, and trustworthy real estate lawyer named Ron Reeves. I liked them all and enjoyed our dinner very much. When, at the close of our meal, Corky offered me the lower-than-market salary of $51,000 a year, $20,000 less than other offers I had in hand, I voiced my appreciation for the offer, but also my concern about the amount. Corky told me to take the offer and trust him that this firm was going to be the quickest to see and reward "your kind of talent." I did trust him, and I decided to accept the offer right on the spot.

I quickly learned that, despite my youth, I had more trial experience than any attorney in the firm. This experience gave me a lot more courage than the others. They thought taking a deposition was some kind of war tactic, where I saw it as a simple necessity. They thought bringing motions to dismiss was a tactic to be used sparingly, where I thought it routine. They used interrogatories and requests for production of documents carefully and judiciously, where I used them liberally to get any and all information that would help me to learn about and win my cases. They thought of a trial as some far-fetched possibility that would only happen if all else failed during the litigation process. I knew from day one that if my client was in the right, I was going to trial for sure unless my opposition quit the fight. Unwittingly, I'd become a bit of a warrior, all while thinking myself to be a very peaceful person.

It turned out that years of practicing law in LA had forever changed me. I'd had the unfortunate but very educational experience of being opposite some of the least ethical, nastiest, most dishonest lawyers on the planet while practicing law in Los Angeles. These people were angry, hateful, dishonest, and took no prisoners. You could never count on their word. I'd been to war in LA, and the practice of law in Colorado was gentlemanly by comparison. Fortunately, I had never compromised my ethics, and although I always practiced in an honorable way, I was no pushover. I had become, unbeknownst to myself, a strong trial lawyer. Like a boxer who had been fighting cage fighters, I knew how to win.

Corky had promised me over dinner that he would reward my kind of talent, and he did. After only a year or two at the firm, he promoted me to head of litigation and gave me a huge office in our twenty-fourth floor office atop a Denver skyscraper. This was pretty funny since I wasn't even a partner yet. To the contrary, I was one of the newest and youngest lawyers in the firm. I thought it was a gutsy move by Corky, but he had no doubts and made no apology about vaulting me into a position of authority. When a few of the other lawyers questioned him, he told them exactly how I had earned this office and title. He encouraged them to work more like I had, and they too would rise up in the firm. Corky made it clear to all of us that he would reward only the activities that provided value to the firm. He was all about recognizing merit. He didn't care about age, seniority, or politics. He wanted his lawyers to be productive, and he didn't leave any doubt about who he thought was adding value. I learned a lot from Corky. I learned the value of building a meritocracy, and also the value of being extremely clear about expectations.

As I continued to work extremely hard, I achieved strong

results on my cases. Word spread, and more and more people were asking me to help them with a myriad of legal matters. This was such a satisfying time for me. I felt so happy and proud that my services were in demand! I worked harder and longer, and I came in earlier and earlier. I figured my wife and kids were sleeping anyway, so there was no harm in leaving for work earlier and earlier in the morning. But the demands on my time and my work hours became absurd. I needed help. With only so many hours in the day, something had to give. It turned out that the "something" was my own fear of letting go.

## LEARNING TO BUILD TEAMS

When clients came to appreciate me and wanted me to be personally involved in their cases, it felt good. But, at some point, it became unsustainable for me to be personally involved in every case. I realized I needed to get clients to accept associates doing their work, so it would not all fall on me. But when I delegated increasingly more work to junior associates, clients called me to complain. They expressed concern that I was not doing their work myself, and were worried that I didn't care as much about them. They thought I was "pawning them off" on younger associates.

The truth is that, initially, their complaints warmed me. I felt wanted, needed, and important. Of course I did! That's human nature. It felt good that these clients wanted me to be personally involved. But needing to be personally involved with all of these cases was exhausting and ultimately unsustainable. To carry on like this would mean I had no time to build a team, train associates, or continue my own development as a lawyer and as a person. My own desire to be wanted and needed was holding me back. I couldn't move on while I was still tethered to doing the same things with all of my time. Once I came to realize that I was the cause of my own dilemma, I knew I had to change. I had to let go.

But it's hard to leave behind something safe and secure, something you are good at, love to do, and for which you are praised and rewarded. In fact, most people in this world are working to find a situation where they feel this way. It seemed silly to want to move on from this comfortable and enviable place. But I had to do exactly that if I wanted to grow, and if I wanted to help others grow as well.

Once I decided to get out of my own way and accept that I could not and should not try to do it all, I set about building a team of lawyers who could do the work without my constant oversight. Soon, my desire to be the most sought after lawyer gave way to a much more powerful and fulfilling desire—the desire to build an incredible team. To become a leader.

This was something completely new to my way of thinking. I always strived to be the best at what I did. I thought it a high calling to be strong and needed. But suddenly it occurred to me; it's much better to help others to be strong and needed. Rather than being the strong one, it was more effective to be a catalyst who leads others to be strong.

I soon realized that building a team of top-performing lawyers was incredibly rewarding. Hiring superb people, and training them to be at their very best, was something I found challenging and exceptionally satisfying. I took pride in teaching the new lawyers how to write legal briefs, take depositions, and prepare for hearings. It was thrilling to watch others grow. To watch them develop relationships with the clients. To see the look of satisfaction on their faces when they began to realize their own potential. I realized at last that it is far more satisfying to become someone that helps others to be at their best than to simply work on one's own personal advancement.

I suppose this was the first time in my life that I contemplated the concept that my greatest satisfaction would not come from my own advancement as an individual, but from helping others. That is a core reason I'm writing this book.

## THE POWER OF HIGH EXPECTATIONS

After a couple of years heading up the litigation team in our downtown Denver office building, and with the firm thriving, Corky started to look for a building to buy. In 2001, he found a beautiful, historic building in the exciting lower downtown (LoDo) Denver neighborhood, which, as fate would have it, happened to be right across the street from the office building that Chipotle moved into five years later. We bought the building and moved our firm into it. Corky entrusted me with the work of designing our office space and began to give me even broader responsibilities running the law firm, and I eagerly worked to reward his faith in me. Part of my responsibility was overseeing the hiring of all new associates at the firm.

I began to learn more and more about the kinds of people that could be a successful part of the new kind of culture I was building, and the kind who could not be. Specifically, some worked hard to be exceptional, and others were less interested in mastering the job. I spent significant time and energy trying to train the latter group to possess the attributes of the former group, and my inability to do so taught me an important lesson. I realized that while skills can be taught, personal characteristics are almost impossible to teach once someone is an adult. So if I had the right person, I could teach them legal procedures, advocacy, strategy, how to write great briefs, try cases, and how to effectively advocate for their clients. But I could not teach someone to be motivated, conscientious, ambitious, enthusiastic, curious, hospitable, honest, or smart. After months and even years of trying to teach people these characteristics, there were some people I had to terminate. Firing people was very hard for me, so I committed to hire much more carefully. I'd have to hire people who had the very important traits that could not be taught.

The key to building a strong firm was finding excellent people who could understand and get excited about my vision, and then training them to perform excellent work in an environment which supported their continued growth, such that they would remain satisfied, driven, and loyal to the firm. If I could accomplish this, I would be able to say yes to more new cases, master new areas of law, grow as a leader, and spend more time building a great firm, instead of toiling just to get the work done. To attract and retain these top performers, we'd have to become the kind of firm that deserved them. A firm where the best people could become great lawyers, learn to lead others, perform meaningful work, develop their careers, and be financially rewarded. So I set about building such a firm.

One of the key things I did along the way was set very clear—and very high—expectations.

I learned at a young age the power of setting high expectations. In high school, I had some very tough teachers who expected excellent work. My math teacher, Mrs. Margorie Sauer, became a strong force in my life. Once she had graded exams, it was her practice to walk through the rows of seated students and place the graded tests, face down, on each student's desk. But when she passed my desk, she made a quiet disgusted sound as she handed mine out. It was a sort of grunt/groan, as though she had just remembered something unpleasant from her past. It was audible just to me. I turned the test over. I'd gotten a 90 percent. I took her disapproving noise as an invitation to see her after class.

I approached her desk and said, "Hey, Mrs. Sauer! I got a ninety! Why did you make that sound?"

"Because I expect your best work in my class, and that is *not* your best work!"

"But it's an "A," isn't it?"

She corrected me, "It's an A-*minus*! And Monty, you know better than to have missed those problems. Why aren't you trying your best? Do I not deserve your best effort?"

I don't remember what I said. But I do remember how I felt. I was embarrassed. I was ashamed. I felt that I had let her down. The idea of her feeling that I didn't think she deserved my best was totally unacceptable to me. Here I thought that my "A-" was a good result, and she made plain that it was unacceptable. But I understood what she meant, and I didn't slack off anymore in her class.

I had plenty of teachers who didn't take special notice of me, and I was still immature enough to put in a mediocre effort in their classes. I don't remember them, and they likely don't remember me. But I did respond quickly to those who called me out on my laziness. And gradually, the lessons taught by the few who really cared bled into the rest of my classes, causing me to increase focus and effort. It was a lesson I would apply again and again as a leader.

## WORK-LIFE BALANCE: A DAFT CONCEPT

Corky was very satisfied with the way I handled the additional leadership responsibilities he gave me and he frequently complimented me on my vision and the kind of culture I was building. The lawyers were having more fun, working harder, and displaying more enthusiasm and energy. Corky supported me as though I were his son, brother, and best friend wrapped into one. It was a magical time. My work was exactly what I wanted to be doing with every waking hour of every day, and I loved it.

Around 2000, Corky and Ron Reeves asked me to become CEO (aka Managing Partner) of Messner & Reeves, LLC. I was touched and grateful that they believed in me, and I eagerly accepted my new role. Their confidence in me fueled me to strive harder than ever. I was bristling with energy, waking up between 3:00 and 4:30 a.m., wired with motivation, completely alert, and with a totally clear picture of what I wanted to accomplish. You'd have thought someone had injected me with a triple shot of espresso, but I never touched coffee. I awoke clear, bright, and focused. I was driven to build a kind of law firm that no one had ever seen before, and that every lawyer and client would want to be a part of. I scrambled into a rushed shower, threw on my clothes, and merged onto the empty dark freeway for my daily commute to Denver, with goosebumps of excitement for what I would accomplish each day.

Working the way I did, I never thought about work-life balance, largely because I never figured out what that meant. During my time at my law firm, we had a team of people working extremely hard. Those outside the firm labeled it a sweatshop and made comments about how hard we worked, but within the four walls of our sweatshop, we were delighted. We worked hard, laughed hard, did things that mattered, and loved being together. We had a blast. I would bet that all of us who were there would say it was one of the most invigorating times of our lives. Was that work-life balance? Who cares?!

Some people really want to work around the clock. They're passionate about their work, and there is nothing they'd rather spend time on. For them, life seems out of balance if they are not working nearly all the time. To them, work is their life, and a good work-life balance would take place if you'd stop talking to them about taking time off and let them get back to work.

On the opposite end of the spectrum, some people really don't like to work. In their minds, what they really want is to win the lottery and sit on a beach somewhere, drinking cocktails. To these people, the real balance they seek is not to work at all. Allowing these folks their appropriate work-life balance would mean they'd get nothing done at all. In short, you can't give these folks what they want anyway.

Of course, most people fall in between these extremes. For these people, there are still widely varying definitions of the term. I strongly recommend leaders avoid getting caught up in any concern about establishing a work-life balance for their team. Instead, focus on building a team of top-performers who are empowered to achieve your vision (I write about doing this later in the book). If you succeed in doing this, you will end up with a team so enthusiastic and passionate that none of them will talk about daft concepts like work-life balance. Instead, they will be enthusiastically working towards something they are excited about, and they will love how they spend their lives.

## THE NEED FOR MENTAL SPACE

While I don't subscribe to concerns over work-life balance, I do find it essential to create some mental space. I learned this by the example my parents set when I was growing up. Dinners were sacred in my family. Mom cooked a great meal, and to prevent any interruptions, my dad took the handset of the telephone off the cradle and put it in a drawer filled with dish towels in order to muffle the obnoxious off-the-hook tone that came loudly out of it in those days. As he put it in the drawer, he nearly always cursed it first. "I'm going to put this damn phone in the drawer," he'd begin, then finish his sentence with a bold declaration such as, "Phone, you shall interrupt us no more!" and he'd thrust it in the drawer with great satisfaction, as if he'd singlehandedly brought it to justice. This was a nightly wrestling match between my dad and the phone. Dad always won. Then, candles were lit, and mom and dad would say grace, or ask my brother or me to say it. If there was meat on the table, the grace always involved thanking the animal for giving its life to us, a gratitude that I've carried on silently in my mind throughout my life. There were no distractions during these dinners, no interruptions. We were completely together as a family.

I loved these dinners. We were encouraged to eat slowly, and our manners were noticed and corrected if necessary. We'd speak one at a time, and we all shared the same conversation. It felt good, warm, close, and important. Being in my family felt like being part of something special, and these dinners were the epicenter. They were a nightly ritual of respect, awareness, gratitude, and warmth. I believe my parents' example, in creating some space for our family to simply be together without interruption, helped me to understand the importance of this ritual, and how creating some mental space allowed for depth of being to arise.

Once you are in a leadership position, you will find many competing demands for your time. In modern society, we are even proud of how busy we are. We boast about it and feel important that we have no spare time: that we had such a busy day. The problem is that when we don't allow for mental space, while we may be very productive in terms of getting things done, the quality of our actions is sometimes not what it could be. This is because when we don't pause to clear our mind, we tend to operate more out of our weaker conscious mind, and less out of our much more powerful subconscious mind. When I use the term *subconscious mind*, I am referring to the deep inner workings of our mind which we are often not aware of, but which contain our deepest intelligence, including vast historical information and the wisdom of our instinct. The subconscious mind is much more powerful and intelligent than our conscious mind, as a much larger portion of our brain is devoted to it. For this reason, we want to find a way to listen to it and benefit from it. It is what provides the intuition often referred to as our gut feelings. In my experience, gut feelings are very seldom incorrect.

It is very important to give our subconscious mind the time and space to operate, to give it room to blossom and listen to what it's telling us. In my twenty-two years as a CEO, I found this very difficult and even became rather addicted to simply getting things done. I'd jump between phone calls, texts, emails, and rushed meetings, checking boxes in my mind. I'd even put off going to the bathroom until it became urgent. But there was something that saved me, and it arose from my desire to stay physically fit. A few times a week I ran or swam laps at a health club on the way to work. During this time, I didn't talk (it's very hard to while swimming), and there was room for my subconscious mind to operate. I'd find that my best ideas came at such times: they'd just pop into my mind. When I was running, I would often stop just long enough to write them down. What was amazing was that these ideas came without any effort. Indeed, they came precisely because there was no mental effort! The powerful wiring of my subconscious was allowed to flourish.

It is essential to be completely present in order to allow ourselves to be connected to an innate, infinite, and timeless intelligence that surpasses all of our conscious thinking. If we allow time and space in our lives, whether through sports, meditation, or a hike alone in the mountains, we can create space. Only in that space will our subconscious intelligence have room to arise. Only by not trying can we gain access to a more powerful version of ourselves. Ironically, that more powerful version of ourselves is not really ourselves at all. Instead, it is us being connected to and partaking of that which is much greater than ourselves. It is us tapping into thousands of years of instinct, and the truth that is love, and is God. We are blessed with enormous innate, instinctual intelligence, and a number of delicate senses that allow us to partake of intelligence and knowledge that is far greater than that which we can learn in this short lifetime. But to access it, we need to practice quieting our minds.

Once we learn to quiet the incessant, repetitive, and often unhelpful or even dysfunctional thoughts that paralyze our connection to a deeper intelligence, we create space. Since "nature abhors a vacuum," our innate and instinctual intelligence arises in the space we've created. This intelligence is the place where genius lives. Brilliance does not come from our conscious mind; it arises in that place where our subconscious is allowed to translate the wisdom of the ages into a form we can communicate to others.

Finding space is essential to our ability to partake of and express genius. It allows us to momentarily sip from the wisdom of history. There are many ways to do this. One can run, swim, meditate, or take a quiet stroll in nature. Others prefer yoga, climbing cliffs, or martial arts. There are many ways. But only by occasionally leaving behind our conscious mind for the greater wisdom of the subconscious will we bring our best wisdom to bear on fulfilling our vision.

## THE POWER OF SHARING A VISION

After my promotion to CEO of Messner & Reeves, LLC, I started calling the entire firm together weekly for a short meeting to share my excitement and clarify and illustrate the vision so that it became our mutual vision. At first, I saw mostly amazement in my colleagues' eyes for my level of excitement and ambition. But soon, their eyes started to light up as well. They became enthusiastic and saw that what we were creating was going to be something real and powerful. In these meetings, I explained that while lawyers were often maligned for being expensive and for taking advantage of clients to make money, we'd do the exact opposite. We would find smart ways to solve people's legal issues and leave them in a better place than we found them. We'd be counselors to them. We'd add more value to their businesses and their lives than the value of the dollars they paid us. They'd count us among their friends. We'd measure our success by their success. To accomplish this, we would employ only excellent lawyers, and then we would work harder than anyone else and be invested in each other's success. We would build this place together, a team that loved and cared for each other, doing something we'd be proud of. We'd commit to each other's success, and have the time of our lives becoming the best version of ourselves. This was going to be awesome!

Soon, the vision was no longer mine. It was ours. I was no longer the only one arriving at 5:00 in the morning. The place was abuzz with excitement. It felt warm and collaborative, smart, addictive, and fun.

People walking in often noticed right away that the place was special. Our associates had bright eyes, intensity, and a fast pace. Meeting rooms were filled with eager people, leaning forward in their chairs. We attracted great lawyers, and when they walked in for an interview, they saw and felt something utterly different than anything they'd seen before. I explained to them that we were building something special, and I'd make it clear we'd only hire those who'd ensure our success in doing so. I'd say things that scared some people away, and that was intentional. "We work very, very hard here," I would tell them. "We care about what we're doing, and we're going to be the best at it. We're going to build the best law firm ever!" I would explain that we were looking for a certain rare type of person with certain characteristics. The right lawyers were attracted to this sort of talk, and the wrong ones weren't. Soon, we'd recruited a superb team.

Keeping such talented people was simple; we needed to be the very best place for them. Our firm had to capture their hearts, their minds, and their ambitions. It needed to bring out the best in them by challenging them, teaching them, and helping them grow into great leaders. It needed to be fun, encouraging, exciting, and financially rewarding. To accomplish this, we needed to be different than every other firm; better than any other firm.

The most successful firms become profitable by attracting and retaining the best clients, who have a lot of work that needs to be done, and are willing to pay high billable rates. The lawyers who are most adept at attracting such clients are known as rainmakers, and these lawyers make partner quickly. Traditionally, the rainmakers are the partners, but junior lawyers (associates) do the hard work while the partners take the credit and maintain the relationship with the client. In this way, the partner ensures that when the client needs help again in the future, they call on the partner, not the associate. Most partners discourage their associates from contacting clients directly, for fear that they could lose the client to the younger lawyer.

For our firm, I chose to stand this age-old tradition on its head, and do the exact opposite. I decided to show confidence in my young lawyers by giving them client contact as soon as possible. It seemed clear to me that associates would work harder to serve a client they knew personally, so I introduced them and encouraged them to develop direct relationships with the clients. This saved time, empowered our associates, and saved our clients' money. I concluded it was a good thing if I lost a client to a young lawyer, as long as that lawyer remained at our law firm, which I knew they'd do if it remained the best place for them. To make sure it was, I trained our lawyers well, showed gratitude for their work, let them know that they were needed, challenged them, and developed them. I worked tirelessly to make them better, and they noticed. They knew there was no better opportunity for them anywhere else, and we were committed to keeping it that way.

This philosophy worked beautifully. Our associates felt wanted, needed, and important. They knew they were central to the clients' and the firm's success. They stayed, and they worked extremely hard. Together we built a place that we all felt ownership of, were proud of, and were loyal to. The firm grew quickly, and our profits shot skyward. We enjoyed each other, and it felt like home. We were copilots on a critical mission. And when a bunch of smart people are passionate about doing excellent work, success seems to chase them down. It chased us, and it caught us.

It was an incredibly exciting time. I loved what I was doing and loved what we were building. Yet, I was about to get an opportunity to build something much, much bigger.

# CHAPTER 5

# CHIPOTLE

I HAVE APPRECIATED GOOD FOOD AND WINE SINCE I WAS too young to legally drink alcohol. My mom was, and is, an excellent cook, and my father was brilliant in his knowledge of wine and quick to pour me a small glass with dinner from the time I was about ten years old. Between the two of them, I came to understand and appreciate a great dining experience at a young age. This appreciation continued during my years at the University of Colorado, but I didn't have the money to support my love for great food, let alone great wine.

One day a friend told me I had to meet his friend, Steve Ells, who he said was a great chef. A week later, I attended a dinner party at Steve's small Boulder apartment. Steve was busy in the kitchen, and when he finally brought dinner to the table, the result was absolutely delicious. The pork was medium rare, perfectly seasoned, and plated with such care and respect that it seemed a shame to take a bite. Steve himself ate remarkably quickly. It seemed to me that the act of cooking and presenting the food was where all the magic was to Steve, and he excelled at both.

The way he ate seemed to be more of a confirmation that he had gotten it just right (and he had), than a celebration of how delicious the food really was. To this day, I feel that I loved eating his food even more than he did!

Steve could tell how much I appreciated his cooking, and he was kind enough to invite me to many, many more such feasts over the coming years. But I didn't just stand by and watch. I became an eager student of Steve's and learned all I could every time I joined him in a kitchen. He really was a master.

Steve had learned from watching cooking shows as a young boy and from helping his mom cook family meals. He honed what were already very strong skills when he attended cooking school at the Culinary Institute of America in Hyde Park, New York. Then he advanced his art even further when he went to work for Jeremiah Tower at the famous Stars restaurant in San Francisco.

While working on the line at Stars, Steve often visited burrito restaurants in the Mission District, where customers selected ingredients along a service line, and the staff rolled them into thirteen-inch tortillas, making huge, inexpensive burritos. He began to envision combining this idea with what he had learned at Stars, and making his own burrito restaurant. He told me about this idea, and it sounded good to me. But he wanted to test it first. One night, Steve invited my dad and me to come to his house for dinner to try his idea out on us and a few other good friends.

He slow-roasted a pork shoulder in the oven and diced it up. He made a delicious corn salsa with cilantro, citrus juice, salt, and jalapeno peppers; pinto beans with bacon, and cilantro-lime rice. He grated cheese and whipped some crème fraîche so that it was the consistency of pancake batter. Once every ingredient was ready, he wrapped them in heated flour tortillas and handed each of us a burrito in a basket. They were amazing. Something simple, elevated to the extraordinary. Steve was really on to something, and we were all sure Chipotle would be a hit.

My dad asked if he could invest, but Steve already had received an $85,000 loan from his father, Bob Ells, after putting together a simple business plan. Later, Bob invested a bit more in exchange for a sizable piece of the company. It turned out to be the best investment Bob Ells ever made.

At this time, I was living the California dream—playing volleyball and surfing daily on the beach in front of my Manhattan Beach apartment and practicing law in downtown Los Angeles. But on my many weekend visits to Boulder, I'd check in on Steve's progress. Soon, he built his first Chipotle—a tiny, 840-square foot restaurant. Somehow, he managed to equip the place with a full kitchen, service line, and a few tables. He'd hired a contractor to build it but ended up doing a lot of the work with his bare hands in order to stay within budget. It turned out to be a great location, just off the DU campus in Denver. A bunch of the DU students made Chipotle a part of their daily ritual, and Steve was there behind the counter, making burritos that were honestly so good that you'd feel guilty swallowing them. They were somehow magically much better than the sum total of their parts. I brought my dad, my friends, anyone I could. I was not the only one. Everyone was finding out about this place. Steve had launched a winner!

The very first Chipotle, Evans Street, Denver, Colorado, 1993

## EARLY WORK WITH CHIPOTLE

I often saw Steve when I returned to Boulder to visit my parents, either at Chipotle, or at a dinner at his house. I came to understand that Steve is not just a good cook. He looks at meals with the eye of an artist. He selects ingredients with great care, has incredible *mise en place*, prepares everything meticulously, and cooks superbly so everything is ready at the same time. (*Mise en place* is a French term, common to the world of fine dining restaurants, meaning everything in its place. Picture an incredibly well-organized workstation.) He tends to the entire environment where the meal is to take place—the light, the temperature, the utensils, the glassware. He selects the wine well in advance, decants it when appropriate, and ensures it's at the perfect temperature when the meal is served. In this way, the entire experience is elevated. Dinnertime is his most important and sacred ritual.

By the time I moved back to Boulder in 1996 and began working at Messner & Reeves, LLC, there were eight Chipotle locations in Denver and Boulder. When Steve asked if I'd be willing to do the legal work to help Chipotle lease real estate for new locations, I was eager to help.

As I began this work, the future looked bright for Steve's young company, then called World Foods, Inc., and my goal was simply to be as helpful as possible. Steve, for his part, was energetic, fun, and had a sharp and intelligent sense of humor. He made it a priority to come over to my law office to spend time together. He seemed more comfortable in my law office than in his office, and frequently complimented me on what he felt was an incredible culture that I had built as the CEO of the firm. He asked me how I did it, and listened carefully to my description, but I couldn't help but see that he wanted me to give more attention and focus to Chipotle than I was giving already. He wanted my help running the company, not just advising as a lawyer. I could tell this by how many meetings and lunches he'd invite me to—occasions where a lawyer wasn't needed at all. He brought me to look at kitchen equipment that he was considering. He brought me on a private jet to Morelia, Mexico to look at how Chipotle's avocados were grown. He brought me to every board dinner, and to meet every executive he was considering bringing on board.

Steve trusted me and asked for my advice about almost everything going on with Chipotle. He asked me to help decide who to hire, who he could trust, who should get stock awards in the company and how much, and how to handle the many challenges that confront a young company struggling to make its place in the world. Being his go-to guy and his good friend made me feel special and rare. He'd ask me tough questions, and he'd listen intently to my answers. I felt incredibly appreciated and valued, and this helped us form a strong bond of friendship. It was satisfying to work so closely with him, and simultaneously to be running my law firm as its new CEO. Each of us grew to trust each other deeply, and we shared a mutual concern for each other's success, as we both endeavored to execute our CEO roles to the best of our abilities.

When I first started negotiating leases for Chipotle when there were only a handful of restaurants, I agreed to do the leases for a $1,200 flat fee. This included all the environmental site assessments, exhibits, letters of intent, and a fleet of other related documents. This rate turned out to be much too low for the number of hours it took me, but I was committed to helping Chipotle at a time when funds were scarce. There was a little problem, though. I had no real estate experience, beyond my law degree. Unfazed, I decided to become an expert overnight. I checked in to the CU law library for a week, emerging occasionally for food, water, and sleep. I read major treatises on commercial real estate law and quickly became very knowledgeable on the subject. Also, Ron Reeves, one of our partners, was an expert in real estate law and there to help me.

Chipotle's director of real estate eventually asked me if I would be willing to give a speech at the company's annual development conference in Vail. "Of course!" I replied. But somewhere back in my mind, I heard a loud, *"Oh, shit! How am I gonna pull that off?"* Fortunately, I had two months to prepare. I committed to making it a great speech. In those days, every officer attended the real estate retreat, and I wanted to impress them.

In preparation, I went back to the library and learned everything I had learned before, but in greater depth. I wanted to give an interesting and informative presentation. I wanted to be as knowledgeable as possible about real estate leasing and real estate law, so that I could answer questions about landlord disputes, differences in the laws of different states, financing, tenant improvement allowances, subordinations, estoppels, non-disturbances, subleases, and ground leases. I used all of my spare time for two months to prepare, intent on demonstrating to everyone at Chipotle that I was the right guy to help them. It was also a chance for me to learn a lot more about real estate law, which would help me for the rest of my career.

The speech went better than I could have imagined. I spoke for an hour and a half, then answered loads of questions. I was elated. Afterward, many people came up to me, complimented my knowledge of real estate law, and told me I had made what should've been a dry topic very interesting. I was proud! My hours of study had made me so interested in the subject, that I think it was contagious! They told me they'd never seen someone so passionate and knowledgeable about the law. After that time, the Chipotle employees forever teased me for being a guy who could talk forever about a subject that they thought would be boring. Subsequently, I was invited to countless company meetings, dinners, or golf outings. The Chipotle guys would rib me at all these functions, saying, "Don't get him started about real estate law!" It was fun and led to many friendly relationships. From then on, whenever they had any need, they'd always want me involved. I became the go-to legal guy, and received many calls every day from someone at Chipotle.

The considerable exertion that I put into this speech highlights a critical lesson for anyone trying to become a leader or trying to build a portfolio of business. Put simply, the lesson is to take full advantage of every opportunity given to you that provides an opportunity to be helpful to your boss or your clients. Keep in mind that I didn't bill a dime to Chipotle for the weeks I spent preparing for this speech. And there was no guarantee I'd get anything out of it. But I was invited to present to a lot of people, and I was going to make it worth their while. I didn't do it for money or because I thought I'd get more legal work. I did it because they asked me to. But the result was that it put me on the map. It advertised my expertise and competence, and made it clear to a lot of people that I was someone worth getting involved with.

Over the following months, as I grew our culture and my practice at Messner & Reeves, LLC, the people at Chipotle came to like and trust my work, and they asked me to do more and more for them. There were landlord disputes, lawsuits, disputes with vendors, liquor licenses, government agencies, neighborhood associations, and contracts to be negotiated and signed, and people got me involved to help overcome these obstacles. Often I had to research what to do, but this learning on the fly was fun, and I learned so much helping to solve these problems for Chipotle. I made sure to never bill any of my time spent learning something that I felt I should have already known, so I'd remain a bargain to the company.

My strong desire to please, which probably originated with my efforts to be worthy of my father's time and attention, was a quality that drove me to work very hard. But I also felt so grateful that people trusted me to be able to help them.

To this day, when people ask me the secret of my success, and how they can get ahead in life, I tell them, "Don't worry about getting ahead. Totally focus on what you are doing right now. Do it very well, with all your passion and energy. People will notice, and when they do, they'll want more of your time. Then, soon, they'll want even more. Eventually, they'll want more than you can give. At that point, you'll need a team to help you, and you will need to lead that team."

## MCDONALD'S BUYS IN

In 1998, after I was well entrenched as Chipotle's counsel, Steve was confronted with a new and exciting development. McDonald's was interested in buying a percentage of the fledgling company. The deal would instantly make Steve a millionaire, and would give McDonald's a pathway to a majority ownership stake in the company. For this deal, Steve enlisted the services of a large law firm and an attorney who had been a longtime friend of Steve's father. As Chipotle's general counsel, I was involved every step of the way.

Later in 1998, McDonald's completed its purchase of a minority stake. Steve was suddenly wealthy, and he quickly bought nice cars, beautiful artwork, and began to design a spectacular house near the Denver Country Club. We were all proud of Steve, and I certainly thought he deserved every penny.

Months later, McDonald's hired a new general counsel named Jeff Kindler. In my mind, Jeff was a big shot—a Harvard lawyer who had clerked for Supreme Court Justice William Brennan and who was hired to transform the legal department at McDonald's. Soon, Kevin Reddy, Chipotle's COO, told me that Jeff wanted to meet with me to discuss the best direction for Chipotle's legal work. As soon as I heard this, my heart sank. I thought I was going to be fired in favor of some larger firm that had a long history of doing work for McDonald's.

While I was nervous, I wasn't going to give up. I did everything that I could to prepare for the meeting. I calculated my firm's effective hourly rate for Chipotle to show how economical we were. I made lists of accomplishments. I was able to clearly articulate my philosophy as general counsel and how this benefitted the company. I knew everything going on at Chipotle, and I had a good relationship with everyone in its corporate office.

Jeff turned out to be one of the smartest guys I'd ever met. After Harvard and his clerkship, he became a litigator with the prominent Washington, D.C. firm Williams & Connolly, and then went to work for the iconic CEO, Jack Welch at GE. By joining McDonald's as general counsel, he made clear his ambitions of stepping swiftly into the CEO role. Our meeting was framed by Jeff's superb questions, my quick answers, and a lot of passion. I loved my role as general counsel, and I truly believed the value we provided to Chipotle was irreplaceable. I'm sure my passion was clear to Jeff. He asked if just the two of us could go to lunch. I've no idea where we went or what we ate. All I remember was a long conversation about the legal function, my partnership with Messner & Reeves, LLC, my fellow lawyers there, and my plans to fulfill Chipotle's legal needs. When our lunch finished, I felt I had made a friend, relieved and happy that this impressive man seemed to appreciate and understand me.

As it turned out, I didn't get fired! Instead, Jeff asked that Chipotle formally name me as its general counsel and give me a business card and an office at Chipotle where I'd be asked to spend at least sixteen hours a week. Jeff felt that Chipotle would benefit greatly from me being on-site, and I'd be closer to the inner workings. I was excited and relieved that the man whom I'd so recently feared was suddenly my champion.

About a month later, a lawyer at McDonald's who I'd become

friendly with leaked a letter to me. It was from Jeff, written to a whole slew of lawyers at McDonald's. In it, Jeff explained that he had evaluated the team of lawyers providing legal services to Chipotle and had researched the allocation of legal work. It went on to say that "having met with Montgomery Moran and his partners at the firm of Messner & Reeves, LLC, and having been favorably impressed, I'm now directing that all of the legal work be directed to Messner & Reeves, LLC."

What tickled me so much about this was that Jeff had never met with any of the lawyers at my firm, only me. He'd never even been to our law office! So I knew his decision was based on our meeting, and the endorsement of the Chipotle team, for whom I would have broken bones to deliver the smallest bit of service. What a victory! I felt valued and understood. To this day, Jeff remains a friend.

## SHOULD I BE CEO?

From then on, I was treated like an officer of Chipotle. Steve asked for my involvement with every major decision, and he asked me to join the leadership team and attend all board of director meetings. People started to whisper that Steve was grooming me for a bigger role. I didn't know if that was true, initially. I just wanted to do the best job I could. But soon, he did start to ask me questions about coming to Chipotle full-time. I said I liked it the way it was, but before long, he asked me if I'd be willing to come on board as CEO. He told me he was tired of running the company, and said: "Chipotle needs the kind of leadership I know you can bring." He wanted me to come and build the kind of culture I'd built at my law firm. I was tremendously honored and promised to think about it.

Chipotle was growing rapidly and required many additional capital contributions by McDonald's, the primary investor funding this growth. Each time McDonald's made a capital contribution, they were issued additional shares of stock, which diluted the shares of Steve and the original investors. By the time Steve first asked me to come on board as CEO, McDonald's owned 87 percent of Chipotle's stock. This meant it was really McDonald's company. I hesitated to accept Steve's offer, knowing that at any point in time, McDonald's might decide to exert control. I was not interested in working for McDonald's. I had enjoyed a degree of freedom as CEO of my law firm, and I didn't want to feel that my future was in McDonald's hands.

But Steve was persuasive. He even had Jeff Kindler, (who, at that time was the chairman of Chipotle's board of directors, in addition to being the general counsel of McDonald's and the CEO of Boston Market Chicken, which McDonald's had recently purchased), fly out to meet with me, to convince me that coming to Chipotle was the right move. Jeff, after all, had made the jump from a law firm to the business world when he joined GE, and Jeff wanted to explain to me in person why he thought it best that I come to Chipotle. At that time, they were asking me to become the CEO because Steve wanted to step down, but didn't trust anyone besides me to take over the job of leading Chipotle. After much handwringing and a very persuasive dinner with Jeff, I decided to make the leap and become CEO of Chipotle. I told Steve, and he was delighted. A day later, McDonald's sent me an offer letter. Things were moving fast! I was to receive a large salary, as well as a generous grant of McDonald's stock options since Chipotle was still a private company, and there was no market for Chipotle's shares.

The next night, I got the strangest phone call from Jeff, calling from his Chicago office. I knew, by the way he was speaking, that Jeff was not at liberty to tell me everything he wanted to. But one comment in particular let me know he was quitting his position at McDonald's. He said, "I just wanted to tell you that if I got hit by a bus, there are a lot of people at McDonald's who would resent a young person who is not from McDonald's running Chipotle." He went on to describe that he felt it would be very difficult for me politically in that situation, and that "he just wanted to make me aware of that," since he "hadn't mentioned that before." I called Steve and told him that I had changed my mind and wouldn't take the job.

Days later, it was announced that Jeff had accepted a position as the general counsel of Pfizer Inc. It was a huge job, probably the largest in-house lawyer position in the world at the time. I felt thankful to Jeff that he had done his best to warn me, and I returned happily to my work at the law firm, as well as my role as general counsel of Chipotle.

This went on until the end of 2004, when Steve once again encouraged me to come run Chipotle. But by then, I was hearing credible rumors that McDonald's was going to take Chipotle public. Chipotle was going to be an independent company, no longer owned by McDonald's. This meant that I would not be working for McDonald's if I accepted the role. I'd be my own boss. Also, if I came on board in 2005, I would lead the team that would take Chipotle, now a company with more than 300 restaurants and 8,000 employees, public. This was very exciting to me because leading Chipotle would give me an opportunity to test my ability to build a corporate culture on a much larger scale, with the potential to positively influence thousands of people and to change food culture.

Steve fanned the flames of my enthusiasm by telling me,

"You're a great lawyer, but that's not your greatest strength. Your greatest strength is that you are a great leader." But by then, my law firm was also doing extremely well, and I loved what I was doing. It would take quite an offer to convince me to make the move. That offer came.

I was to be Chipotle's new president and COO. I told Steve I'd rather him keep the CEO title for the time being, to make for a smooth transition, and also to allow me an "out" if I didn't like the job and decided to return to my firm. McDonald's and Chipotle's board of directors offered me 470,000 shares of Chipotle stock (pre-IPO stock which was then valued at around $1 a share), a salary and bonus, and a company car. At the time, my new salary was less than a third of what I was making at the law firm, but money wasn't my primary concern. I was excited about the possibility of leading such a large team of people. It would give me a chance to make a positive impact on their lives while also changing the way people think about and eat fast food.

Before the offer could be made final, Chipotle's chairman, Mats Lederhausen, wanted to spend a couple of days with me. Mats was a senior executive of McDonald's. We flew to the ski town of Telluride, Colorado for a couple of days. Mats and I got along wonderfully. After a long day of skiing followed by a sushi dinner, we ended up talking philosophy late into the night. We both shared a passion for the notion that one could achieve business success while simultaneously improving the environment and people's lives. Mats told me he thought Chipotle would benefit hugely with me at the helm, and having his support and confidence meant the world to me. I left feeling invigorated about my new path.

Before I officially accepted the offer, I asked that I be able to bring Betsy Hobson, my wonderful legal assistant for ten years, with me. Betsy had made it clear to me she wanted to work for me forever, and I wanted the same. (As I write this today, in 2020, Betsy still works for me, twenty-three years after I hired her at my law firm!) When that was agreed, I accepted the offer and started the difficult and melancholy job of transitioning my legal cases to other lawyers.

It was sad to leave my law firm. For ten years, I'd been completely devoted to my associates, partners, and clients. But on March 5, 2005, I became president and chief operating officer of Chipotle. A tear rolled down my cheek as I steered my car to the right into Chipotle's underground parking structure that morning, instead of left into my law firm's garage. I reassured myself that leaving a wonderful past was necessary to be reborn into something new and mysterious. With this sentiment in mind, I felt the elevator gently lift my feet up into the historic brick and timber building of Chipotle's lower downtown Denver headquarters. Awaiting me were warm handshakes, hugs, and words of congratulations and excitement from many of the 100-plus employees that worked at the corporate office. Any sorrow for leaving my past quickly transitioned to a feeling of freshness and excitement.

## CHAPTER 6

# FIRST DAYS

YOUR EARLY DAYS LEADING A NEW ORGANIZATION ARE A UNIQUE opportunity. A blank slate. What you do and how you do it will set the tone for years to come, and everyone is watching to see how you take the reins. I ended up doing a lot of unconventional things—many by instinct—that became representations of how I led. It began on my first full day in the office when I said something that would become foundational to the way I ran the company.

My first day on the job, before I could begin to wonder what I was actually going to do in my new position, Steve grabbed me, brought me downstairs, and asked me to speak to a large team of area managers who had traveled to Denver for an all-day meeting. I hadn't been given any notice of the meeting, nor even a minute to prepare. I didn't even know area managers were in town. I'm sure they were as caught off guard as I was. It turned out no one had even told them Chipotle was hiring a new president!

I introduced myself, relaxed, and just started talking. I told them I was excited about my new position and couldn't wait to get to know them. I explained that I'd never run a restaurant company and that I'd need a lot of help from them because I "didn't know what the hell I was doing." That instant, they let their guard down and accepted me. They were visibly relieved. *"Wow!"* they seemed to be thinking. *"He said he needs us! He said he wants to get to know us! He wants our help!"* I felt vulnerable and chose to let it show. Like my dog Chelsea, I completely exposed my soft underbelly, revealed all my weaknesses, and was completely myself. This was disarming to them. They let down their guard and began to accept me.

I said some things during that talk that ended up being of critical importance to my next twelve years leading Chipotle.

First, I said that "the restaurant general manager is the most important position in the company." Since my audience contained no general managers but instead was composed solely of the area managers to whom the general managers reported, I saw them wince a bit. I explained, "It's like Tiger Woods. He is the most important person since he's the one playing golf, but even Tiger needs a coach! So, the rest of us are important because we can coach these general managers to be at their very best!" This explanation seemed to resonate. They knew I valued them, and that is what they were most concerned about.

Second, I went on to describe the culture we'd built at Messner & Reeves, LLC, and how I'd like to do the same at Chipotle. The foundation of that culture, I explained, was "that each of us will be rewarded based on our effectiveness in making the people around us better."

I'd never said this quite this way before, but I liked it as soon as I said it. So I repeated it a second time, slowly, "Each of us will be rewarded based on our effectiveness in making the people around us better." It was a mantra that came to me in an instant, but has remained with me forever.

They seemed to understand this concept right away. At the end of my speech, many area managers came up to speak to me. I promised to visit them in their restaurants and get to know them better. It went marvelously well, and I felt liked, understood, and accepted as their leader.

These two statements became foundational to the culture we set about building:

*"The restaurant general manager is the most important position in the company."*

*"Each of us will be rewarded based on our effectiveness in making the people around us better."*

These concepts immediately started to catch on and provided a change in direction for Chipotle's culture. Over time, they became a powerful engine driving our success. Everyone quickly came to realize these were not just words. I wanted everyone in the corporate office and the field to understand that our best path to success was to serve the needs of our restaurant general managers, and make sure they were the best they could be. But also, since we were a growing company that needed to develop more leaders, I wanted everyone to realize that their success would come from their effectiveness in making others better.

I explained that "If everyone at Chipotle is pulling for you, then you have thousands of people on your team. But if each of you is trying only to advance your own agenda, then you have only one person on your team: yourself!" I asked them which they thought was more powerful. They understood. This was important for Chipotle since we were growing quickly and needed thousands of new crew and general managers. It was critical to encourage and reward people who would teach, train, elevate, assist, and empower others.

We changed the way we made decisions. Every raise, promotion, demotion, and personnel decision was made based on how effective someone was at making the people around them better. Those who did this best were promoted and celebrated. They were our heroes. By celebrating these people, others quickly became aware of the importance of leading by making others better, and leaders started to work diligently to empower the people around them. They came to understand that the path to success was not to focus solely on building their own reputation and skills, but to instead do that for others.

Amazingly, that first day might have been the most important day I had at Chipotle. During those few hours I planted not one, but two stakes in the ground. I led the company from these two principles for the rest of my time there.

As I said in chapter 2, the ideas and concepts in this book are intertwined. I could not have arrived, seemingly spontaneously, at the idea that "each of us will be rewarded based on our effectiveness at making the people around us better" without years of building a culture at Messner & Reeves, LLC that celebrated that. As I leaned in to my new job, I found myself pulling on many lessons I learned as a child or as a teen working in a variety of service jobs, or from taking depositions.

In the chapters that follow, I'll describe how I put meat on the bones of these early ideas. I will show you how I figured out what to prioritize in a fast-growing company of thousands of employees. How I developed the signature one-on-one interviews that characterized my hands-on leadership, and the Restaurateur program that celebrated our most important employees, the very best general managers. I'll show you how I went deep into the ingredients of leadership that I laid out at the beginning of this book and how I redefined what empowerment means so that everyone in our company was able to row in the same direction. Finally, and importantly, I'll discuss the craft of excellent communication, the foundation of our human interactions.

But first, I will tell you the story of how I went undercover.

## GOING UNDERCOVER

If, as I had just announced, "the general manager is the most important person in the company," then I had better understand the general manager's world. What better way than by becoming one?

Of course, I couldn't waltz into a Chipotle as the new president and COO and say I wanted to be trained as a GM. That would distort everything that happened in the training. I wanted to experience GM training the way our managers did. I spoke to our regional director in Denver, a wonderful person named Gretchen Selfridge, and asked if she could place me as a general manager trainee without giving away who I was. She loved the idea and was eager to help pull it off. Ultimately, she placed me in a Thornton, Colorado Chipotle restaurant with an excellent training manager named Kay Geist, and my training began. While Kay did know my real position with the company, she was sworn to secrecy and made sure that the crew believed me to be a "regular" trainee. We kept my identity a secret. That would have been tougher today, with social media and smartphones. But this was 2005, and the smartphone had just been invented—few people had one yet. Also, only 5 percent of Americans were on social media then. My secret remained safe.

At this time, Chipotle's manager training program was called the "MIT" program, an acronym for Manager in Training. These MITs were hired off the streets, usually due to their experience at one of the better known fast food restaurant chains. In MIT training, I worked each position, learning managerial tasks such as placing food orders, performing inventories, calculating food costs, hiring new employees, writing schedules, and managing labor costs.

At my training restaurant, I quickly saw the beauty of our incredible crew members, most of whom were Hispanic immigrants. Few spoke English fluently, but they were incredibly eager to teach me the art of preparing vegetables, achieving perfect cut sizes, how to clean and organize the equipment, and how to cook the food. They were excellent. They worked hard and were proud of their jobs. I really enjoyed being with and learning from them. I loved these people. They cared for me, empowered me, and taught me so much. But I noticed that while these crew members were incredibly skilled and capable, very few of them were being promoted into manager positions. Instead, nearly all of Chipotle's general managers were white and were hired from outside the company. This made no sense to me. It was so clear to me that these entry-level employees would make excellent future leaders of the company. Any effort we made to give them a path to rise would deliver an enormous return on investment, in the form of a strong bench of future leaders.

The MIT trainees, some of whom trained alongside me during my time as an MIT, were all recent hires, chosen by our HR team. Apparently, the "best people they could find." But best at what? Most were low energy, had little sense of urgency, and weren't particularly eager to learn. Why would we choose these qualities?

Part of my training entailed reading training manuals. But to my dismay, I found Chipotle's manuals to be condescending, uninspiring, poorly written, and designed to appeal to low performers. They did not reflect the sort of ambitious goals that would attract top-performing talent to Chipotle. Soon after my training, we set about rewriting these, and it made a huge difference in our operations.

My many weeks of training were very informative. I discovered dozens of ideas for how to quickly improve the company. I also learned that much of what we were teaching was not consistent with what I had learned from cooking with Steve and had to be changed. But perhaps most importantly, I gained an enormous appreciation for the skill, talent, value, and authenticity of the hourly workers in our restaurants. I saw them as an enormous resource and began to envision how we could better empower them and improve their experience, while providing a better restaurant experience.

At the close of my six weeks of training, while I was competent at each task, I was expert at none. It occurred to me that the crew members who trained me would be more effective managers if they were given the same training, since they were already experts at all the underlying tasks. So, this begged the question: why have an MIT program where we hire outside candidates? Why not just train our crew to be our future managers?

This question was burning in my heart. I knew that the way Chipotle was training its employees was not the answer, and it bothered me so much that I couldn't sleep. It seemed an emergency to me. I saw that we were actively seeking the wrong people to be our future managers, while overlooking the talented people who were already working for us. Absurd! Why not cultivate our future managers from this class of excellent, loyal, tested, proven, and skilled people who we'd known for years? If we trained our crew to be our managers, wouldn't our restaurant teams celebrate and rejoice that we recognized their talent, believed in them, and bet our future on them? Wouldn't we then attract better crew candidates, since they'd know that Chipotle was the place with the most opportunity?

There were other questions as well. Why were we paying outstanding GMs the same wage as our mediocre ones? Why were we promoting our best GMs out of the store into the ill-defined and ineffective position of area manager? Why would we set up our company to have our best managers aspire to not be managers anymore?

To most of these questions, there were no good answers. Chipotle had "just always done it this way." No one questioned it. It was the traditional fast food human resources recipe. To the questions that did have answers, none of them satisfied me. The reason our MIT candidates were mediocre was that our HR team had decided we needed people with fast food experience. But what is fast food experience? To me, and to most others, fast food meant dirty, rude, disorganized, unhealthy, and uninspiring. Why look for people who had that training to lead great restaurants? Moreover, the fast food workers we often hired were *unemployed* fast food workers! That's right. We were selecting folks who couldn't keep a job at McDonald's or Taco Bell, and training them to manage our restaurants!

The next question I asked was why wasn't Chipotle promoting its existing crew people? No one had an answer. But as I dug deeper, I found the reasons. First, there was no path to a promotion: no training program to help crew members become managers. The only management training we had was our MIT program, which was geared towards outside hires, but not generally available to those who already worked for Chipotle. So there was no practical way for crew members to work their way up. Also,

## DON'T OVERVALUE EDUCATION AND EXPERIENCE: VALUE CHARACTER

Over and over, when hiring, I see leaders overvalue the experience of a candidate and overlook character flaws in order to get the experience that they think is so essential. But more often than not, this is a mistake.

First, often the experience people come in with is poor experience. You will have to spend time to help them unlearn what they learned in their former position, so you can show them a better way.

Second, often getting a new employee the experience they need is not particularly difficult. They can quickly learn it on the job.

Third, people with prior experience usually want more money in consideration for their experience. But, oddly, a person with excellent character usually doesn't command more money for their characteristics, even though excellent characteristics are *not* trainable, and experience *is* trainable!

For this reason, it is most often a better decision to hire someone with excellent personal traits and character, and train them to do what's needed, than to spend more money hiring someone with the experience you think they need. The "experienced" person's experience may not be what you'd hoped for. But good character will almost certainly be something you'll appreciate for years to come.

there was no expectation to move up, and so few crew members thought it possible. I learned this when I asked questions of the people who were training me.

"What do you see yourself doing in five years?" I'd ask.

"I like this job pretty well!" they'd answer.

"Yes, but would you like to become a manager?"

Then they'd give me a suspicious look, as though I'd asked if they wanted a million dollars. Their eyes said, "Are you messing with me?" I learned from this that we'd done nothing to give our crew any expectation that they could be managers. They assumed there was no real chance to advance. I found this totally unacceptable. People will grow and learn much more quickly and effectively if there is a clear path for them to follow to advance their skills.

In 2006, we created a brand-new career path, designed to promote our crew into management positions. The problem with the old system was that people came in as crew, but there was no position between the entry-level position and a supervisor role. The supervisor role was responsible for managing the entire restaurant, including opening in the morning, closing up at night, making bank deposits, and hiring and firing. The supervisor position was just too big of a leap for these employees to take, so they weren't motivated to try. There was also no training program in place by which crew could learn the supervisor role.

We immediately created new positions that carried very specific descriptions and constituted a very logical progression by which crew members could work their way up to management positions. Then, we created specific training for each position. We called this logical progression the career path, and it worked like this. People would come in as crew, and if they were doing well, they'd be asked to train for the kitchen manager (KM) role, which was responsible for limited managerial tasks, such as ordering food, taking inventory, and food safety. Once they'd mastered this position, they'd be able to train for the next position, called service manager (SM). Service managers learned additional managerial tasks such as cash handling, how to give excellent customer service and deal with complaints, how to run the service line and deliver great throughput, and how to run the second "make line," which we used for online orders.

Once successful in the SM role, people could then train for

the apprentice role. The apprentice did all the tasks of a full general manager and was formerly called the assistant manager. I changed the title from assistant manager to apprentice because I wanted to be sure that no one stayed in this role for long. If they were good, they should quickly become a GM!

Finally, our apprentices would immediately be working to become a GM in their own restaurant. This career path worked wonderfully, and suddenly caused thousands of crew to move swiftly into manager roles, and build great careers with Chipotle. This career path was a home run because it drastically dropped our costs to train a new manager, while dramatically improving the competence of our managers, lowering turnover, and attracting much better candidates to crew positions at Chipotle. Put simply, we became the place to work for entry-level employees, and we began to mint future leaders, which we needed for our rapid growth.

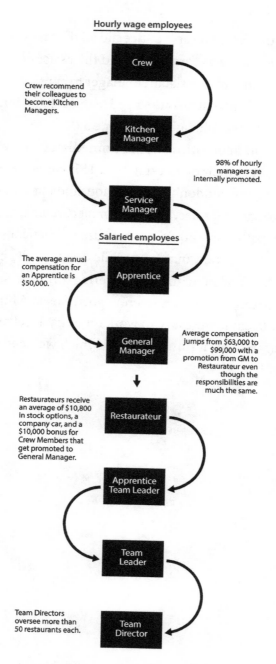

Hourly wage employees

Crew

Crew recommend their colleagues to become Kitchen Managers.

Kitchen Manager

98% of hourly managers are internally promoted.

Service Manager

Salaried employees

The average annual compensation for an Apprentice is $50,000.

Apprentice

General Manager

Average compensation jumps from $63,000 to $99,000 with a promotion from GM to Restaurateur even though the responsibilities are much the same.

Restaurateurs receive an average of $10,800 in stock options, a company car, and a $10,000 bonus for Crew Members that get promoted to General Manager.

Restaurateur

Apprentice Team Leader

Team Leader

Team Directors oversee more than 50 restaurants each.

Team Director

The career path Monty implemented, which gave every crew member an opportunity to become a future leader, reduced training costs, and lowered turnover. Credit: "How Chipotle transformed itself by upending its approach to management." Max Nisen, *Quartz Magazine*, March, 2014.

## FOCUSING ON WHAT'S MOST IMPORTANT

It was clear immediately during these very first days working in the restaurant that much had to change. This was exciting because I saw that I was going to be able to help Chipotle become a much better company with better operations and happier people! This motivated me to work very, very hard to immediately solve what I saw as obvious problems in the way the company had been run. During my first few weeks on the job, I concluded that we needed to focus on three core things, which I discuss below.

It seems obvious that a leader should focus on those things that are most important. But what is less obvious is how powerful it is to focus on only the very top priorities, all of the time. The top few priorities, in my experience, tend to be more important than all the rest put together. In other words, failing to advance one of the top priorities, and getting the next twenty right, is usually a worse result than getting the top few right, and nearly ignoring the next twenty.

The key when picking priorities is finding the things that, if done well, will affect the most positive change in all areas of the company. Also, it is important to pick priorities you know can be improved, and will have a long runway. In other words, things that, if continually improved, will have a compounding positive effect on the business.

At the same time, it is also important to avoid pursuing objectives that, even if successful, won't help the business much. Surprisingly, lots and lots of such ideas surface, and an important skill of the CEO (or leader) is to have the courage not to chase them all. It reminds me of a saying that I heard: "Something not worth doing is not worth doing well."

I think it's funny but also true. So, pick things that are worth doing, which, if achieved, will have a huge and broadly positive impact on the business. Ignore distractions that will take up resources, detract from top priorities, and not help much.

A worthwhile exercise is to write down the top ten things that you think you can do to improve your business. Then, take the time to prioritize them in terms of their potential impact. Look to see if any of them, if completed, would advance other priorities on your list. For those, put them at the top. Once they're in order, you should devote your time to the top two or three. When you invest a lot of work into the top two or three, it will have a huge impact on the business. Then, after working on those priorities for a time, do the same exercise over again. Make a list of the top ten things, and boil it down to the top two or three most important ones. It's perfectly likely that the top two or three most important ones are the same, over and over again, and that's OK! Just keep assessing and keep focusing on the top few.

I quickly settled on my top three priorities at Chipotle.

## Hiring the Right People

The first priority was hiring the right people and then promoting those people to manager roles in the company. I was certain that training our existing crew would be vastly superior to hiring from the outside. To confirm my decision, I went back to the corporate office and pulled data. I looked at the performance of the few crew members who had been promoted from crew to manager, and compared it with the MIT managers who constituted the vast majority of our GMs, and had been hired from the outside. The data revealed that managers who came from crew positions ran much better restaurants, and were four times less likely to quit than the MIT managers.

After seeing this, I announced that we would increase our

internal promotions from about 30 percent to 100 percent in two years. If someone was going to be a Chipotle manager, they were going to come in as crew, and earn it by demonstrating their ability to build a great culture, create a strong team, and run a terrific restaurant.

## DON'T FOCUS ON THINGS YOU CANNOT CONTROL

There are things that you can control in business, and there are things you can't. Any effort focused on the things you can't control is wasted effort.

Likewise, leaders often focus on sales and revenue as if talking all day about higher sales and higher revenue will somehow cause them to happen. This seems an obsession for leaders: "If we can get our sales up by 20 percent this year, that'll get us to profitability!" Well, any such talk or handwringing over getting sales up is a waste. Instead, leaders need to ask themselves, "What action can I take today that will cause us to give a better product or service to our customers?" Then, they need to powerfully and swiftly take that action.

I'll never forget a time at Chipotle, when our stock was white hot and probably overvalued by an investing public that thought we could do no wrong. Around that time, our CFO showed me a video clip of a leader at a competitor, complaining that his company deserved a higher share price than it enjoyed, given its financial results. He droned on about this. I think he even complained about how Chipotle's share price didn't deserve to be so high. But really, who cares? That is just useless whining. What if this leader had instead spent that time talking to his employees or customers, learning what they enjoyed and appreciated, and what could be improved, so that he could improve their experience in his restaurants? That would have been a much better use of his time, which would've ultimately led to higher sales, higher earnings, and a better stock price. Instead, he spent time bemoaning something that he could not control.

Anytime you're spending time on something, make sure it is a top priority, and make sure it is something you can control. If it's not both of these, there is a better use of your time.

Also, we were no longer going to hire for experience. Instead, we were going to hire for character—for this critical aspect of personality that cannot be taught. After all, what fast food experience did we really respect? Was there a fast food restaurant that we felt did an excellent job with training? That we envied, because their people were great, talented, and happy? The answer was "Heck no!" Most fast food restaurants were poorly run, and had poorly trained people who were not inspired with a vision that would lead them to care about their jobs. We didn't want to hire people who had learned the wrong habits, or who had low expectations for customer satisfaction. It would be far better to train someone new.

Next, we were going to quickly construct a clear and easily understood path from crew to restaurant management, so that our people knew exactly what was expected of them to ascend the ranks. Then, we were going to create a compensation system that rewarded top performers much more than low performers.

I found the reasons to promote from within almost absurdly obvious. We would attract more top performers at the crew level, as word would get out that our crew members were slated for management positions. Our existing crew would be motivated, knowing we believed in them, and that they had a bright future. Our GMs would be much better, as they would have deep knowledge of every position, and more experience at creating excellent operations. We would create optimism, as our teams would witness the ascent of their deserving peers. It would eliminate the frustration our teams had when they saw someone coming in, as their boss, who knew far less than they did about Chipotle. It would demonstrate that we cared about and were investing in the people we already had. Our managers would hire more carefully since they'd know they weren't hiring just to fill a position, but instead were hiring a future general manager. Knowing that there would be these benefits and many more, I couldn't stand still. We had to get this new, better way of building teams in place immediately.

## Ensuring Excellent Operations

The second priority was to ensure excellent operations within each restaurant. My revelations from MIT training were not just about the team. I also had many ideas as to how to drastically improve the customer experience, both our customer service, and the quality and taste of our food, and thereby maximize our success. The most significant of these was to speed up our throughput—the time it took a customer to get through our line and receive their food. During my training, we had huge lines. Most Chipotles did, at both lunch and dinner. I saw that our employees were proud of our lines, because the lines meant people liked us.

But many customers decided not to wait. Those sales were lost forever. We had upset those customers who might decide not to bother coming next time ("Their lines are too long!"). Even for those who chose to wait in line, it was the least positive part of their customer experience, and faster throughput would solve that. But improving throughput did so much more for our business that you'd hardly believe it.

I knew that if we really improved this one aspect of our business, it would simultaneously cause many other aspects of our operation to improve. At first, not everyone saw things my way. One of our board members, a smart and talented man named Matt Paull, who at that time was CFO of McDonald's corporation, challenged me on my desire to speed up our service line. "Won't people feel rushed? Won't this degrade the customer experience?"

"Actually, Matt, speeding up service will have exactly the opposite effect," I answered. "It turns out that the very things that constitute great customer service are exactly the same things that speed up our service line. For instance, when customers walk in, they feel most welcome if we notice them and greet them right away. But this greeting also gets their attention so that we can quickly get their order started. Once they are at the service line, we need to make great eye contact to hold their attention and make sure we understand what they want, so we can make their order correctly. This same eye contact makes them feel important, seen, cared for, and happy!

"Then we need to speak clearly and loudly so that there are no miscommunications. Customers appreciate this clear communication. It gives them confidence that their order is being correctly made, and it also allows the next employee on the service line to hear what the customer wants, so that we are not annoying the customer by asking them to repeat themselves as they shuffle down the service line. All of this allows us to make their burrito quickly, which ensures we roll it up while the food is still hot, and get it to them right away, so they can begin to enjoy it, or get back to work if they're taking it to go."

Needless to say, Matt was convinced. But more importantly, the initiative to improve throughput was the gift that kept on giving.

In order to go fast, we needed excellent *mise en place*. We needed to have extra service spoons ready, all the baskets cleaned and ready, the foil wrappers separated so they could be quickly taken out and used, and buckets with clean towels ready to clean the line between guests. We needed each person on the line to know exactly what their role was, such that they were as efficient as possible during peak hour. Getting all this ready helped us understand and deploy our labor better, so that we had exactly the right number of people in exactly the right roles, which saved millions in labor costs and also helped us to make job descriptions clearer, which was empowering to our people. But also, our teams loved it. They said going fast made them feel proud and skilled while making their shift fly by faster. Our people became experts at their positions and had friendly competitions with other stores to see who could go fastest.

Meanwhile, our customer service comments became more and more positive. When I started working at Chipotle, we had very few comments about our service. Instead, most comments were about the taste of our food. But in time, the number of positive customer comments about our great service just exploded. We even began posting, in each store, the number of days since the last negative customer comment, and many stores had numbers in the hundreds. Keep in mind that most fast food restaurants get mostly negative comments. People seldom are moved to write unless they were somehow offended. But we turned that around. The vast majority of our comments raved about our customer experience.

As our teams got better at throughput, they were simultaneously tackling most of the other aspects of a great operation—a cleaner, better organized store, with better food, and better service. Our managers needed to write good schedules, to ensure their "A-team" was on the line at peak times, and that led to better labor management and lower labor costs. By moving faster, we were increasing our sales dramatically, with little additional labor, and with no added restaurant costs (other than food and packaging) so our margins increased dramatically, as did our profits.

By focusing on just one initiative (throughput), we were improving literally every aspect of the customer experience and our entire business model. For this reason, this initiative remained a top priority at all times.

*Creating a Strong Culture*

My third priority was to create a culture throughout Chipotle like the one I'd created at Messner & Reeves, LLC—a place teeming with hard-working, passionate people, who were at their very best, invested in each other's success, and driven to give a great customer experience. I wanted it to be fun, addictive, exciting, and positive. I knew that to create this kind of culture, we needed a clear vision that people would be excited about, and we needed to hire only the very best people to join our team.

I decided to sit down, one on one, with everyone who worked at the home office—over 100 people. I asked them many things, but started with nine basic questions designed to find out who they were, what they did, what they liked and did not like, and get a deeper understanding of the entire corporate culture. The questions were:

1. What do you do? (50 percent of the one-hour meeting was usually spent answering this simple question.)
2. Who do you work for (what's it like working for them, are they a good boss)?
3. What do you like most about your job?
4. What do you like least about your job?
5. What do you like most about Chipotle?
6. What do you like least about Chipotle?
7. Out of all the things that you spend your time on, where are we as your employer getting the greatest bang for our buck?

What is it that you do that is of the greatest value to the company?

8. Of all the things that you spend your time on, what time do you feel is giving the company the least value?

9. What should I do (as Chipotle's new president/COO)?

I was amazed at how powerful these meetings were. So much so, I kept doing them. During my time with Chipotle, I had over 20,000 one-on-ones with crew members in our restaurants, and hundreds in the corporate office as well. People often asked where I found the time to talk to them, get to know them, and understand them, with such a big company to run. But the reality was, I had such a big company to run that I could not afford *not* to sit down and talk to them. Caring for, understanding, and knowing our people gave me a reputation for caring deeply. And while I could never meet with all 70,000 of our employees, this reputation spread, and engendered incredible loyalty on the part of our people, and led them to devote their full energy to their work.

From my first round of one-on-one meetings in the corporate office, I gathered six major takeaways.

First, people were elated that I was even having these meetings: that I was talking to them in the first place. They told me that no officer had ever spent time to get to know them even though they were the very people who were tasked with the company's growth and success! Instead, they'd been largely ignored. (While low performers like being ignored, top performers don't). In fact, the most common answer I got to my last question, "What should I do?" was, "This! What you're doing right now, talking to us!" The hunger people had just to be spoken to, cared for, understood, and valued was amazing.

Second, I learned that we had some very promising people,

but also some people who were obviously not going to be able to help us achieve our mission.

Third, I learned that the communication in the company was very poor. People were not open with each other, didn't feel at liberty to speak their minds, and didn't trust each other or the company's leadership.

Fourth, there was a lot of waste. People were pursuing projects and working on tasks that were not helpful to the company.

Fifth, many of the senior executives provided no real direction and were doing very little work.

Sixth, people didn't feel at liberty to innovate, feeling that their ideas were not valued.

Basically, while Chipotle had delicious food and an exciting future, it was poorly led. Most of the leaders did not have clear goals for their teams, and the corporate staff wasn't empowered, motivated, or working with urgency. The things most employees reported liking best about their job at Chipotle were that they got free food (everyone was very proud of our food), could dress casually, take long weekends, bring their dog to work, and that no one held them accountable. In other words, people were happy with their job not for what they could do, but for what they didn't have to do.

## ELIMINATING CORPORATE OFFICE DYSFUNCTION

From my point of view, the corporate office culture was dysfunctional. At a minimum, it was incredibly undisciplined. Many employees regularly left the office shortly after lunch for happy hour at a bar downstairs and drank themselves dizzy on their Chipotle credit cards. The office was closed on Fridays in the summer so that everyone could enjoy long weekends during Colorado's beautiful summer months. Of course, this hurt the 99 percent of Chipotle's employees who worked in the restaurants, who were without support on Fridays, which, along with Saturdays, were our busiest days. The department leaders regularly scheduled team-building exercises, which included rafting trips, golf outings, and getaways to expensive hotels and resorts around the country, which were usually useless boondoggles. Dogs were allowed—encouraged may be more accurate—in the office, where they would bark, run around, defecate, and distract everyone from getting work done. Their owners would routinely leave their desks to feed and water them, walk them, or to chat with other pet owners about their dogs. There was a ping-pong table, with regular tournaments, and other games and activities.

Before 9:00 a.m. and after 4:00 p.m., you could have safely fired off a cannon in the office without hurting anyone's ears. There was almost no one there. It was fun in many ways. It felt like a nonstop fraternity party. But the primary focus in the corporate office was certainly not about building a culture of top performers or achieving high restaurant standards.

Ineffective getaways, unfocused or ineffective people, and needless distractions were all examples of precious company resources that were being wasted. Precious time and money going straight out the window. This observation led to an ongoing effort on my part to hunt down and eliminate waste, a dangerous cancer that bleeds the life out of organizations and leaves them tired, weak, and lifeless.

In their personal lives, people are careful with money. They care about every penny. But, magically, as soon as money is placed in the name of a corporation or other legal entity, people seem excited to part with it. They hire more people than they need. They don't ensure that those they hire are adding value.

They willingly pay more for products and services. They buy stuff they don't need—luxury boxes at sporting events, expensive dinners, swag, and all sorts of junk. It is even worse when a company becomes successful. When that happens, people spend money like they're angry at it. Like they want to get rid of it. Like drunken sailors! It's shocking, really. There is also a tendency for people to assume that if time and money are being spent, there must be a net positive outcome. But this is often not the case. Having the discipline to carefully look into this is critical. It's essential for a leader to notice when there is waste and put a stop to it.

Accomplishing this starts with having one-on-one discussions with people in every department of the company, to learn how they are spending their time, what tasks they are working on, and what their goals are. They will readily share with you loads of valuable information. They'll tell you if there are more productive uses for their time, whether certain activities are helping the business, or whether time and money are being wasted. You need to quickly reallocate people's time and energy to things that have the greatest possible positive impact.

Your job is not to make sure that everyone is working hard and doing something useful. That is not enough. Your job is to shepherd all of the organization's resources (people's time, effort, and money) in a way that provides the maximum possible benefit to those few top priorities that are going to lead to success.

As you hunt down and eliminate waste, don't just look for people wasting time and wasting money. Look also at everything that is being done in the company and ask if it is important to achieving one of the company's priorities. If it is not, strongly consider ceasing the activity. Also, look carefully at the people in your employ. Are they all working efficiently? Are they in the right positions? The answer, the vast majority of the time, is that they aren't. This needs to be rectified.

Mike Caro, a famous poker player, likes to say, "Money you don't lose buys just as many things as money you win."

This is such a helpful thing to remember. If we know we are beaten in a poker hand, putting in even a small amount "just to see what the other player has" is a mistake. It is throwing money away. Likewise, throwing the second-best hand away instead of throwing in that last twenty dollars (and then losing to the best hand) is just as powerful as winning twenty dollars.

In business, this is even more true, since businesses need to pay tax on money they make, but don't always get a deduction on the money they spend. Also, when a leader makes a decision to save money, or not to spend money on unneeded tools, headcount, or technology, there is usually a recurring savings since tools, tech, and headcount require ongoing maintenance payments for as long as you have them. And, just like taxes or government entitlements, once a new tool, or luxury, or headcount is in place, it is very hard to get rid of it without creating friction with someone on the team!

### MAKING AN IMPACT

I believed that work should be fun. We had a great time at Messner & Reeves, LLC. But the fun we had at the law firm flowed from excitement about what we were accomplishing together. Similarly, I believed Chipotle should be fun, but the enjoyment should arise from the satisfaction of building an incredible company together, not by the relief of avoiding hard work.

Through these one-on-one interviews, I noticed that most people fell neatly into one of two buckets: those who liked their work for what they were able to do for the company, and those who liked their work for what they didn't have to do for the company. Put differently, some described the contribution they were able to make in terms of the advancement of and betterment of the company's goals. Others described with pride all the ways the company's culture allowed them to avoid working. Needless to say, I wanted to build a culture that promoted the former, not the latter.

There was a longer-term lesson here for me, and it is applicable to every business in which I've been involved. There are people who measure their job satisfaction by how powerfully they can contribute, and there are people who measure it by what they are able to extract from their job. As a leader, it is critical to surround yourself with those who like their work for what they are able to do for the company.

Learning so much in these first weeks after joining Chipotle led me to feel a heightened sense of urgency, an excited impatience, and I immediately set out to make things better. These initial observations set the stage for much of what I worked on for my next twelve years at Chipotle. We set about creating a special culture that appealed to top performers and repelled low performers. We made sure only excellent leaders remained in place, and put them in positions that allowed them to have the most positive impact possible. We redefined roles and responsibilities to maximize productivity and impact, and eliminated overlapping job responsibilities so that it was always clear what everyone's responsibilities were. We eliminated low performers and positions that were hindering us from achieving our goals. We even eliminated a whole department that was counterproductive! Finally, we taught our leaders how to build teams of top performers, empowered to achieve high standards in our restaurants, and in our field teams.

My new direction was not always smooth sailing, and this new kind of culture, which was about hard work, clear communication, making others better, and empowering top performers, did have its detractors. For example, one man who reported to me, whom I'll call Doug, went to Steve and complained that, "Monty is running this company like a law firm!" Steve called me to tell me this when I was off-site in a meeting with our CFO, and I was immediately concerned.

"Did he elaborate?" I asked Steve. "Because I'm not sure what it is about running it like a law firm that is bad."

"Not really," said Steve. "He just said that what you are doing is not the Chipotle way. That it is changing our culture. He threatened to resign."

This comment shocked me, mostly because Doug was someone who expressed great affection and admiration for me on nearly a daily basis. He'd often come up behind me, put his hands on my shoulders as I sat at my desk, and say, "Monty, it is incredible what you're doing for this company! I'm so glad that you are here." He would daily support almost every move I made, and never gave me the least bit of criticism. In fact, just the week before, Doug had asked me to be tougher on him and to give him clearer direction since, in his own words, he "lacked discipline and needed a clear path to perform at his best." But when Steve shared that Doug had threatened to resign, I was secretly a bit pleased, since I had long thought (before even starting in my new role at Chipotle) that Doug was not a top performer and was doing little to benefit Chipotle.

"I'll come back to the office and talk to him right now," I said.

I drove back to the office and set up a meeting with Doug right away. As he entered the room, he looked nervous.

"Steve explained to me that you had concerns about my

leadership," I began. "I'd really like to understand what it is that concerns you, so I can do the best job possible." Doug started to shake his head in denial, but I continued. "In particular, Steve explained that you felt perhaps I'm changing the culture here, and while I don't doubt that is true, I just want to get your perspective."

"No!" Doug exclaimed. "No! I told Steve that what you were doing was good. It is Steve that's acting differently. He is making it uncomfortable here lately." Doug went on to cite many examples of how Steve had changed recently and how it was making him feel less able to be effective in his role.

I was dumbfounded. Doug had made it clear to Steve that I was the problem. Now he was making it clear to me that Steve was the problem. "I'll tell you what," I continued. "Let me ask Steve to join the meeting, just so we are both clear what you are saying."

"No!" Doug said. "No, I'm not comfortable with that."

"Well, Doug, what concerns me is that what I am hearing from you and what I heard from Steve is completely inconsistent. Don't you think it is critical that we get to the bottom of this?"

Doug begged me not to bring Steve in. He admitted that perhaps he'd not been clear with Steve about the real reason for his concerns. He told me that he wanted time to think about what to do. I agreed and told him that we'd speak the next day.

After the meeting, I spoke with Steve, and we agreed that, if Doug threatened again to resign, we'd immediately accept his resignation. As it turned out, Doug called Steve and resigned that very evening, and Steve and I both felt it was the best outcome for everyone.

While this story illustrates that there was some friction in instilling a new culture of hard work, discipline, and vision, it also illustrates another critical point: that low performers will not like it when you create a culture that appeals to top performers. I address this in more depth in the coming pages.

Friction notwithstanding, things were going beautifully well. I had spent only a few months as Chipotle's president and chief operating officer, but by late 2005, Steve started to tell me that I should replace him as the CEO. "You're better at this than me," he would often say.

But I have a lot of experience reading body language, and I could tell that while his words were flattering, he was feeling conflicted, maybe even threatened. I quickly set to work complimenting Steve and trying to build him back up, to make him feel good again. I reacted much more strongly to his disapproving eyes than I did to the complimentary words that accompanied them. I was so grateful to Steve for seeing and valuing my skills as a leader that I felt I owed him. I felt I owed him my loyalty. I felt I needed to make him feel good about himself.

I had so much to accomplish and a full wind in my sails. I shared my new thoughts and ideas with Steve constantly, and I could tell he was swept up in my excitement. He was so happy and grateful for my work, and he would boast about my great ideas and brilliant curiosity during board meetings. I beamed as he told others, as well as my fellow executives, how "Monty has discovered this," or "Monty has figured this out." I felt fulfilled, loved, and valued, and that all my hard work was being recognized and appreciated. This was made all the sweeter by the fact that Steve was, like my own father, extremely hard to please, but when he approved of me and recognized my talent, I felt my deep insecurity and self-doubt fade. I felt, for a moment, at peace.

But beyond pleasing Steve and the board, my work in those first few months quickly began to pay off in other ways.

When I first started at Chipotle in March 2005, our same store sales increases were at 5 percent. In other words, the sales of all of our stores that had been open for at least twelve months were 5 percent higher than they were the previous year. While that is a good number, I was not satisfied. I believed our sales could be growing much faster if we were operating our restaurants like I knew we could. Six months after we instituted our throughput effort and new cultural changes, same store sales jumped over 14 percent for the last quarter of the year, which was strong evidence that our new direction was paying off. Same store sales comparisons (also known as comp sales) are probably the most important indicator used by analysts to evaluate the strength of a restaurant company's leadership. Most companies are delighted when their comps are even a single percentage point positive. Numbers in the double digits are extremely rare in larger companies. So when our comp sales leaped into the double digits, it was a big deal. But at the same time, our costs began to decrease, which boosted our restaurant margins and our profits.

Our throughput sped up rapidly, which increased sales. Our crews got better, cooked tastier food, and delivered better service. Our employee satisfaction got better, and we lost fewer crew members and managers—turnover among managers dropped 12 percent in a year. We went back to hand-cutting our ingredients, which made them taste much better than when we used a machine, and we committed to using superior ingredients: naturally raised chicken, beef, and pork, more organic produce, whole-head Romaine lettuce instead of pre-cut, brown rice, and fresh-squeezed citrus. I pushed for the food to be like it was when Steve cooked it himself at the first Chipotle, and these efforts paid off with better tasting food. Our internal promotions (the number of crew people who were being promoted to manager positions)—a big initiative—nearly doubled in a single year. And, on the technology side, we launched our first digital ordering system—a huge innovation. Remember, this was 2005, two years before the iPhone was invented!

As another way to increase throughput, I directed that we add a second *make line* in every Chipotle, which would allow us to avoid slowing down our main production line when a customer ordered food by phone, fax, or via our online ordering platform. The second make line was absolutely critical to our ability to service our online orders, which grew to an incredible 2,000,000 orders by 2008. That was before our iPhone app, which came in August of 2009, only one year after the launch of the app store in July of 2008. Chipotle was one of the first companies to let you pay for your meal directly on the iPhone app.

Meanwhile, Wall Street became very interested in us. The time was ripe for our company to take the enormous step of becoming a publicly traded company.

An early version of the Chipotle App, released August 2009, was touted as groundbreaking. This, along with building a second make line in each location, caused Chipotle to be well ahead of the competition in the rush to prepare for online ordering.

# CHAPTER 7

# PRIORITIES

IN THE EXCITEMENT AND ANXIETY OF ACCEPTING A NEW job or leadership role, our desire to differentiate ourselves and make an immediate difference is a wonderful instinct. But it may cause us to become disorganized or overwhelmed. We may find ourselves jumping right in and working on whatever first confronts us. We reason (as I often have) that if we just work hard enough, we can do it all, and that we'll have time to fix anything and everything that needs improvement. As one person, though, we cannot personally clean every restaurant, check the taste of all the food, or make sure that every customer interaction is a good one. In my new position, I realized, even more dramatically than I had at the law firm, that I had to leverage my team. But also, I needed to focus on those things that would have the most profoundly positive impact on the business.

I pondered this question: "What can I, as one person, do that will change all 400 of our restaurants to make them lastingly better?"

I also asked myself: "What is one action I can take that will simultaneously improve all of these detailed observations I am making, all at once?"

I came up with the most important priority. I decided that if I could ensure that we had a great general manager in each of our restaurants, that would cause all of our operational details (like throughput, cleanliness, and great tasting food) to improve. After all, great general managers would hire great people, train them well, run a great operation, and have a clean place with delicious food and great service. They would basically take care of every detail.

So to answer my question about "the one thing," I set my focus on the general manager position. I asked myself how we could attract a better pool of applicants for this position, select the very best, train them to perform excellent work, retain them in their restaurants, and create a system of rewards that would bring out the very best in each of them such that they would run terrific restaurants. I could not imagine any other priority that was as important as this one.

This single priority—having great general managers—governed the majority of my actions from then on. Among the early actions I took, I:

- Acknowledged publicly, and to all of our leadership team, that the general manager was the most important position in the company.
- Created the Restaurateur Program, which I describe in detail in chapter 8, to ensure our best GMs were acknowledged, rewarded, and empowered to build great teams.
- Made sure it was clearly understood what the Restaurateur position entailed and what it took to earn it.
- Made sure we had appropriate financial rewards for our best GMs.

- Made sure we hired GMs from within, since this attracted stronger candidates, and data showed that our GMs who came from within were much better and less likely to quit.
- Made sure we gave our GMs the best tools with which to do their jobs.
- Listened to the feedback of our GMs and made sure that we were acting on that feedback.
- Ensured that the corporate office staff was aware that their primary responsibility was to take care of our GMs, and to give them the tools, data, and support they urgently needed to do their jobs well.
- Publicly sang the praises of the best GMs, and celebrated their success throughout the company, so that everyone knew what we were looking for and could strive to achieve it themselves.
- Created an excellent field leadership system to support our managers and our restaurant operations.
- Scrutinized every facet of our restaurant operation to improve food quality, taste, safety, and every aspect of the customer experience.
- Revamped our training systems and tools to make sure that our people were confident in their ability to do great work.

When I first joined Chipotle, things were very different. There were really no operational priorities that the whole company was focused on. Rather, there were a few dozen field leaders who oversaw multiple restaurants, who were largely left on their own to keep their food and labor costs near certain targets that were set for them by corporate. The problem was they were all focused on different things. There were no clear standards for how all of our restaurants were to be run. Senior leadership was not effectively leading the teams in the field. Even the financial targets, such as food and labor costs, were not good ones. The targets were set based on what poorly trained teams were accomplishing, rather than being set on what was possible with a well-trained, strong manager and team.

As employees would transfer from one restaurant to another, as they very often did, they would be saying, "Oh, we don't do it this way in Dallas." This led to wide-scale conflict and disorganization in our operations. It was a mess. It led to regional differences, politics, and infighting among people around the company. It set people on a course to prove that their way was right, rather than trying to do what was actually the most effective thing for the business. It was divisive and disempowered our teams.

By focusing the whole company on the most important things—hiring the best from within; having great GMs who run great operations; having clear operational goals and standards; and building a great culture of empowered top performers, we brought consistency, and we started to see what was possible.

Our very best stores set the example and taught the rest of our teams how to be excellent. A natural, fun competition emerged as each team tried to deliver the fastest throughput in the company. As a result, our customer service scores improved dramatically. As I mentioned previously, where most of the positive email comments we received had been about food, we started to see more and more about our great service. Soon, the most common positive comments were about service. Simultaneously, our food was much better, because better teams make better food, and when throughput is fast, our food is fresher, cooked more often, and hotter. Every aspect of our business improved. It was also fun!

During analyst calls in later years, we were often asked about what changes we were working on. Will we add new menu items? A loyalty program? A dessert? Perhaps drive-through stores? Will we franchise?

For a decade, I realized that none of those things, even if successful, would be nearly as effective in improving the customer experience, sales, margins, and profits, as focusing on having better general managers, and the resulting better operations. These better general managers would hire better people, train them better, empower them, retain them, improve throughput, serve better food, and improve every aspect of the dining experience upon which all of our success depended.

## THE ROAD TO GOING PUBLIC

Even as I was focusing on developing my key priorities inside the company during my first few months, my attention also was being drawn to the task of taking Chipotle public. One reason I'd agreed to come aboard was that McDonald's was preparing to do just this. McDonald's would be selling their shares, resulting in Chipotle being an independent company. In my new role, I was thrown into the middle of those preparations.

Public companies are those that are traded on a public stock exchange, such as the New York Stock Exchange (NYSE), and this allows the stock to be readily bought and sold by any investor. We began to undertake the work of getting ready for our company to be listed on the NYSE, such that we could undergo our initial public offering (IPO). An IPO is the process by which a company becomes public, and it involved our management team (Steve, our CFO Jack Hartung, and me), traveling extensively throughout the country to meet with potential investors to gauge their interest in buying our new stock. The process of traveling to these many meetings is called a road show, and ours was a very exciting time for all of us.

While our company staff undertook the enormous effort of performing the immensely complex work to comply with government regulations for public companies, our management team began to prepare a presentation to help educate the large investment firms about Chipotle Mexican Grill, to help them evaluate their level of interest in becoming shareholders.

The road show was an incredible adventure. It was led by two separate investment banks, Morgan Stanley, and SG Cowen, each of whom stood to split a commission of approximately $7 million for their work in taking us public. Part of their job was to set up meetings throughout the country, as many as twelve in a day, with investors. It was an exhausting but exciting process, and the investment banks spared no expense taking care of us as a team, and making sure that we made it to as many meetings as possible. They put us on a chartered private jet, with our own flight attendant making delicious meals for us in flight. We went to many states in a single day and wound up having elaborate dinners until late at night with the bankers, followed by collapsing in the most absurdly luxurious hotel rooms the banks could find. There was even a Morgan Stanley employee whose sole job was to go ahead of us on a different airplane to inspect our hotel rooms and get us checked in so that we wouldn't be troubled by having to wait for a room key upon our arrival.

The dinners were outstanding, and since each bank hosted dinners on alternating nights, they seemed to compete to see which could treat us to a more elaborate experience, with outstanding wine and food. While it felt like the life of a rock star, it did get exhausting. On one night, I even complained to Steve how all I really wanted was to go up to the room, eat a hot dog, and rent a movie. Steve was shocked and offended at the notion of me wanting to skip another enormous feast. He was *actually* mad at me, and so I quickly dropped the idea, and reluctantly joined for yet another spectacular meal.

During this whole time, Steve and Jack and I got along very well. Our relationship felt so close. We laughed, joked, teased each other, and had a lot of fun, even as we worked tirelessly to represent our company excellently to the prospective investors. On other occasions, I saw flashes of conflict.

One day in early 2006, while we were flying, I showed Steve a new organizational chart I had devised for our leadership team. I had worked hard on it, and was excited that this new direction would be great for our company. I asked Steve if he'd take a look. He paused his work on his *New York Times* crossword puzzle and said, in a warm tone, "Sure!" But as Steve looked at it, his face dropped in what looked to me to be disappointment and frustration. My heart sank, and I felt butterflies in my stomach. "This is great work," he said, "and *this is CEO work!*"

While Steve's words were clearly complimentary, his tone was not. He sounded immensely frustrated and even offended. This left me deeply confused.

"Don't you want me to do my best work?" I replied.

"Yes, but I'm the CEO! It makes me feel useless when you are the one having these ideas! It makes me wonder why the hell I'm even working here anymore!"

His tone was angry, and I felt threatened. Nonetheless, my instinct was to try to rescue him from his negative feelings. To again reassure him that he was smart, valuable, and wanted. So I quickly shifted into that same mode I used on my father to earn his admiration, and calmed and reassured Steve that both of us brought different strengths to the table, and that there was no need to believe that my good work in some way diminished him. I desperately wanted him to feel good again. As Steve and I settled into our relationship over the years, I came to understand that he both valued me and was threatened by me, and I would have to navigate that in order to lead the company. But, on this occasion and always, when he calmed down, he assured me that he did not want me to do anything differently, that these insecurities were his problem to solve.

While I appreciated him saying this, I still remained a bit nervous about doing my best work, for fear that he'd feel threatened by it. This was a challenge I had to work constantly to overcome during my years as co-CEO, because these feelings were very disempowering to me.

During the road show, there were no such conflicts. We were all floating on a cloud, as analysts and investors kept telling us that we were the strongest management team in the industry. We were warmed by this, and we all felt so proud to be part of such great success. It felt like the garden of our lives was in full bloom on a perfect spring day. Every day brought more good news, statistics bearing out the brilliance of our new strategies, higher sales, better profits, improvement on literally everything we could measure. These were golden years for all of us, and we were all grateful.

When the IPO was finally upon us in January of 2006, we traveled to New York City, and went to the floor of the New York Stock Exchange to watch as Chipotle became a publicly-traded company. We all stood together on a stage overlooking the trading floor, with TV cameras upon us, and rang the bell to set the day in motion.

Chipotle pre-IPO stock had been sold at $22.00 per share to the investors we'd met with on the road show. But when we rang the bell and trading began, trading of our stock was delayed for over an hour, because no one would sell their IPO shares for this price. In fact, the very first Chipotle share ever traded on the NYSE traded at $44.00, an increase of 100 percent! That meant that instantly, in one second, every one of our investors doubled their money.

Monty, Steve, and members of the Chipotle team celebrating the listing of Chipotle on the New York Stock Exchange, New York City, 2006

Looking back on these days is surreal. In retrospect, it seems everything rolled out so quickly and naturally that it appeared almost effortless, even though I was working all day, every day, to do all I could to make Chipotle the greatest restaurant concept in the world. That September, Steve told me that he was leaving Chipotle "in your hands." He moved from Denver (where Chipotle was headquartered) to begin a new life in New York City.

Throughout 2006 and 2007, Steve often told me that he felt I should take over as CEO. He was spending little time in Denver, and it seemed he very much enjoyed his life in New York and the freshness of his newfound freedom. To reduce his travel to Denver even more, we occasionally held board meetings in New York. At one such board meeting in Steve's home in the West

Village in December of 2007, Steve suggested to the board that it was time for him to step down to an executive chairman role and hand the CEO title to me. The board agreed so enthusiastically that I was concerned Steve might be offended. Nonetheless, everyone congratulated me on what they saw as a well-deserved promotion. We were to announce my new title in three months by a press release, right after the next board meeting.

To my disappointment, just before that change was to formally take place, Steve got cold feet. Apparently, a friend of his told him he'd have to "answer to Monty" and, as he reflected, this made him nervous. So, just before the March 2008 board meeting, he asked me if I'd be willing to be his co-CEO, instead of CEO.

If I'd known then what I came to know later, I would have agreed to this arrangement. But at the time, I just thought Steve needed a little more time to feel comfortable adjusting to the thought of stepping down. I declined his invitation to share the title, instead telling him I'd wait until he felt good about making the promotion. But soon, I concluded that Steve had no need to ever give up the title. The company was doing so well that there was no scrutiny as to his level of involvement, so no one challenged him.

About a year later, when Steve apologetically asked me again if I would like to be his co-CEO, I decided I'd be a fool to say no again. The reality was that the promotion would literally double my compensation, and yet would not change my role or responsibilities at all. Not even a little. I'd already been acting in the CEO role since the day I began, and that never changed during my dozen years at Chipotle.

I tried not to let the disappointment get to me, and just focused on making Chipotle the best company it could be.

# CHAPTER 8

# THE RESTAURATEUR PROGRAM

THE RESTAURATEUR PROGRAM WAS FOUNDATIONAL TO Chipotle's spectacular success, and the idea for it hatched during my MIT training in April of 2005. It grew out of my unflinching belief that the general manager was the most important position at Chipotle, and my knowledge that if every GM was a great leader, we would have profound success on every critical operational standard and financial metric.

Chipotle's general managers had a huge amount of power over the restaurant experience. They were responsible for hiring the crew, training them, setting the standards for cleanliness and food quality, and setting the tone for customer service. Also, the positive and negative characteristics of the manager were readily apparent in the mood of the crew members—their degree of happiness, vitality, *esprit de corps*, and desire to work hard. If there was a strong leader in the general manager role, everything in the restaurant would go well. They'd hire great crew members and take care of them, cook delicious food, keep the place spotlessly clean, give great customer service, and take great care of the restaurant.

Since the GM was the most important person, GMs became our top priority. We needed to ensure that we had the right GM in every restaurant and then set them up for maximum success. But how? We'd have to promote the best candidates into the role, and then train them how to build excellent teams, and run great restaurants. Next, we'd have to reward them well. Finally, we'd have to make sure that the position was a prestigious one, not just a stepping stone to the ineffective area manager position, but rather a prestigious and valued position in its own right.

I decided that the best way to accomplish this was to create a new position—one that everyone would aspire to achieve. A prestigious position with a new title that would be awarded only to our general managers who built extraordinary teams, and empowered them to achieve excellent restaurant standards. I settled on the name "Restaurateur." This name had a prestigious ring to it and sounded like something excellent, and worth working for.

As another way to ensure the prestige of the Restaurateur position, I suggested what was initially thought of as an outrageous idea. Each person selected for this position would be interviewed and promoted only by me or by Steve. After all, if the position was the most important in the company, shouldn't it be hand-selected by the top leaders?

As a final way to secure the prestige of this new position, we explained that this position would be a prerequisite to future executive leadership positions at the company. If you wanted to rise up at Chipotle, you must first master your leadership skills in the restaurant by becoming a Restaurateur!

## HOW WE STARTED THE RESTAURATEUR PROGRAM

Even though the Restaurateur program spelled a massive change in direction for our company, it was unusual in one very important way. Unlike almost any other major company initiative, this one cost almost nothing to roll out, and carried virtually no risk! All we had to do was announce it, explain it, and start the process of training our leaders how to identify the kind of excellent leadership we were looking for. There was no downside since the leaders needed this training anyway. Despite costing nothing to roll out, the potential savings were enormous. Our ineffective MIT program cost millions of dollars a year. Specifically, in 2006, each MIT candidate cost Chipotle $5,750 for air travel and salary for their six weeks of training. Additionally, each of our senior restaurant managers who were training the MITs trained ten MITs per year, and their salaries were $70,000, meaning their time cost Chipotle $7,000 per MIT trainee. When you added in the salaries for our field recruiters (we had eight making $70,000 a year and would need none of them if the Restaurateur program worked), advertising costs to find the MIT candidates, job fair costs, and other costs associated with hiring and onboarding these trainees, the cost just to hire and train each MIT was over $25,000 per person. And in 2006, we had 450 of them! That is $11,250,000 per year!

Conversely, we calculated the cost to train someone from within to be $2,100. When you consider the potential power of getting much better managers for less than a tenth the cost, with 75 percent lower turnover and a much better message for our crew ("you guys are our future managers"), the potential impact of this program was astounding. But it was even more of a home run when one considered the high costs of the poor operations and lousy customer experience caused by constantly losing managers and hiring new ones, the huge increase in crew turnover caused by high manager turnover (crew leave when they come to like a manager and then that manager leaves), or the distraction to our area managers who had to scramble around to patch holes in our teams. In short, the Restaurateur program solved dozens of critical problems, while causing almost none.

We launched the program in late 2005 and began interviewing candidates. The way we chose the first several Restaurateurs was, upon reflection, a bit silly. We asked area managers and team directors to recommend candidates, and we flew them back to Denver to interview them. We picked our first eight to ten Restaurateurs this way, but it was ineffective because without visiting the restaurant and meeting the crew, it wasn't possible to evaluate the type of culture a manager created. Additionally, our field leadership at the time still didn't understand what constituted an excellent restaurant culture, or how to go about creating one. This concept was totally new, and it would take time before I was able to effectively teach the concept to our hundreds of field leaders, and thousands of managers and crew throughout the country.

I quickly decided we'd interview all future candidates in their restaurants. I knew that these travels would take a great deal of my time, but I concluded that the effort would pay off. It would allow me to evaluate our managers and the field leaders that the managers reported to, as well as the executives who oversaw them. I would become intimately familiar with the state of our restaurant operations nationwide. It would also allow me to teach my vision directly to our leaders throughout the country. Quickly, the wisdom of this plan became obvious.

Restaurateur candidates were first nominated by their area managers. Once nominated, I visited Restaurateur candidates in their restaurants throughout the United States—and eventually in Canada, England, France, and Germany, too, when we came to have stores there. These visits were unannounced, which meant that sometimes the general manager whom we were there to interview was not present. But this wasn't a problem. We could tell whether the manager had earned the promotion to Restaurateur by interviewing the entire crew in the restaurant, and ascertaining whether they were all top performers, empowered to achieve high standards. In some ways, we even got a better idea if the manager was absent, since a well-led team will perform extremely well in the absence of the manager. We were specifically *not* looking for managers who could get the team to perform well only while the manager was in the restaurant. Instead, we were looking for leaders who could create a sustainably great experience by empowering a team of top performers to consistently be at their very best.

Over the years, I was able to more crisply define the Restaurateur position and how one could most efficiently achieve it. But in 2005, at the outset of the program, I came up with this one-page definition of The Chipotle Restaurateur that we distributed throughout the company.

This one-page summary stood the test of time and remains a very good description of the culture our best managers were able to create. But in time, I decided to write a very brief definition of Restaurateur, so that we'd have a shorthand way to refer to what it took to be promoted to this elite position.

That definition was:

*A Restaurateur is a manager who creates a team of Top Performers, Empowered to achieve High Standards.*

# THE CHIPOTLE RESTAURATEUR

**First Impressions.** Within seconds of walking in, a Restaurateur restaurant will capture our attention. The music is at the right level, the dining room is perfectly clean, the temperature is right, and friendly, positive energy emanates from the crew.

**The Crew.** The crew in a Restaurateur restaurant is empowered, and has a sense of ownership. They feel a deep sense of pride about themselves, the food and service they provide, and the cleanliness of the restaurant. Their manager regularly sits down with each of them, and has one-on-one conversations with them. They have a development journal with specific and meaningful entries, demonstrating our commitment to their development. There is a sense of camaraderie and cooperation: a team spirit. No one on the crew is working solely for a paycheck. The crew is inspired by the vision of having a team of top performers, empowered to achieve high standards, and they are aware that the result of such a culture is an extraordinary dining experience and an extraordinary customer experience.

**The Kitchen.** The kitchen is impeccably clean and all of the equipment is working well and properly calibrated. The team is mindful in their preparation of food to be certain it is delicious, the team avoids waste, and demonstrates respect for our high-quality ingredients from the moment they are delivered through the time they are served. All cleaning and food handling procedures are well understood and adhered to.

**Overall Restaurant Cleanliness.** The whole restaurant, including the dining room, drink station, restroom, kitchen, walk-in and back office, is extremely organized and clean. The whole facility is in good shape with no signs of neglect or abuse.

**The Food and Front Line.** The crew understands that to cook Chipotle food correctly, they must focus on all of the details. The food on the line looks perfect: fresh, hot, colorful. The team frequently tastes the food to ensure it is delicious. Everything is spotlessly clean, and the team is attentive and ready, and is at ease interacting and communicating with customers.

**Hospitality.** The team is welcoming and hospitable toward their customers. They treasure them and enjoy them, as they would guests in their own home. They greet them warmly, and show their gratitude to them.

**The Business.** The manager and team have an entrepreneurial spirit and work hard to increase sales in their restaurant. They write great schedules, maintain the labor matrix, deploy their people effectively, and have excellent food cost numbers and cash handling. They know what it takes to run a profitable restaurant, and they know how to use their financial tools to understand their restaurant's performance. They achieve financial success by providing a great dining experience, but also through getting involved with their communities by doing fundraisers, hosted lunches, and donations.

**Vision.** Our Restaurateur teams have achieved their vision of having a team of top performers, empowered to achieve high standards. It is our vision that one day all of our managers will be Restaurateurs. We know that the customer experience in every Chipotle restaurant will be elevated as we push towards this goal and that, as the customer experience is elevated, the success of our company will follow.

After creating this concise definition, I defined the key terms used in that definition as well:

- A **Top Performer** is someone who has the desire and ability to perform excellent work, and through their constant effort to do so, elevates themselves, the people around them, and Chipotle.
- **Empowerment** means feeling confident in your ability and encouraged by your circumstances, such that you feel motivated and at liberty to fully devote your talents to a purpose.
- **High Standards** means creating an excellent restaurant experience for each one of our guests and crew.

These definitions became extremely important to creating the culture which led to Chipotle's outstanding business results, as I will explain in great detail in the coming chapters.

During my travels, I wrote emails to the whole company sharing what I was doing, what I was learning, and what I thought we should do differently. I'll share one such email, which I believe effectively summarizes the essence of the Restaurateur program.

## LEADERSHIP AND THE PATH TAKEN (EMAIL TO FIELD, SUNDAY, MAY 7, 2012)

*Hello, Everyone:*

*The other day, on a beautiful spring morning, I went jogging on a dirt path that led me out to the plains that sit just below the mountains in Boulder, Colorado. Cool air awakened me, and the golden morning sun was intense in color, but gentle on my eyes. The path took me past rabbits and birds, wildflowers, and prairie dogs. It was a magical time, and it made me wonder why I did not do this every morning!*

*As I ran, I thought about how none of this would have happened without this path. I mean, I certainly could have gotten out on the plains without the path, but I wouldn't have. I could have stumbled over the bumpy ground, stepped over yucca plants, and found my own way. But the bottom line is that the reason I was having a great experience this morning was because someone created this wonderful path. The path helped me to know that it was OK for me to go out there. It suggested the route that I took. And it made the running easy, so that I could enjoy the incredible scenery.*

*It got me thinking about how important paths are. They almost never take us somewhere we could not have gone, but yet they so often take us somewhere we would not have gone. They give us confidence, showing us that others have made the journey before us.*

*When you get to the trailhead, there is usually a sign, and it gives you an idea what to expect. It says what's at the end of the path, how far it is, how steep it is, what sights might be seen, and what to look out for. It might even warn you to take an extra bottle of water, or to wear good shoes. But at the end of the day, it is really up to you where you go, what you see, whether you make it the distance, and whether you enjoy yourself. The sign simply does what it can to equip you for success, and the path allows you to make the journey a bit more smoothly. But neither the sign, nor the path, takes you anywhere that you cannot go yourself.*

*It occurred to me that there was a lesson here about leadership. In essence, great leaders are guides. They take us to a trailhead, and they suggest a path for us. They don't shove us down it, nor do they carry us. But they give us a vision of why it is worth taking those first steps. They get us excited about what we might experience along the way. They give us confidence that we can make the journey. They suggest good shoes, and the right kind of equipment that will make our journey easier. But we have to have an interest in making the journey, or the leader's efforts will be wasted.*

*This is why our Restaurateurs are so successful. They assemble a team of ambitious people, who have the desire and ability to make a journey, and they provide them with a vision. They tell their people what the path is like, what they'll encounter along the way, and why the journey is exciting and worth the effort. They tell stories of others who have made the journey, and how wonderful it was. They walk alongside their teams, and give them the tools and encouragement to keep walking. They celebrate milestones, and rejoice in the success of their people. They commit to make the journey with their people, and by doing so, maximize the chance of their team arriving somewhere very special together.*

*I want to encourage all of our managers and field leaders to consider these things. Is your team full of people eager and able to make the journey? (Do they have the desire and ability, and are they willing to put forth the effort?) If so, have you shown them the path, what to expect along the way, and where it can lead them? (Do they have a vision for what it will be like to be part of a Restaurateur culture?) Do they have the tools they will need to make the journey? (Do they have the knowledge about our high standards, and do they have the right tools to make great food and give great service?)*

*As leaders in this company, we can provide a path and guidance to allow many wonderful people to make a journey that they would not have otherwise made: a journey that will change their lives. By showing these people the way, you will achieve something truly special for yourself, your team, and for Chipotle.*

*Thank you, and I hope you all enjoy the journey!*

*Monty*

My presence in the field, as well as messages like the one above, led our leaders to quickly see that our restaurant teams and operations were my primary focus. For this reason, they redoubled their focus on their restaurants, which was an excellent result.

This latter point illustrates a critical lesson for all leaders. It is essential that a leader understands that everyone is watching how you spend your time, and they will conclude that whatever you spend your time on is what is most important to the organization. Where a top leader places attention, the rest of the company will place their efforts. If leaders spend all their time crunching numbers, those reporting to them will do the same. For example, my predecessor at Chipotle was always talking about sales. As a result, that is what the area managers, team directors, and regional directors were focused on when I took over. The problem was that talking about sales is not inspiring. It does not cause people to do the things that lead to better sales. However, when a leader spends time focusing on people and great operations, their teams will focus their efforts on improving these critical aspects of the business.

Merely by making great teams my primary focus, I was injecting new enthusiasm into creating better food and service at Chipotle. The result, as you might guess, was that sales, margins, and profits soared, as did our stock price. After increasing 100 percent on our first day of trading as a public company in January 2006, it was 200 percent over the IPO price by May 2007, 300 percent by August 2007, 400 percent by September 2007, and 500 percent by November of that same year! But that wasn't the end. After the great recession of 2009, Chipotle's stock kept shooting skyward and stood at an incredible 3,400 percent over its IPO price by August of 2015! This 500 percent increase in twenty-two months and 3,400 percent increase in nine years was driven by the enormous rise in our sales, which soared from $672 million in the year ended March 31, 2006, just after we went public to $1.575 billion in 2010, to $4.574 billion in 2015.

In a few short years, our company was enjoying meteoric success, and it didn't come by talking about sales! It came from focusing on the behaviors that lead to great sales, specifically creating empowered teams, since empowered teams cook better food, give better service, and do all of this more efficiently.

My travels around the country allowed me to meet thousands of our crew and managers, and learn directly what working in a

Chipotle restaurant was really like. I learned why they came to us, why some left, what was great, what wasn't, what motivated them, what made them feel empowered, and what kind of leaders were most effective. It allowed me to get to know and relate to our field leadership—area managers, team directors, and regional directors. The relationships I formed with them taught me a great deal, and I learned which leaders were most effective.

I saw hundreds of different restaurants: how they prepared vegetables, cleaned their restaurants, treated their equipment, wrote schedules, managed labor, and hundreds of other data points that were critical to running a great business. I got to see what worked best and what was ineffective. I taught the best techniques to everyone, and I put a stop to the ineffective stuff.

My credibility as a leader skyrocketed. I had an incredibly broad and deep knowledge of what was going on throughout the company. The regional directors knew it, my fellow officers knew it, the managers and crew knew it. Even the Wall Street analysts knew it. Chipotle and I were featured in numerous magazine profiles, which touted our culture and way of managing people as "brilliant." All of this gave me more confidence to make sweeping changes that would help us build an even stronger culture and company.

## GREAT CULTURE, GREAT RESULTS

Getting our field leaders to understand the difference between a good manager and a leader was difficult. It was inconsistent with what they'd been taught before. Once, prior to joining the company, I attended a leadership meeting at which Steve told the team that "In the best Chipotle restaurants, you can always tell right away who the general manager is." I completely disagreed, although at that time, I did so silently. Now that I was leading the company, what I was proposing to cultivate and reward by creating the Restaurateur program was exactly the opposite. What Steve had described was a good manager, not a good leader. What I wanted was a restaurant experience that was so good that it would be impossible to tell who the GM was, because the whole team was terrific, talented, excited, and acting with a sense of ownership.

People started to do more of what worked and less of what didn't. Our restaurants flourished.

When I started working as general counsel for Chipotle in 1997, we had a dozen restaurants with annual unit volumes (gross sales per store) of around $800,000, with nearly no profit. By 2015, when the Restaurateur program became well established, we had over 2,000 restaurants with average sales of over $2.4 million per store, and enormous profits. Our restaurant level margins became the highest in the industry, hitting an incredible 30 percent, and our average restaurant had a cash on cash return of over 100 percent. This means that our average restaurant was contributing cash to the company of around $800,000 a year. Amazingly, this meant that each Chipotle restaurant, on average, earned back more than the entire cost to build it, each and every year it was open. By this time, Chipotle had sales of about $4.5 billion per year and was serving more than 1.5 million customers every single day.

It wasn't all smooth sailing, though. Like many companies, we hit a big bump in the 2008 financial crisis—at least our stock price did. Our stock, which had already traded up to $148 a share, fell to a low of $38 per share in 2009. But the reality was, our company fundamentals were extremely strong (despite a reduction in consumer spending, we never had negative same store sales growth, even as nearly all other restaurant companies struggled) so I wasn't concerned. Nonetheless, since others were concerned, I chose to use this time as a way to get even better. I didn't want this crisis to go to waste!

As I was reviewing industry data in the midst of this 2008 recession, something caught my eye. I noticed that our competitor, QDOBA, had average annual sales volumes (usually called AUVs, meaning Average Unit Volumes) per restaurant of about $1,000,000, whereas we had AUVs of approximately $1,700,000. But QDOBA was happy with these volumes, and could make a decent profit from these restaurants, whereas in the few Chipotle stores where we had volumes as low as QDOBA's average store, we were barely breaking even. Why could our competitor make money at low volumes, but we couldn't? I decided to investigate. Some of the difference was that we were buying better (more expensive) ingredients. Another difference was that we had more people working in our stores, which created better customer service, but did cost more in labor. We also spent a bit more to build our stores. But overall, I still believed we should be able to make a good profit on lower volume stores.

If we could only be profitable at very high AUVs, that meant that the number of stores we could build would be severely limited. However, if we could demonstrate that we could also build less expensive stores that could be profitable at lower volumes, we could dramatically increase the number of stores across the country. This would allow us not only to better achieve our vision of changing food culture, but it would make our company much more valuable, and our share price much higher. I decided we needed to pursue this strategy immediately, and I felt that a recession was the perfect time to unleash it!

This new strategy was not going to interfere with the strategy we already had in place for building new stores. It was going to be a new, incremental way of adding value to our company. I called the strategy our A Model strategy. First, we would find real estate sites that were less expensive to rent (thereby lowering our occupancy costs), and then we would spend less money to build them (thereby lowering our construction costs). Then, we'd staff them with one less manager, and take other measures to lower our operating costs. This combination would allow us to derive a favorable profit margin even if we had lower sales.

The results were terrific. These stores dramatically exceeded our expectations, had much higher sales than expected, huge profit margins, and allowed us to credibly forecast a much larger number of Chipotle restaurants in the future. When these began to roll out over the next several years, our stock price exploded upward, reaching $758 in 2015, and we learned lessons about how to build all of our stores more economically and intelligently, so that our whole company became much stronger. It was another home run!

## THE RESTAURATEUR INTERVIEW

Our CFO, Jack Hartung, often boasted to our analysts that our Restaurateur program was what allowed Chipotle to retain these powerful financial returns for our shareholders, instead of having to franchise our stores to owner-operators like nearly all of our competitors found necessary. So, with the whole company strongly believing that this culture was critical to our success, I continued to invest as much time as I could in making sure it was pervasive throughout Chipotle. The power of having the officers completely buy into building this culture in our company was extraordinary.

Field leaders were eager to get interviews set up for managers they felt were ready. The resulting Restaurateur interview would last around three hours with the GMs and their teams in the restaurant, but I could tell in an instant what the answer was. If it was a Restaurateur restaurant, the place would feel alive, filled with optimism, joy, excitement, and a camaraderie that felt full, fresh, and inclusive. But still, I'd spend hours talking to each and every crew member, in order to teach the people who accompanied me how to interview our employees, while simultaneously making sure the team was all empowered top performers, and that the operation was excellent.

Walking towards a store to perform a Restaurateur interview, I'd usually be spotted by members of the team from inside the restaurant, and I'd hear screams of excitement well before I reached the front door. Walking in, I'd see nothing but beautiful smiling faces and tears of excitement, as the whole team greeted me with hugs and shrieks. Right away, they'd pull me by the arm back into the kitchen to show off their restaurant, which they were so proud of. Excitedly they showed me around, introduced me to the team, and proudly pointed out how excellent their restaurant was.

The whole team took such ownership of the store that I was often deeply into a tour before I even realized who the GM was. As I'd turn to greet individual team members, they'd often burst into tears of gratitude as they explained what their team meant to them, how they "loved this place." They'd share how it had changed their lives and what the Restaurateur culture meant to them, their team, and even their families at home. When I'd sit down with each of them, they'd tell me how they used Restaurateur principles in their family to raise happier, more fulfilled children and even to improve their marriages. They thanked me for believing in them, caring for them, and for creating a culture that brought out their best.

If the interview was successful, the GM was promoted to Restaurateur on the spot, and the whole team would just explode. Everyone would erupt in tears of joy and gratitude for each other and what they had accomplished. People routinely told me that becoming a Restaurateur team was the most significant and important accomplishment of their lives. And while the person actually promoted was the GM, you would never know that from the celebration which immediately followed. You would've thought every one of them had been promoted. They were all crying, running around, and hugging each other, thrusting their hands in the air in celebration, and emitting screams of victory. They would hug tightly and give thanks to each other in loud whispers as they embraced, for helping them get to this unique and magical moment in their lives. These moments were so special that my words simply can't do them justice. People felt the overwhelming emotional culmination of so much hard work and so much gratitude for each other, their leaders, and everyone on the team who owned this accomplishment. It was a validation for each of them as being an indispensable part of a beautiful whole. Instant validation of a victory and success that already existed before I even walked in the door.

The celebration did not stop at the team. Customers would often approach saying how they knew this team was special, and that they clearly deserved whatever promotion they had just received. Many asked questions and were pleased when I took the time to explain the Restaurateur program to them. "I knew there was something special about how you treated your people," they'd say.

I was proud to hear that the culture was experienced so positively by our customers, who, after all, were the final judge and jury of how well we were doing things at Chipotle! The customers would go on and on, telling me about how much they loved the team, naming certain crew by name, bragging about the restaurant experience, and the awesome service and food. They'd boast to me about how many times they came to eat, but also about how many friends they'd introduced to Chipotle. The sense of ownership that these customers had was amazing. They really felt that it was "their Chipotle." Because the teams were so happy and inclusive and cared about their guests, customers often felt like part of an extended family. Analysts and reporters also began to take notice of our special culture, which soon became the subject of many articles. A large number of reporters and thought leaders began to interview me to learn more about this unique culture that we were building.

Monty was invited many places to speak about how Chipotle empowered its employees. Left, with Bill Clinton, Denver, Colorado, 2014. Right, with His Holiness the 14th Dalai Lama, Tenzin Gyatso, Washington, D.C., 2015.

The Restaurateur Program was the engine for Chipotle's future since it would provide us with the teams we needed to run great restaurants and rapidly expand. Most other restaurant chains don't own and operate their own restaurants, but instead sell them to franchisees in exchange for a royalty, often around 7 percent of the gross sales, such that most of the profit goes to the franchisee. This is true for McDonald's, Taco Bell, Arby's, QDOBA, Burger King, and most others. In our case, we owned and operated all of our restaurants, allowing us to keep the enormous return, which was around a 30 percent restaurant level margin for our average restaurant. It'd be a pity to give that away!

Beyond our wild financial success, our employee surveys showed how incredibly happy and empowered our population of crew and managers were, so much so that the survey company told me they'd never seen anything like it. Labor costs decreased, since top performers got more done in less time and with fewer people. Food waste decreased. Our facilities were better cared for and maintained. Positive customer comments skyrocketed.

People wanted to learn more about how to create Restaurateur cultures, and asked to join my restaurant visits to learn how this was done. I welcomed this and made it my general practice to always bring others along, to teach them to create these cultures. Steve Ells's praise for my ability to do this was very affirming, and he even insisted that the entire board of directors come to witness a couple of Restaurateur interviews. With the board in tow, we traveled to two of our Manhattan locations and showed them what it was all about. They were blown away. Not one of them had any doubt this was the future we needed to pursue.

There was rising excitement in our restaurants, and everyone seemed to notice. Customers wrote thousands of letters to our website boasting about the "amazing team" in their neighborhood Chipotle, and describing in detail the heroic acts of customer service they'd received. One customer said she'd inadvertently placed her diamond engagement ring on her tray and feared she might have thrown it away with her foil burrito wrapper. One of our crew members went out to the dumpster, got in it, and dug for an hour and a half through garbage and the foul mix of trash and effluent festering at the bottom of the dumpster, found the ring, cleaned it, and returned it to the customer.

Crew members wrote countless emails thanking me for creating a program designed to enhance their careers and help them become leaders. Board members called me to tell me they noticed a huge difference in the operations of the Chipotles they visited. The hundreds of outside guests who, over the years, experienced a Restaurateur interview, such as film crews, members of the media, outside lawyers and vendors, or corporate employees were stunned by the level of love, commitment, loyalty, and emotion present in these restaurants. Nearly all of them made comments like, "Can I work here?" or, "Give me some of what they're drinking!" Everyone was excitedly rallying behind this idea of building teams of empowered top performers. Meanwhile, sales soared.

The people in the corporate office started to hear the stories and see the much-improved restaurant operations when they ate at Chipotle. For this reason, around 2012, they asked me if I could do "Restaurateur interviews" in their departments to help acknowledge and reward them for building excellent cultures. I found it to be a great idea, and we started this process. The desire to have a healthy culture was now everywhere!

By 2015, I had spent thousands of hours teaching what it took to build a Restaurateur culture to everyone, from entry-level employees to officers. It was fun, and extremely effective, leading to empowered, delighted employees, well-run restaurants, and terrific financial results. It was a win-win-win-win situation. We had achieved something that very few organizations ever do, which is having everyone in the organization buying into the same vision, and rowing our boat in the same direction. We were a completely united team, all working together in unison.

## MONEY IS NOT THE MOTIVATOR YOU THINK

When I first created the Restaurateur program, in addition to a $10,000 bonus for developing managers from crew, we also paid a bonus of 10 percent of the amount by which a Restaurateur increased the comparable sales target of their restaurant beyond its plan. In other words, I gave them a very clear cash incentive to increase the sales of their restaurant.

Guess what happened? It had no positive effect at all! Now, to be clear, our Restaurateur restaurants did achieve better operational and financial results, but this particular bonus was not the driving factor. When I was in the stores interviewing Restaurateurs, I quickly learned that not only were they not motivated by this potential bonus, they were not even thankful for it. They told me that the reason they had worked so hard to become a Restaurateur was because they believed in our people culture, and they believed in their team. They didn't need to have a bonus to do their best work. They wanted to do it anyway.

Soon, I got rid of this bonus, which was not yielding any results and was difficult to administer. No one complained. Of the 300 Restaurateurs, not a single one complained. I kept the $10K "people development bonus" in place, though, because I believed it reinforced the importance of developing people. But in truth, even this bonus failed to correlate to a greater number of GMs developed. But, the people development bonus communicated something important: that developing people was a top priority. This was good, because nothing increased sales faster than a great, committed team, and we needed good GMs to accomplish that!

With the exception of simple, repetitive tasks (like picking fruit), it turns out that when you try to use money to get someone to do more of a certain activity, while it may have an initially positive effect, over time it actually causes the person who is being rewarded to lose their own motivation to perform that activity. If you still doubt the truth of this, I recommend you read Daniel Pink's book, *Drive*, wherein he gives a very clear, compelling, and well-researched description of this phenomenon. So, if you are interested in increasing someone's motivation to be a better leader, it is not effective to concentrate on monetary rewards to do so. Instead, you should concentrate on giving them a vision, a reason why it is important to achieve the goal, and then make sure they are confident in their ability and encouraged by their circumstances, such that they feel motivated and at liberty to fully devote their talents to the purpose.

## THE RESTAURATEUR PATH

Becoming a Restaurateur was an extremely important milestone in people's lives. It meant the world to those who achieved it. The profound meaning had very little to do with the financial aspect of the promotions. What moved these leaders was our validation of the excellent leadership they'd provided and the strength of the team they'd assembled, trained, and led to greatness. After all, the financial aspects of the promotion were not particularly significant. GMs promoted to Restaurateur were not even given a raise.

Being promoted to Restaurateur was, in itself, a huge accomplishment and honor. But some of these newly minted Restaurateurs would have the capacity to do more. They could mentor another nearby restaurant, since their own store was functioning flawlessly with little further effort on their part. So we wanted to reward these people and maximize the benefit of their leadership. To do so, we asked these Restaurateurs to help a GM in another restaurant understand what he or she needed to do in order to hire a team of all top performers and empower that team to achieve our high standards. The Restaurateurs would be uniquely qualified to do this because they'd just accomplished this in their own restaurant and knew the pitfalls and difficulties. Those mentoring a second restaurant were designated an "R2." These R2s were still responsible for their original restaurant, where they'd continue to develop more leaders from their crew. If they successfully promoted a GM to run another nearby Chipotle, and if both of their stores were still excellent in terms of operation and culture, they'd be allowed to mentor a third Chipotle as an "R3." If they could do it again, they could become an "R4."

When they got to the R4 level, they were showing a propensity to be an excellent multiunit manager and would become eligible to be promoted to what we called an Apprentice Team Leader position, which was a leader who oversaw up to eight restaurants. This position was very prestigious, and our senior executives saw these people as the future executives of Chipotle. The promotion to ATL was very significant, and we wanted to be sure it was not given lightly or incorrectly, so it required a visit by me or one of Chipotle's officers who were qualified to evaluate and recognize a person's readiness for this position.

By 2008, we had fully built this new field leadership structure, which was designed to promote and elevate our very best leaders into positions where they could do the most good and create better restaurant experiences. What was so brilliant about the structure was that it made it clear that the path to becoming an executive at Chipotle was rooted in creating an excellent restaurant experience and excellent team—first by becoming a Restaurateur, then by developing others to do the same.

Quickly, the success stories of the managers who accomplished this spread, both from word-of-mouth and from the hundreds of emails that I sent out to the field acknowledging these new elite leaders. But what was also great was that our promotions no longer had anything to do with politics or whether your boss liked you. It was all based on the excellence of your leadership and how powerfully you made others better.

People who joined me on Restaurateur visits were visibly moved by the level of love, loyalty, and devotion that our people had for this culture. It was unlike anything they'd ever seen before.

But while the team members showed such love to me, the feeling was mutual. I saw these people as beloved family members, and I delighted in seeing them immersed in restaurant cultures where they felt valued and capable of anything they wanted to accomplish. Over and over again, I learned and relearned the lesson that the most powerful thing any of us can do in this lifetime is to help others shine as the most authentic and powerfully positive version of themselves. This was the gift I gave to Chipotle. And this was the gift the people of Chipotle gave to me.

If there was any shortcoming, it was that we were not promoting Restaurateurs fast enough. All of us wanted every team to reach this elite level. Solving this problem was a top priority, but doing so was going to require a lot of leadership and effort. It would involve teaching hundreds of leaders how to create healthy and inspirational cultures. The question that plagued me was how to make this transformation happen faster. Answering this question was always the subject of my speeches in Las Vegas at our biennial leadership conferences, where we brought together thousands of our leaders to focus on building these elite teams and restaurants. During these conferences, we'd bring 3,500 managers, assistant managers, and field leaders to Vegas, and steep them in all aspects of building cultures of empowerment. My speeches formed the backbone of the lessons there, and people took the information home and eagerly applied it to their restaurants. Beyond these conferences, I used every opportunity I could find to reinforce the message about the critical importance of building this culture.

One might wonder how I was able to lead such a large organization while spending so much time in our restaurants. But there was no better place for me to learn what our company needed than to be constantly on the front line. After all, it was our restaurants which either drew customers in or repelled them; where we'd either be efficient, fast, skilled, and exciting, or slow, dull, and unimpressive. This was where I could discover inefficiencies and weaknesses in our operations and immediately envision how to improve them. In fact, during nearly every restaurant visit, I'd make calls to various department heads and leaders, asking them to consider changing various aspects of our operation. With the power of a smartphone, I'd be in touch with dozens of my colleagues during the drive between each restaurant I visited. And, on my hundreds of flights around the country, I worked feverishly with a fire in my belly to improve many things I had just witnessed in our restaurants. In hindsight, my hours in the corporate office were seldom as productive as the hours spent in the field. So, I would be quick to recommend to CEOs of large, multiunit organizations to maximize their time in stores. It's where they'll learn the most, see the most, and come up with their very best ideas to advance and grow the company.

CHAPTER 9

# EMBRACING EMPOWERMENT

IN 2010, JOHN MACKEY, THE FOUNDER AND CEO OF WHOLE Foods, asked if I'd meet him for breakfast at Boulder's Dushanbe Tea House. John said that he had heard about the people culture I'd created at Chipotle, and he wanted to pick my brain about it. We sat on a flowered outdoor patio, with a stream running by, and had a long discussion. John was fascinated by our Restaurateur program and by my philosophy of leadership. I spoke about our promote-from-within philosophy, how we empowered our people, and other critical strategies we implemented to make Chipotle special and successful. Towards the close of our breakfast, John asked if I'd be willing to come give a keynote speech at the upcoming Conscious Capitalism Conference that he was hosting in Austin, Texas, where he promised I'd meet many other people trying to make a difference in the world. I told him I'd be delighted to.

John told me he thought my approach to creating a healthy culture was brilliant, and that much of what I described would work well at Whole Foods. Then he asked me a question that he told me had been burning in his mind: "How does your co-CEO relationship with Steve work? Is it healthy? Is it an advisable way to run a company?"

"The co-CEO relationship works well for us at Chipotle," I began. "But I believe our situation is unique." I went on to describe in detail the very close personal relationship I had with Steve. How I knew him like no one else knew him in terms of how he thought, his frustrations, his strengths, and weaknesses. I shared how we had learned to communicate very well together and work through the many moments of friction. Importantly, I described my incredible loyalty to Steve, which drove me to work hard to help him feel comfortable with me taking the reins leading the company. I explained how I stayed in constant communication with Steve to keep him informed as to my leadership of the company he founded.

The truth was, Steve and I knew each other very, very deeply. Each of us had insecurities, and we both looked to each other for approval, validation, and support. Each of us knew the other's preferences and personality quirks. We confided in each other and trusted each other. I knew how to take care of Steve's feelings, and I knew that a big part of this was to diminish the importance of my role as CEO and make him feel secure about my contribution. This was difficult sometimes, as when our national training director insisted that I speak first at the All Manager Conference. I told her how important it was to Steve to speak first, but she pushed the issue with him at the conference in Las Vegas. She quickly regretted her decision to challenge Steve. In front of a large group of meeting organizers, he made it clear to her that he would have none of it. He was the founder, and he was going to speak first. After this, she was ashamed and crestfallen, and soon left her job at Chipotle.

While I was the one primarily leading the company, I constantly endeavored to hide this, which I could tell Steve appreciated. Often, when I articulated the company's vision to our teams or to investors and analysts, Steve would tell me afterward that what I said was exactly what was in his mind, but that he could not communicate it as well as I could. In the early days, he acknowledged this frequently and complimented me on my intelligence, leadership ability, wisdom, and ability to unite people. I felt warmed by his confidence in me, but unfortunately, I often sacrificed my own needs or interests to continue to earn his approval. In hindsight, my desire to earn his approval led me to take many actions to earn his loyalty, even when such actions hurt my own progress, growth, or ability to lead as well as I could. I spent considerable energy trying to keep him happy and secure. But, when I did this right, I was rewarded not only by his continued warmth, trust, and loyalty, but also with the latitude to lead Chipotle the way I knew it needed to be led.

While sometimes difficult, my relationship with Steve was also great fun. He made me laugh so hard sometimes that it was painful. Even in the midst of board meetings, sometimes he'd send a text, usually only a single word, or a few words, that would cause me to erupt in waves of almost uncontrollable laughter. We came to know each other so well that we could communicate whole paragraphs to each other with a single glance. With us, everything was an inside joke. Everything we did caused others to view us as incredibly close and aligned. And, in most respects, we were extremely close. We spoke nearly every day, and our contact was always as much personal as it was professional. Neither of us seemed to really separate our personal lives from our work. If one of us was having a hard time in our relationship, we spoke about it. After all, it would affect our motivation and our work if something had us feeling down. In a way, we became each other's therapists.

These questions about the co-CEO relationship had come up many times from analysts and investors throughout my time at Chipotle. But this time was different. John's question felt personal. I could tell he was considering whether he should ask Walter Robb, his second in command, to become his co-CEO. In John's eyes, I saw the same struggle that I'd seen in Steve's eyes since I had joined Chipotle years before. Like Steve, John was struggling mightily with the notion of letting go of the CEO title that had come to feel inseparable from his very identity. He feared losing control, but also knew that Walter deserved the promotion to CEO. Since John's question was personal and heartfelt, I slowed down to really think about it. I wanted to provide him with a really good answer.

What I was trying to convey to John was that if Walter was really going to be the acting CEO, and John was merely reluctant to let go of his CEO title, he'd better be sure that Walter was as committed to him as I was to Steve. Unless he and Walter had such a deep connection as Steve and I, the co-CEO arrangement wouldn't work. John shared with me that his situation was, in many ways, very similar and he thought the same arrangement might work for him and Walter at Whole Foods. As history would have it, Walter did become the co-CEO of Whole Foods in May 2010.

That conversation helped me realize how hard I'd worked to thrive inside the complex relationship with my co-CEO. In truth, I'd been exploring relationships and how to get and give the most in them since I was a child trying to get my father's attention. Once I got into the job market as a teenager, I had the opportunity to dive deeply into many different kinds of relationships. Many people go to business school to get their master's in business administration, or MBA. I got an incredible business education starting from a young age from a combination of my many minimum wage jobs, my vulnerability, and my intense curiosity.

I was pretty much born curious. As I mentioned earlier, it drove my dad nuts. But vulnerability was something I have actively cultivated since childhood, largely because my mother so intensely valued my emotions and feelings. She always taught me that there was no such thing as bad feelings or wrong feelings; simply that we all have many feelings and they are all valuable. They should all be respected and honored. Throughout high school and college, while I had a lot in common with other kids, I differed in how uniquely vulnerable and open I was. I got to know people quickly, easily made deep friendships, and was quick to share anything about myself, particularly my weaknesses. To this day, I am very open and transparent and want to be seen for who I really am, even when I am scared, nervous, embarrassed, or ashamed. What's nice is that once I open up, people seem quick to open up to me too. This vulnerability, to me, is a key ingredient of rich relationships and a rich life.

When I was a student at the University of Colorado, I was a member of the Alpha Tau Omega fraternity. Under pressure from the guys, I agreed to be the fraternity president. I took this position seriously and worked to create a special culture in our house. The idea was that each of us would become the very best version of ourselves, and treat others well, such that our house stood out as something special. Of course, we also aimed to have a lot of fun. We had a members' meeting every week, which felt sort of sacred, and we worked out all the issues confronting our fraternity or the members in it. It was a special time, and I felt honored to be leading such a great group of people.

Being the president of ATO taught me a great deal. I learned how badly people want to be led. Most people, in my experience, are eager to follow someone who sets an example that appeals to them. I also learned how powerful hard work is in creating a bond of unity and respect among a group of people. The hard work of pulling together as a team to accomplish a common goal formed a strong bond among all of us and made us very proud to be members of the fraternity. I have since used this knowledge many times, such as at my law firm, when I let prospective new employees know that we worked hard and that our firm was not for everyone. At Chipotle, I again used this knowledge when I declared that we were going to build a culture that appealed to top performers and repelled low performers. The Restaurateur program, of course, was rooted in this concept. All of it ties back to lessons I learned early in my work life.

## CURIOSITY AND CONNECTION

On my fifteenth birthday, I landed a job at Dairy Queen. I was paid minimum wage, $2.85 an hour, which seemed mighty decent to me, especially since they offered free food, and I had an insatiable appetite. This was the first of several jobs I had in my teens—as a fast food worker, a janitor, and at an automobile repair shop, among others.

At Dairy Queen, I took pride in cooking burgers exactly right: juicy and delicious. I snuck mayonnaise onto all orders, knowing that anyone in their right mind would enjoy the addition of this magical condiment. I'd cook the fries until they were perfectly crispy, and salt them just so. I'd add extra pickles and mayo to the chicken sandwiches every time because they were best that way. As I worked at my post back in the kitchen, sometimes customers would yell back, "tasty burger" or "great fries." I beamed. Such a compliment was unheard of in the fast food world.

I learned some unexpected lessons at Dairy Queen. There were slow times when there was only one or two people in the dining room, wrapped around a cup of coffee. Often these customers had come from a nearby mental health treatment facility. In time, I recognized them and started to spend breaks listening to their stories. I came to know many by name, and soon I seldom spent a break without at least one of my new friends across the table. I was fascinated by their stories. They'd often had difficult lives and found themselves alone and homeless. I'd ask questions, trying to find out where and whether their choices and actions had led to their present situation, and what could be done to improve things. I'd ask why they smoked cigarettes when they had so little money. I'd ask why they chose to eat ice cream and drink coffee when they were not very healthy. While these questions may sound judgmental or offensive, the opposite was true. I actually cared about them and wanted to better understand them. They knew I cared, as they could hear it in my voice and see it in my eyes. So, they would answer me with total authenticity. Rather than being offended, they were touched by my concern, and they felt honored to be seen and understood as having important information to share with me. I truly wanted to learn from them. As a kid who'd grown up in very different circumstances, I was fascinated to learn the many lessons they could teach me about a very different world. I looked up to them; they had seen and been through a lot more than I had.

Will, for example, always took six creams in his coffee. He'd sit in a booth, wrap his hands lovingly around the warmth of his coffee cup, and stare into it as though the secret of the universe was somewhere deep within it. Carefully and very slowly, he'd peel the foil top off a plastic container of creamer, and watch as the cream clouded the dark coffee. Then, he'd repeat the process five more times, stacking the empties inside one another and setting them neatly aside. While he took only occasional sips, each seemed to nourish his soul and calm his mind.

Before I met him, I seldom saw his face. He was usually looking sharply downward. But one day I greeted him, and he quickly looked up and motioned for me to take the seat across from him as if I were a guest in his home. I noticed for the first time his steely-blue eyes, and ruggedly handsome face. I began to ask him questions, and his posture straightened. When I looked into his eyes, they quickly became glassy. Tears formed as he felt the loving warmth of someone looking into his heart. There was deep wisdom in his gaze, but also pain, suggesting that he may at any moment, be moved to tears. He began to recount aspects of his history that had touched his heart, and I was mesmerized. I saw his deep intelligence, and I began to understand the road he'd traveled. As my break ended, I hated to interrupt our time together.

I got to know many people in this way. It was remarkable to see how the simple fact that I was interested in them—that I cared about them—lifted their spirits. They instantly seemed lighter and happier. Some even quit smoking, or, on subsequent visits, bragged to me that they chose a chicken sandwich instead of ice cream. My coworkers questioned why I spent my time with these folks, as they thought them somehow undesirable. Some people still stigmatize people they consider homeless. I never understood that reasoning. I just enjoyed their company and learned much from my many discussions with them.

I learned from these new friends the power of simply seeing someone. I learned the power of caring for and valuing someone. The power of listening with a curious heart. I'd cry with them and laugh with them. They were my teachers, and I was theirs too. They made me a deeper and more understanding person. I learned that what people want more than anything in the world is to be seen and understood and to be accepted and loved for exactly who they are. As I've grown older, I've found no exceptions to this rule.

The skills I learned from these interactions served me well later in my career. I became very comfortable speaking with people from every walk of life. The incredible diversity of people I interacted with helped me to understand many different backgrounds, challenges, and histories so different than my own.

I spent my first high school year, at fifteen years of age, at Fountain Valley School, a boarding school in Colorado Springs, a hundred miles from my home. Sometimes on weekends, I took the Trailways bus home to Boulder. Once, while in the station waiting for my bus, I sat next to a man who weighed over 500 pounds. I introduced myself to him—his name was Tom—and asked him where he was going. He was headed to Denver for what he described as a stomach-stapling surgery to help him control his appetite and lose weight. We had a long conversation about how he struggled with his weight. He shared how it impacted his marriage and his sex life, how he felt ashamed and embarrassed, and how these feelings drove him to the only comfort he knew: food. In his openness and vulnerability, I too found a safe place to share some of the anxiety and fear in my life. I told him that my parents were divorcing, and how I was struggling with the decision whether to return to public school in Boulder with my brother or stay in boarding school alone. Our mutual shared vulnerability led to an instant depth—a true friendship born out of shared struggles. As our conversation drew to a close, I took solace in the hope that his surgery offered him comfort, and I felt such optimism for him that it felt as though he was already getting healthier. I could tell he felt the same way because even though both his eyes and mine welled up with tears as we said goodbye, I was warmed by his broad and hopeful smile as we went our separate ways.

The nearly instant friendship between Tom and me taught me how unimportant the passage of time is in terms of developing deep relationships. Most of the depth of relationships arises not from the amount of time we spend together, but from openness, vulnerability, and presence. When Tom and I were together, albeit briefly, we were totally present, open, curious, and compassionate. This created a wonderful space in which we could rest our concerns and doubts about our own difficulties, and allowed space for a new optimism, a fresh outlook, and a strong bond of friendship to form.

When two or more people trust each other and share their authenticity, open their hearts, and see and feel the other person, the result is something extraordinary. We all share the same human experience: moments of pain and moments of delight. Nonetheless, we tend to idealize others, thinking they have managed to escape having to feel the difficult feelings that trouble us. (They haven't.) Or, at times, we pity others, thinking they have it worse than we do. In truth, we are all inescapably part of the same human experience that always includes many different feelings and sensations. The difference is how we relate to our experience. If we reject our experience, it causes us to suffer. If we can learn to be accepting and gentle with our experience, then a state of grace and peace arises in us. We may feel pain, but we will not suffer. From person to person, we find similar problems, but it is our gentle embrace of these experiences that brings about change and growth in our ability to skillfully navigate our way in the world.

From my discussion with Tom, I learned something about the power of basic curiosity and the power of questions. My questions to him about his situation, his obesity, his discomfort, and why he overate were powerful tools that brought us closer. I have learned that asking questions is a way to invite intimacy with other people. When we avoid questions in an effort to be polite, we are usually depriving ourselves of a chance to get close to someone. The key is that the questions arise not from any negative judgment, but from our loving curiosity: from our desire to truly understand someone. When questions come from this loving place, they are hugely affirming. They are an invitation for intimacy. A welcome mat, placed before the other person's feet, offering a warm place for them to feel seen, accepted, and at home.

My next job was at the Boulder Senior Citizen's Center, where I worked as a janitor. It reinforced my understanding of how hungry people are to be seen, known, and understood. As I listened to their stories, I'd see passion in their eyes. They'd move quickly to tears as they recounted wonderful moments, hardships they'd endured, and family and friends they'd lost. As they spoke, they'd become visibly lighter and happier. More optimistic, open, and friendly. By simply being present with them, and valuing them as I did, they were uplifted. Giving them an audience to share their past gave them belonging in the present moment. In turn, I felt uplifted, wiser, stronger, and more optimistic. The deep contact was enriching and made me feel better about my job. No longer was I merely cleaning up food stains, dirty plates, and feces. I was helping friends. I could feel their appreciation, and I felt honored to be of service. What started as curiosity and appreciation for the seniors I worked for ended up being a gift to me. As some of these friends passed away, I felt grateful that some of their wisdom lived on inside of me.

When I was sixteen, I got my driver's license and (after years saving up for it) bought a used Datsun 260Z. After another year of saving up, I had it painted Ferrari red. It was my pride and joy, and I worked on it all the time. Eventually, to afford the costs of owning and working on it, I found a job at Car Mart, an auto parts store owned by my dear friend, Kevin's father, Jack Breslin. Of course, this was a natural fit. I enjoyed learning more about cars and made enough money to pay for gas and insurance.

Car Mart was a slow business, but I tried to change that by taking great care of our customers. When they'd come in and buy parts, if I had time, I would perform simple repairs for them at no charge. For instance, when someone would buy wiper blades, I'd offer to put them on for them. One time, in a blizzard, I put tire chains on for a customer. I was her hero. It was freezing out and putting chains on a car is not much fun. Sometimes I'd change a tire or add motor oil. I interrupted these acts of service to run back into the store when another customer would walk in. The most complicated repair I did was to disassemble, clean, and reassemble a customer's carburetor, right there in the parking lot. All of these things made me feel valuable and satisfied.

Jack Breslin came to know me as a good employee, and somewhere along the way, he gave me some very sage advice. He grabbed me by the shoulder and said, "Monty, don't ever take another job for an hourly wage. Do you understand?" I did understand. He thought I worked fast and efficiently, and that an hourly wage wouldn't compensate me well enough for what I added to the business.

Towards the end of college, I applied to work at a pizza restaurant called Old Chicago. They had these delicious, deep dish pizzas that helped me keep the weight on, despite my ridiculously high metabolism. I wasn't twenty-one yet and couldn't be a waiter. They hired me as a host, where I seated customers and managed the long waiting list. It was fun, and I met a lot of interesting people.

After hosting at Old Chicago for a few months, I turned twenty-one and was promoted to waiter. What a job! Serving good food and drinks to a bunch of nice, excited people out for a good time was so fun, I'd have done it for free. I often made a hundred dollars a night in tips, and I'd cram all but twenty dollars of it into a beer can in my room. I also moved out of my fraternity and into my dad's house that semester to save money. I got to know my dad in a new way, more as a peer and friend. I also slowed down a bit from the college party scene and managed to do some nonacademic reading.

It may sound silly, but I think waiting tables is an excellent business education. Our best waiters were cool under pressure. They were organized, masters at multitasking, and knew how to prioritize. They made decisions quickly, deftly handled complaints, and were perceptive enough to know when to leave a guest to their own thoughts, or engage them in lively discussion. I got good at this job fast, probably because I loved it and wanted to be excellent. I also enjoyed the instant gratification of earning tips, which quickly found their way into my beer-can piggy bank.

**CHAPTER 10**

# UNDERSTANDING EMPOWERMENT

THE BEST LEADERS SEEM TO HAVE SOMETHING MAGICAL about them. In their presence, teams come alive, work hard, and accomplish amazing things. They have that certain something that allows them to rally people to move mountains. That certain something is the ability to empower the people they lead.

The term *empowerment* is now commonly used in business, but in my experience, it is usually misused, or at least misunderstood. As part of building Chipotle's culture, I focused intently on defining empowerment and making sure it was understood by everyone in the company. Eventually, I came up with this definition, which has stood the test of time:

**Empowerment means feeling confident in your ability, and encouraged by your circumstances, such that you feel motivated and at liberty to fully devote your talents to a purpose.**

I didn't arrive at this right away—it evolved over time. My efforts to define empowerment so carefully were motivated by the many signs I saw early in my time at Chipotle of people who were anything but empowered. As I saw these signs of disempowerment, or misunderstood beliefs about what empowerment meant, I felt a burning desire to fix it right away. It was painful for me to watch as leaders undermined the potential of their teams, or failed to release the powerful force of potential top performers. I'll begin this chapter by describing some of these misunderstandings about empowerment.

Ironically, one place I saw the most egregious misunderstanding of the concept of empowerment was with Chipotle's human resources (HR) department, the very department that should have understood it best.

## ELIMINATING TRADITIONAL HR

When I became president and COO in 2005, the HR department made their decisions out of fear. They felt their job was to avoid getting sued by employees. Avoiding being sued seemed to me to be a weak goal for an HR team to have. It's just not ambitious enough. It's sort of like hiring a landscaping company to make your yard beautiful, and then learning that all they're trying to accomplish is keeping the poison ivy out. You'd want more out of them than that! But even if avoiding suits was a worthy goal, our HR team failed to achieve it. Instead, their efforts to avoid lawsuits ended up causing most of the employee lawsuits against us!

The reason for this stemmed from our HR team's insistence that our restaurant teams catch the person doing something wrong before firing them. This was absurd. It created a situation where, if a manager wanted to fire someone, they'd stop treating them well, stop trying to help them, and wait for them to mess up—the opposite of what I wanted managers to do if they were going to elevate and develop the people around them.

Imagine how you would feel if you were an employee who was suddenly being treated coldly and watched like a hawk by the judgmental eye of a manager who was just waiting for you to do something wrong, so that he could fire you. Imagine how you would feel having everyone betting against you, just waiting for you to fail, and harshly judging your every step. It was awful, and it made people mad—mad enough to call lawyers and pursue claims. And that is what many did.

Some members of our HR team felt they knew better about who should be removed (as well as how and when it should be done) than the very managers who spent all of their working hours with these people. I didn't agree. I gathered the HR team together to explain my concerns. During my time as a litigator, I handled a lot of employment cases, and I assured them there was no legal reason for interfering with the managers' decisions regarding removing people. I explained that we'd be more efficient and fair and have less legal trouble if we just promptly removed low performers without trying to get them to do something bad first. I undertook many efforts to teach HR how to do this better over the years, but while they showed some signs of improvement, I remained dissatisfied with our progress. The biggest problem was with the field HR generalists, known simply as HRGs, who kept interfering with our general managers' personnel decisions. When we finally decided to bring all of our managers together for our First Annual All Managers' Conference in Las Vegas in August 2010, I saw an opportunity to set the matter to rest once and for all.

During this conference, at which every HR employee was in attendance, I offered our teams a new procedure by which to remove low performers. First, I told our teams that it was everyone's responsibility (not just HR's) to make sure everyone on our teams knew what a top performer was. I projected my well-known definition on the huge one-hundred-foot long screen behind me during my speech:

**A Top Performer is someone who has the desire and ability to perform excellent work, and through their constant effort to do so, elevates themselves, the people around them, and Chipotle.**

Second, I told them that if someone was not a top performer, it was our responsibility to communicate that fact clearly to the employee, with a clear explanation as to what we thought about their work, and the reasons why, so that they'd have an opportunity to quickly improve.

Third, I told them that as long as: 1) we'd been clear with an employee about their performance; 2) we'd given them a chance to quickly improve; and 3) their removal could not reasonably be considered by the employee to be a surprise, then the manager was free to remove such low performers immediately and needn't get permission from HR. When I announced this to the live audience of general managers in Las Vegas, they just went off. A huge round of applause exploded throughout the room, illustrating the release of years of frustration, and the relief of being freed of the restrictions placed on them in the past. Fortunately, since the whole HR team was also present, I was sure there would be no confusion. Even so, I repeated myself and invited questions from the audience. I wanted no misunderstanding. Hearing no misunderstanding, I was satisfied that the issue was crystal clear.

It wasn't.

For those who followed this simple new rule, things went well.

But there were members of the HR team who continued to muddy the waters. They inserted their own rules, continued to require write-ups from GMs in their area, and insisted that "I know what Monty said, but he didn't quite mean it like that." But I had meant *exactly* what I said. I called the HR team to another meeting and shared my concern that a number of them were not heeding our new plan. After that, I was certain that the issue was laid to rest and they would stop restricting our managers' ability to swiftly and fairly remove low performers. I was certain that they understood and would adhere to this better way of doing things.

They didn't.

Since HR kept muddying the waters and creating rules that led to the poor treatment of employees, I took what most people would think was an extraordinary step. I eliminated the entire field HR team. To be clear, I did not fire the individuals. I simply found more useful, positive, and helpful positions for them in another area of the company. I decided that having a field HR team was not the best way to handle the critical function of assuring we had excellent teams.

The board was deeply concerned. "What? No HR team?"

"Well," I explained, "I think the HR function is too important for it to be accomplished by a separate team. Instead, I think HR is everyone's responsibility at Chipotle, and it needs to be carried out by all of our field leaders as the most critical aspect of their job."

I went on to explain that all managers must communicate with their people, give them extremely clear feedback on their performance, and commit to their improvement. My litigation background taught me that nearly all successful claims by employees came from mistreatment, and that treating people with dignity and respect had to be everyone's job. It could not fall to a few dozen roaming field people who didn't even work in the restaurants. I further explained that nearly all of the mistreatment of crew happened after HR decided that someone needed to be removed, but instead of just thanking them and letting them go, the HR team insisted on making the manager start looking for them to do something wrong. This was a condescending, nasty, and sneaky process. You would feel watched and nervous, like you feel when a police car is following you in traffic, just waiting for you to slip up! You're bound to drive more poorly because you feel watched and judged. None of us is at our best while someone is waiting for us to fail.

We set up a hotline for employees to call if they needed to speak to someone outside their chain of command, and built a team of very skilled people, who had worked in Chipotle restaurants, to take those phone calls in our corporate office. From now on, the primary responsibility to hire, fire, and ensure a great relationship among everyone on the team belonged to the managers. They were a much bigger team (we had about 2,300 of them), they were in the store, they knew all of the people, knew the situation, and were in the best position to be fair, reasonable, and make excellent choices about their own team. The well-being of these people was their responsibility. The board understood.

The removal of field HR was a triumph. The managers gladly took on this responsibility, and they performed it very well. The number of lawsuits, complaints, and Equal Employment Opportunity Commission claims fell by half over the next five years, as our employees were treated better. We harbored fewer low performers, as they either improved or were swiftly and fairly removed. We also eliminated costly positions and travel budgets at the same time. It was a great success.

## A NICER OFFICE WON'T HELP YOUR BUSINESS

Shortly after I started my new role as president and COO in 2005, we moved to a new office. There was all sorts of talk about how this would help our efficiency, productivity, and ability to motivate our people. We even hired expensive architects and consultants to do the space planning to allow for maximum use of the space. It was a waste. It did no good, cost a lot, disrupted our team, and landed us on the hook for a longer lease term.

People need to be comfortable, have room to do their work, and have the tools they need. But I too often hear people speak about how a new office would enhance productivity, and see leaders justify huge financial outlays for better workspace in the name of increased productivity. The top priority should be building a team of empowered top performers: a healthy culture. The vast majority of companies have failed to accomplish this, and should not be worried about a better office yet. Nicer offices won't make near the difference that a great culture will, so build an excellent culture first! If you manage that, you may find the office wasn't the problem. But, even if you still think that a new office is a good idea, having a great culture will make your company so successful, you'll at least be able to afford the higher rent for a new office!

## HOLDING PEOPLE ACCOUNTABLE IS UNNECESSARY WHEN THEY'RE EMPOWERED

Empowerment does not mean holding your people accountable. This is another term that makes me wince a bit since what it really implies is the absence of empowerment. Any time you hear someone use this term, let a little bell go off in your mind. That person is thinking more like a manager and less like a leader. Anytime you are wondering how to best hold your team accountable, ask yourself a better question: "Why is it that this team needs to be held accountable?" This latter question will send your mind thinking more like a leader. You'll be thinking about stronger and more sustainable ways to lead your team. You'll be wondering things like, "Are they inspired by a vision? Are they well trained? Are they exposed to encouraging circumstances? Are they empowered?" These latter questions are much more helpful and more likely to lead to a sustainable and powerfully positive culture in your organization—one in which no one needs to be held accountable.

Holding someone accountable carries with it the implication that your people won't perform well or will drift off course without your supervision. It also implies that your people are looking to avoid accountability: that they would rather not do what you've asked them to do, and will only do it if you find some way to stay on top of them. Really, I find the term to be quite offensive.

When you build a culture of empowerment, the people in the organization actually take on the vision as their own. They want to do great work and are eager to advance the mission in any way they can, which means there is no need to keep managing them or making sure they do as you ask.

Since all of the above are NOT examples of empowerment, what does empowerment really mean?

During my 2012 All Managers' Conference Speech, I presented a slide demonstrating the difference in how people act when they are empowered, and when they are not empowered. Here it is.

| Not Empowered | Empowered |
|---|---|
| People need constant direction | People act like owners and don't need to be told what to do, or need permission |
| People walk by problems without fixing them | Everyone feels responsible for the whole restaurant experience, and would not walk by a problem |
| People are concerned about seniority or rank | People respect each other, regardless of seniority or rank and are focused on doing the right thing |
| People are nervous, afraid to make mistakes | People have enough confidence to take risks, and are not paralyzed by the fear of making a mistake |
| "That is not my job!" | "I'm responsible for this restaurant" |

Monty giving his keynote speech to 3,500 leaders at Chipotle's All Managers' Conference in 2014.

Empowerment is the heart of leadership. If you can figure out how to empower the people you lead, it will help you lead any organization to huge success. Teaching and learning the art of empowering others can be challenging, and doing it well involves mastery of many interrelated concepts.

As our restaurant managers worked toward their goal of becoming Restaurateurs, empowering every team member was by far the most difficult challenge. During my many Restaurateur interviews around the country, lack of empowerment was the most common reason I declined to promote GMs to this elite position. For this reason, I set about working to find a way to teach people how to empower their team members. This ability to empower one's people to be at their very best is the most important aspect of leadership. Few do it naturally. But, I decided, if a leader is caring and desirous of seeing their people succeed, it is teachable. If someone is not caring and desirous of seeing their people succeed, the best they will be capable of is becoming a good manager. They will not be a great leader.

When I first discussed empowerment with leaders at Chipotle,

I used many words to describe exactly what it was, how it felt, and how it could be created. When I discussed empowerment with our teams in the field, I found that many people used the word incorrectly or misunderstood some aspect of its meaning. Some told me it meant "doing the right thing for the right reason." Others said, "doing your job without having to be told." While each of these describes one manifestation of empowerment, these descriptions are incomplete. I yearned for a definition that could help people to more quickly understand the concept, so that there would be no misunderstanding. I wanted the meaning to be crystal clear. For this reason, I wrote the definition that I referenced at the outset of this chapter:

**Empowerment means feeling confident in your ability, and encouraged by your circumstances, such that you feel motivated and at liberty to fully devote your talents to a purpose.**

After many years working with this definition, which has now been tested and used by hundreds of thousands of people, I remain confident it is excellent. These words not only explain empowerment, but they can also be used as a recipe for creating it. The definition is actionable, and it is prescriptive. One can look at a certain culture, question what parts of this definition are present, and what parts are missing. In this way, they discover what corrections need to be made to make it into an empowered culture.

It is important to understand that empowerment cannot be imposed. Just as one cannot force someone to love another person, one cannot force someone to feel empowered. Once we accept this reality, it will shift how we go about creating empowered teams.

## DON'T FALL FOR THE MORALE TRAP

People sometimes say that morale is low in an effort to convince management to take some action they'd like to see. The problem is that what these improved morale seekers usually want is something like longer breaks, more days off, wage increases, lavish Christmas parties, more sick days, and so forth. But none of these things, once added, actually improves morale or empowers people. People thinking in these terms are usually fed up with their work, and they are looking for some highlights to make it more tolerable. It is like a couple with a boring and tired marriage going on a beach vacation to try to revive the romance and excitement of their relationship. The trouble is, in both cases, once things are back to normal, the same issues which made morale feel low immediately resurface.

When throwing the lavish Christmas party fails to create good morale, I've seen companies take further useless steps. They come up with slogans to remind people to have good morale, or to do a good job. When I worked at Farmers Insurance, the executives held a huge team meeting in a local movie theater where they lavished us with mugs, koozies, and pads of paper carrying the slogan "PRIDE: People Responding In Dedicated Effort." All of us just laughed. I still laugh today! The idea that some mug will remind you or motivate you to do a better job is absurd. Then there are the motivational posters, like "There is no I in team." When that doesn't work, companies buy donuts for the staff. Perhaps they think that obesity and diabetes will bring that absent smile to the faces on their team?

The only way to create a culture that is not in need of morale-boosting actions, is to build a culture of empowerment. There is no shortcut to doing so. One must have a compelling vision, and a team of people who are confident in their ability, and encouraged by their circumstances, such that they feel motivated and at liberty to fully devote their talents to a purpose. When such a culture is truly present, I can promise that there will be little to no talk about morale!

As you can see from the above definition, there are two feelings people must have to be empowered. They must feel confident in their ability, and they must feel encouraged by their circumstances. It is the leader's job to create an environment in which both of these feelings arise naturally in their people.

## FEELING CONFIDENT IN YOUR ABILITY

The easier of these two feelings to create is that of someone feeling confident in their ability. Essentially, top performers will naturally feel confident in their ability when they are well trained, have the tools they need, and know what to do. It's that simple.

The trouble is that most people, when they see someone performing in a substandard way, try to solve the problem by reminding the person to do a better job. Or perhaps warning them. Or by showing them or telling them something that they already know. These are ineffective techniques: a waste of time and effort and very frustrating. Frustrating for leaders, because they keep spending time teaching, but results don't improve. Frustrating for employees, because they keep watching as the leader repeatedly tells them things they already know, which of course is useless and demonstrates that the leader is out of touch, or even condescending.

If you see employees failing to perform their jobs correctly, and you're not sure if they are confident in their abilities, simply ask them if they know the right way to do the job. Have them demonstrate to you how to do it correctly. If you see that they know how to do the job, then they are confident in their ability! Yet most leaders fail to realize this simple fact, and repeatedly teach or coach the employee how to do the job over and over and over until they finally get frustrated and even fire the employee, without ever addressing the real issue—that the person is not encouraged by their circumstances.

The key to empowering a team is to ensure both of the above

two pieces of the empowerment puzzle are in place. From my experience, what's more often missing is encouraging circumstances. Yet the problem managers most often try to solve is confidence in ability. This failure to correctly diagnose the problem causes thousands of wasted hours and a great deal of frustration.

## FEELING ENCOURAGED BY YOUR CIRCUMSTANCES

Creating an environment in which people feel encouraged by their circumstances is the more difficult aspect of creating a feeling of empowerment in the people we lead. To determine how to create such circumstances, it's helpful to understand what causes them to arise.

The short answer is that people feel most encouraged when in the presence of someone who loves them, supports them, and is committed to helping them be the very best version of themselves. The most familiar example of this might be that of a child in the presence of a very good parent. The parent loves and cares deeply for the child, and finds ways to support the child to grow into a healthy, well-rounded, and fulfilled adult. Perhaps another example we can picture is an excellent schoolteacher, who lets you know she cares for you, expects you to do your best, and disciplines you fairly and lovingly when needed.

For a leader to create encouraging circumstances, they need to emulate the feelings created by that good parent or teacher. But how?

The answer is that people will feel encouraged by their circumstances when they are inspired by a vision, when they know that their leader finds them essential to bringing the vision to reality, and when their leader knows them, believes in them, is committed to them, insists on their success, cares about them, teaches them, helps them, supports them, listens to them, and challenges them. These are all concepts that should feel familiar to you by now.

I remember a conversation about empowerment I had with a young crewperson in one of our restaurants named Tim. Specifically, I was talking about creating encouraging circumstances. I asked him, "Is there anyone you can think of who made you feel incredibly encouraged by your circumstances?"

"Yes," he said. "I had a music teacher named Mr. Cheney. He was great."

"What made him so great?"

"Well, he just made me feel like I really wanted to learn music."

"OK," I said. "Let me ask some questions to find out why that was true. I'll bet he wasn't the easiest teacher you ever had, was he?"

"No, actually, he was pretty hard!"

"I'll bet he cared about you and got to know a thing or two about who you were as a person?"

"Yes, he got to know all of us. He really cared about us."

"Did he care a lot about music and give you reasons why it was important in your life?"

"Yes, he was actually pretty funny. He just loved music and thought everyone should love it."

"What if you hadn't cared? What if you hadn't tried hard or not paid attention? Would he have been easy on you?"

"No! He wouldn't let that happen! He would have definitely talked to me to find out what was going on," Tim said, with a tone that made it clear that he wouldn't want to let Mr. Cheney down.

I went on to ask Tim if there were any teachers who did not create encouraging circumstances. He said there was, and coincidentally, the other teacher was also a music teacher. Tim explained that the other guy didn't really care about the kids, was an easier grader, but wasn't that passionate about the music. He didn't care to really know the kids, and he viewed teaching them as just a job.

## DON'T JUST TEACH WHAT YOU LIKE. TEACH WHAT'S NEEDED

When I first started working at Chipotle, I noticed that our area managers had a tendency to teach people how to clean their store, how to prepare their food, and other basics of running a successful restaurant. Because our area managers had all been GMs themselves, they were all fairly expert in how to run a restaurant. Because of this, they were comfortable teaching restaurant operations, and this was how they spent most of their time. The trouble was, this was seldom what the restaurant employees needed to learn. They already knew how to clean, and they knew how to prepare food. In fact, there was very little that they did not know about how to run their restaurants. If they were not doing what they knew how to do, the obvious question should have been, "Why aren't they doing what they know is right?" But no one seemed to be asking this basic, obvious question!

The answer was usually that these teams were not empowered. Or, if they were empowered, they had people who were not top performers. The thing that our area managers needed to learn to teach was the art of selecting a team of top performers and empowering them.

For the entire time I was at Chipotle, I saw this tendency: leaders teaching what they liked to teach, without regard for the fact that it was not what the team most needed to learn.

There is a saying, "To a man with a hammer, everything looks like a nail." I find this funny, but it's also true. Over and over again, people tend to use the tools they are most comfortable with, even when they are the wrong tools for the job. But we will be much more effective if each of us routinely asks ourselves, "Am I teaching the lesson that my audience most needs to learn?"

The lesson I learned from over 20,000 similar conversations was that the behaviors that create encouraging circumstances always have certain elements in common.

- The leader has a vision that they use to excite those they lead.
- The leader knows their people.
- The leader makes their people believe they are essential to carrying out the vision.
- The leader believes in their people.
- The leader is committed to their people and to their success.
- The leader teaches their people and helps them.
- The leader cares and is concerned about their well-being.
- The leader challenges their people.
- The leader legitimately wants their people to be at their best.

Leaders need not look, act, or sound the same. Some are quiet and contemplative, while others are loud and imposing. They have all different styles. It is fascinating that it doesn't seem to matter if a leader is male or female, loud or quiet, tall or short, fat or thin, fast-talking or slow-talking, young or old. What consistently determines whether the leader is successful is whether or not the leader undertakes the actions specified in the list above. Every effective leader I've seen does these things. Every ineffective leader doesn't do them.

The leader's approach has to be genuine and from the heart. The leader must actually care for the person. It is not too strong to say that the most empowering leaders love those whom they lead. Love, as I described in chapter 2, is central to becoming a great leader. Luckily, love is free! Those who lack the capacity to truly care about others, or delight in seeing them at their best, may be able to manage people well, but will not become truly effective leaders. This is why the journey of becoming a leader is also a journey toward self-discovery. It's a journey toward becoming the best version of ourselves. We need to develop the capacity to truly know and understand people, to feel empathy, and to care for them skillfully.

If your people are not encouraged by their circumstances, then you need to find out what is missing. What is missing is one or more of the following:

- People aren't excited or committed to a vision or don't see their role in it.
- People don't feel essential to carrying out the vision.
- People don't believe you really know them.
- People don't know you believe in them.
- People don't feel that you're committed to their success.
- People don't feel you're teaching and helping them.
- People don't feel you care about their well-being.
- People don't feel challenged.
- People don't feel you want them to be at their best.

## DIAGNOSING FAILURES IN A CULTURE

In an empowered culture, the leader stays in touch with their team and knows them well. They are always on the lookout for ways to make sure they have the training and tools they need. They ensure that their circumstances remain encouraging. If the leader sees someone who isn't working hard or is not doing a good job, the leader recognizes that some aspect of the culture is missing and addresses it at that level. The leader diagnoses what is missing. There is either a lack of top performers, a lack of empowerment, or a lack of knowledge of high standards.

After a few years at Chipotle, I created and rolled out what I called the Restaurateur diagnosis and plan tool. It was a tech-enabled tool, which became known as the DPT, which let a leader go into a store, interview the team, check boxes accurately describing concerns that were obstacles to building a great culture, and generate a report. The report created action items describing exactly what the manager needed to do in order to eliminate these obstacles and create a Restaurateur culture.

Field directors told me that this tool helped them and their teams to quickly understand what specific leadership was needed to make sure their restaurants were operating at their best. The tool resulted in every one of our managers, most of whom had never been given a written plan, having a clear description as to how to improve, usually for the first time in their career. Their feedback gave me great hope that perhaps we could more quickly spread this culture.

One advantage of the DPT was that it allowed us to access and study every plan for every manager in the company. Also, it allowed us to see very deeply the cultural condition of every store in the country, and this helped us to judge the progress and skill of our field leaders, and our entire mid-management team. We studied it to find out which themes were most commonly responsible for preventing the formation of Restaurateur cultures nationwide.

When we looked at the top five obstacles to building a Restaurateur culture nationwide, they were: 1) the team lacks a vision; 2) people don't accurately understand what the Restaurateur culture is; 3) managers are not having one-on-one conversations with their teams; 4) people walk by things that they know are not right and don't say anything about it; 5) new hires are not being set up for success.

All five of these most common themes highlighted a failure to create encouraging circumstances. In other words, this tool made clear to me that our leaders needed to get better at teaching their managers how to create encouraging circumstances, so that they could build empowered teams. This reminded me yet again that too often, leaders spend time training people, even when a lack of training is not the issue. Quite literally, our leaders spent millions of man-hours on training that was a complete waste of time, because their people were already trained, but weren't performing because they were not encouraged by their circumstances.

Creating encouraging circumstances requires you to look inward; to be vulnerable, consider your own shortcomings, and be courageous enough to consider if it is you who needs to change. You must diagnose which of the above feelings you're failing to unlock in your people. It is true that it's not always possible to cause someone to feel every one of these feelings. Perhaps some people just can't get excited about your vision or are simply not right for the job. But look in the mirror for the solution first, before deciding that your people are the cause.

I encourage all leaders to commit to mastering these principles. If your employees lack empowerment, diagnose the reason why. If they are not confident, train them. If they are confident, then go through the list above to find out why they are not encouraged by their circumstances, and make a change. If you do this, your team will feel empowered and will fully devote their talents to the achievement of your vision. If you fail to do this, then you're stuck being a full-time manager, relegated to a life of repeating the same stuff over and over and obtaining mediocre results.

A FLICKER'S LESSON

During one of my All Managers' Conference speeches, I told

our team a true story about a bird and myself. It captured much of what I was trying to teach them about diagnosing problems properly.

Several years ago, my house in Boulder was under constant attack by large woodpeckers called Northern Flickers. These birds are actually quite beautiful, but I grew to have a very bad relationship with them.

They'd land on the house at 5:00 a.m. and start loudly pecking huge holes in the siding. By loudly, I mean it sounded like a jackhammer right outside my bedroom window. At the time, we had small kids who robbed us of nearly all of our sleep, and I can tell you, the idea of a dozen of these birds adding their own natural alarm clock to our lives was unwelcome indeed!

My first solution, which I tried about seventy times, was to run outside in my underwear, yelling and screaming, thinking the birds would suddenly realize the error of their ways and pick on someone else's house. I'm sure I looked insane out there. Even worse, it did no good at all. They kept on pecking away. In time, they pecked a hundred holes all over the outside of my house. Each needed to be repaired, which meant trips to the hardware store and hours of my time on a rickety ladder. I quickly became angry and frustrated, but apparently the birds were entirely insensitive to my anger and frustration, because they kept pecking holes.

I looked online for solutions. I found a company that promised their repellent would keep the birds away, and I spent hundreds of dollars having their product applied to the house. It did nothing. Months later, tired of shouting in my underwear, I bought some fake owls and installed them in the areas where the flickers most often pecked. This worked for about a week, until the flickers figured out the owls were plastic, and got right back to pecking.

Worse, in a sign of massive disrespect for both me and the owls, the flickers took to defecating all over the plastic owls. It was frustrating, and quite frankly, embarrassing.

I told my dad, who in addition to being a cell biologist was also an avid falconer, and by any means an expert about birds and my predicament. I went on and on about how I suffered.

"The Flickers are trying to build a nest," he said. "But lucky for you, Moose (my father's lifelong nickname for me), flickers are territorial, so all you need to do is put a flicker house on the side of your house, and they'll move in, and then they'll chase any other flickers away!"

I ignored his advice. The thought of offering a nice comfy room to these rascals, who'd woken me up for a year, didn't excite me much. A while later, my dad even bought me a flicker house and delivered it to my house when I was out of town. It was a large birdhouse, actually designed for a flicker. I let it sit in my garage for months, certain it wouldn't work. I suppose I also remained opposed to providing luxurious accommodations to the very species that saw fit to harass me on a daily basis.

At night, the flickers would sleep, gripping onto the eaves of the house. Some nights, I was actually able to catch them with a net, after which I would drive them miles away and release them. It did no good. They can fly, it turns out. They flew right back to my house and resumed their pecking.

After much too long, I figured I'd try my father's harebrained idea. I installed a flicker house way up by my bedroom, on their favorite pecking spot.

You'll never guess what happened. A pair moved into the house and took to chasing away all the other flickers, and they never pecked again. They're territorial, you see!

Good Lord. I was almost disappointed that the problem was

so easily solved. It was like figuring out, nine hours into a ten-hour flight, that your airplane seat reclines. You are glad for the hour of comfort, but saddened that you missed nine hours of such bliss!

I suppose my many months of suffering were paid back by the significant lesson these birds taught me, which I will never forget. Do not focus energy on chasing symptoms. Instead, focus on solving the underlying problem that is causing the symptoms. Always ask, "What is the underlying problem here?" Where I had been convinced that the problem was that these birds were pecking, keeping me awake, drilling holes in my house, and driving me fully insane, that was not actually the problem. That was *my* problem, but not *the* problem. Instead, these things were all symptoms. The real problem, the problem underlying the symptoms that I found so intolerable, was that these birds were homeless. Once I solved their homeless problem for them, there was peace and tranquility!

The Northern Flicker (*Colaptes auratus*), a worthy adversary

With regard to Chipotle, I used this story to great success, illustrating that the many symptoms shared by poor restaurant operations were caused by a few underlying problems, and that it was these problems that needed to be solved. We'd not find long-term solutions simply by swatting at symptoms. For example, a dirty restaurant, poor food preparation, disorganization, and all of the other indications of a poor restaurant operation were not underlying problems. Rather, these things were symptoms caused by only three possible underlying problems. Namely:

- A lack of top performers on the team
- A lack of empowerment
- A lack of knowledge of Chipotle's standards

I became convinced that these were the only possible underlying problems. With this story, I was able to demonstrate, in a very memorable way, that it is much easier and more powerful to solve the underlying problem, for instance by building a team of top performers, empowered to achieve high standards, than it is to constantly remind, retrain, or criticize the crew to clean things, or cook food better, or what have you. The latter is tantamount to running around in your underwear, yelling and screaming, with no lasting effect.

# CHAPTER 11

# PRACTICING EMPOWERMENT

EMPOWERMENT IS THE HOLY GRAIL OF LEADERSHIP, THE most important and powerful concept of all. In order to be a great leader, you must learn to empower your people. Any time you see a poorly run restaurant, retail store, or organization, empowerment is missing. Anytime you see a super well-run business, it likely results from one or more empowered people.

During my many years teaching people to create empowered teams, I was always working to explain things more clearly and more concisely. I'd draw diagrams, make lists, underline things, and create tools. I wanted to give details about how to empower a team that people could keep and refer to.

One example of such a tool I created was something called the "5 steps to creating a culture of empowerment." They are:

- Connect with your people
- Inspire them with a vision
- Instill confidence in your people
- Teach them to make each other better
- Share what is going on

## CONNECT WITH YOUR PEOPLE

Connecting means more than talking to someone. It means sitting down and creating a two-way dialogue. It means getting to know them personally and showing an interest in their well-being, not just in the ways that affect their job. It means learning what is important to them in their lives. It means being vulnerable with them, and by doing so, encouraging the formation of a bond between the leader and the person.

It is easy to know when you make a connection, but it is hard to define. It is something you can just feel. The feeling is warm, feels inclusive, and safe. Sometimes, with people who are shy, or slow to trust, it takes considerable time to make a connection. Other times, the connection is nearly instant, and takes little to no effort. But it is seldom the case that a leader just can't connect with someone. No matter what style of person a leader is confronted with, the leader's mere effort to really connect is powerful and important. Above all, it must be a genuine and sincere effort. It can't be rushed, and it can't be just another project on the leader's to-do list. Real connections are born out of creating space—creating a moment in time that is devoted to another person.

## INSPIRE THEM WITH A VISION

A vision has to be something inspiring and worthy of a person's effort. It must be more than something that the leader wants to accomplish for themselves. The vision has to be something that, once achieved, makes a real difference in the life of the person being asked to achieve it.

Inspiring someone requires more than sharing a vision. It requires explaining how a person fits into the vision, how it will affect them, and how achieving it will help them to advance a part of their life that is important to them. Inspiring someone with a vision also means that they need to be able to see exactly how the application of their effort will cause the vision to come to life. They need to see how they can personally help bring about the vision.

At Chipotle, we had articulated a vision for our company of "changing the way people think about and eat fast food." I cared about this vision, as did many of our employees. But this broader, company-level vision was not enough, because most people couldn't understand how they could personally make this vision happen, or how achieving it would directly affect their lives. This is why it was important to create the vision of building a Restaurateur culture committed to creating "a team of top performers, empowered to achieve high standards." This latter vision was something they could accomplish, and once accomplished, would change their lives by surrounding them with an elite team who cared about them and would do anything to help them. This vision mattered to them. They wanted badly to achieve it, and when they did, it changed their lives! It also advanced the company's broader vision of changing food culture.

Leaders need to make sure their people have a vision they can relate to. One that they can realistically achieve and which will change their lives.

## INSTILL CONFIDENCE IN YOUR PEOPLE

Instilling confidence means making sure your people feel confident in what they are doing, and that they understand how they fit into and are a critical part of the overall team. It means challenging them as much as possible with new tasks and trusting them to take more and more responsibility. People thrive on being challenged and being entrusted with more. As long as they are not pushed beyond their capabilities, this creates more confidence.

Few things instill confidence more than being given a challenge and succeeding. The best leaders continually look for ways to push their people and teams to the next level. One great way to do this is to start making leaders out of your team members. Give them a specific responsibility to achieve and ask them to organize a group of people to achieve it. Help them become leaders in their own right and teach them the methods of empowering the people whose assistance they call upon to achieve their goals.

Confidence is a virtuous cycle. Confidence begets more confidence. You have to start somewhere. You have to begin by creating a win worthy of celebrating. For example:

> "Sara, I asked you to clean the kitchen and you did a terrific job! Having a clean kitchen is critical to our mission, and I would like to ask if you'd be willing to take on a larger role. I'd like to put you in charge of training all new employees how to properly clean the kitchen, so that all of them can benefit from your leadership. Would you be willing to do that?"

Constantly noticing great work and asking for more in a way that honors your people demonstrates their importance to you and to the mission. It's extremely powerful. When you ask more of your team and help guide them to success, they can feel their own growth and advancement, which instills confidence. A good leader is always looking for opportunities to do this.

## TEACH THEM TO MAKE EACH OTHER BETTER

Having an empowered culture means everyone is empowered. Creating such a culture is difficult if one leader has to do it all by themselves. You must teach every person on the team how to make the people around them better.

To accomplish this, teach each person how satisfying and rewarding it is to help others and how, by doing so, they become an indispensable part of the team.

The best way to do this is to identify what people's strengths are and then challenge them to teach this to others. Constantly look for opportunities to help your people help the people around them. One effective way to do this is to watch yourself carefully. Each time you find yourself about to teach someone something, stop and ask instead, "Is there anyone else on my team who I can ask to teach this lesson instead of me?" Doing this repeatedly demonstrates your confidence in those whom you ask to teach others (which is empowering to them), provides a chance for them to realize their own value to the team (also empowering), teaches the task to a new person (a wonderful result), and it creates a deeper bond between the teacher and the student, which leads to a stronger team. It also sets an expectation that each person on the team should always be looking for an opportunity to teach and help others. As these behaviors become habitual, your people feel enriched and important, they share knowledge, they uphold higher standards, and you have a lot more time to do something else besides manage people!

## SHARE WHAT'S GOING ON

Have you ever discovered that someone had a party and you were not invited? Maybe you returned to school or work one day and someone said, "Wasn't that a great party?" You ask yourself, "What party?" It's happened to most of us, and it doesn't feel good being left out.

As a leader, sharing with your people what is going on in the workplace means making sure no one ever has that feeling. But it's more than that. When people are empowered, they feel like they are a critical part of the organization. They feel like an owner. It is essential to treat your people like owners, so they will feel and act like owners. This means letting them know every significant development—why we're firing someone, why we're hiring, what other changes we can expect, and any other subjects that may affect the workplace. Everyone feels more valued when they are in the know.

One of the most important and significant events for any team is the hiring of a new person. For this reason, everyone on the team should be involved in this process. Each team member should meet the new prospective member, have a chance to talk to them, and be able to voice an opinion about the wisdom of hiring them. There are a number of advantages to doing this:

- It shows your team that you value their opinion, which is empowering.
- It allows your team to teach you something, which is empowering.
- It demonstrates to the new candidate that we value our employees' opinions, which signals to the candidate how special the culture is.
- It ensures better candidate selection.

- If the new person is hired, it causes your team to work harder to ensure the success of the new hire, because they vouched for them to be hired. This empowers the new hire and makes them feel a sense of belonging.
- It gets the team thinking about the types of things that leaders need to consider, which starts their education towards becoming leaders themselves.
- It takes some of the responsibility of team-building off of your busy shoulders.
- It causes everyone on the team to start thinking about what a team of all top performers looks like.
- It teaches your team to communicate better, which they will need to learn to become leaders themselves one day.
- It gets your whole team thinking about and discussing the mission. What are we trying to accomplish and who will help us get there?
- Your team gets to know the company better, as they answer the many questions posed by the candidate.
- It dramatically increases the sense of ownership that your team feels toward the workplace, which will soon be filled with the people that they selected.

With all of these advantages, why would you not do this? This is an example of a single act that accomplishes many different desirable results. It is what I am always looking for when creating priorities.

Another important event to discuss is promotions. Who is the next manager and why is that person being selected? Obviously, promotions are a very important development in a workplace. When a leader explains their reasoning, it highlights to everyone the traits and behaviors that the leader values and intends to reward. It also encourages a conversation between the manager and the team member about where that particular person is on their journey to management. These discussions are essential to empowering the whole team.

## TACTICS TO CREATE A FEELING OF EMPOWERMENT

As a leader, you must work every day to empower your employees. Here are twelve things I have learned to do that contribute to empowerment, the holy grail of leadership:

- Be quick to take responsibility for your failures.
- Reveal your weaknesses to others, but let them discover your strengths.
- Make HR everyone's job.
- Watch how you spend your time; everyone else is!
- Teach that all satisfaction comes from helping others.
- Bond through hard work.
- Follow up on all requests, especially from junior employees.
- Be there for your team.
- Connect deeply with everyone you work with.
- Understand the power of sitting down.
- Embrace fear and conflict head-on.
- Keep it simple.

### BE QUICK TO TAKE RESPONSIBILITY FOR YOUR FAILURES

Early in my career at Messner & Reeves, LLC, I made sure I always took responsibility for anything our team did that disappointed a client, and I also gave others credit for excellent results.

After all, if I blamed someone else, a client might think less of my firm, and it would be very hard to repair that damage. But if I readily admitted that any mistakes were mine and mine alone, I would simultaneously demonstrate integrity and protect the reputation of my team.

This benefitted me in more ways than I could have imagined. First, my employees knew I had their backs and would never throw them under the bus to preserve my own reputation. Their trust led me to be much more effective as their leader.

Second, my employees had higher job satisfaction since they felt happy and empowered that I had sung their praises behind their backs.

Third, my team would work harder than ever to avoid a mistake, since they knew I would take the fall for it. No one likes to see their boss face criticism for their mistake.

Fourth, my clients came to believe we had an excellent law firm (since nothing was ever the fault of the firm) and started recommending me to other people and companies. We became busy and grew quickly.

Fifth, my team started to follow my example and took responsibility themselves, which conferred on each of them and our firm these same benefits.

Sixth, my team became incredibly loyal to me. They didn't want to work for anyone else. This was especially true for the people who had come from other companies or had other bosses. They appreciated that they had a good situation.

Seventh, taking responsibility is just what the person in charge does. By always doing it, I made it clear that I was the leader. I was in charge, and the buck stopped with me.

And finally, it was the right thing to do.

Yet I have found that very few leaders follow this rule. I often see people in leadership roles try to pass off the responsibility for bad results while claiming responsibility for good results. Doing this is poor form and a clear sign of weakness. It is pathetic, really. Smart people figure it out, and eventually, it erodes the credibility of the leader. As a leader, you are no better than your team and no better than their results. You may as well stand tall and own it!

## REVEAL YOUR WEAKNESSES TO OTHERS, BUT LET THEM DISCOVER YOUR STRENGTHS

As Chipotle's CEO, when I started spending a lot of time interfacing with investors, board members, and analysts who were looking to understand the company and what its strengths and opportunities were, it became helpful to be an open book about my weaknesses and the weaknesses of the company. Each quarter we held public phone calls called Quarterly Earnings Calls to announce our results for the previous quarter, give some texture on the road ahead, and take questions from investors. We started with a prepared statement and then took questions. I always wrote these prepared remarks with the goal of being totally honest and crystal clear. I never wanted investors to be overly optimistic after reading my comments. If they were, that would send the share price up more than was warranted, only to lead to disappointment later, accompanied by a falling share price. It could also lead to lawsuits if any investor later thought we overstated the likelihood of a positive future, leading them to make an investment they later regretted. I wanted none of this. I wanted people to have all the information to know exactly where things stood, so they'd never feel duped or hoodwinked and never feel that they'd made a mistake investing in Chipotle.

I wrote all of the disappointments right into these prepared remarks, and I answered questions asked by shareholders directly and honestly. What was really fun, though, was telling them how much better we should be doing. I focused on what we were doing wrong. I spent very little time talking about our financial accomplishments. They knew all about that anyway.

For instance, I'd share with them that our Restaurateur stores had better same store sales, margins, food costs, and labor costs than the rest of our stores. Then I'd share with them our disappointment that we only had Restaurateurs in 25 percent of our restaurants. I told them the mere fact that 75 percent of our restaurants did not have these elite managers running them was a failure of our leadership and that we had to change that. I'd also tell them that our fastest restaurants put 300 people through the line in one hour. Then I'd share that our average store only put through 110 an hour. I'd tell them this meant we were well short of where we should be, operationally. But by doing this, rather than cause them to think I was a fool, they grew confident that I had my finger on the pulse of what we needed to do to keep growing and improving. It was obvious I was not resting on my laurels, waiting for time to make things better. I gained immense credibility with our shareholders, analysts, and our board.

So many leaders sugarcoat results. It is so daft, I cannot understand it. All that does is temporarily pump up the stock (if even that), erode the leader's credibility, and cause investors to question if the leader really knows what's going on. Investors will usually figure out how good you are, but by telling them what's not going well, you'll gain their long-term respect. Then they will sing your praises much more loudly and credibly than you ever could. The worst kind of leader is the one who expresses more confidence in themselves than the situation merits and acts like everything is excellent. Those are the ones who lose credibility.

By failing to see their shortcomings, they tend to fail to do what is necessary to improve themselves or the company.

The Bible contains a related reference to this topic. It says, "For those who exalt themselves will be humbled and those who humble themselves will be exalted." This is a good rule to live by. There is nothing to lose and everything to gain by humbling yourself and revealing your weaknesses. It tends to keep you hungry to improve, learn, and grow so that you can give more of yourself.

## MAKE HR EVERYONE'S JOB

As I discussed above, at Chipotle, I ultimately found that having a traditional HR department involved in hiring and firing and disciplining employees caused more problems than it solved. While HR can be effective at the administrative aspects of hiring, onboarding, assembling pay and benefit packages, and other administrative tasks, they are often very poor at building strong teams. But that is OK because building strong teams is too important to delegate to any specific department. It should be everyone's job.

## WATCH HOW YOU SPEND YOUR TIME—EVERYONE ELSE IS!

While nearly every leader knows that people are listening to what they say, many forget that everyone is also watching what they do. As the old saying goes, actions speak louder than words. And if you are in the position of leading others, your actions are even more scrutinized.

If top leaders spend their time in the ivory tower crunching numbers and reviewing spreadsheets and financials, the field leaders will follow suit. The team will aspire to be like the people at the top. Just before I started working at Chipotle, the COO spent his time looking at numbers and talking about finance. He created all sorts of goals, seeking to hit this or that financial target. He went on and on about these goals to our employees, our board, anyone who would listen. No one cared. Talking about numbers didn't motivate any behavior at all, of course. Why would it? One goal that I remember in particular was the COO's repeated proclamation that we'd hit a target for our Denver stores of "a million and four in '04!" This silly rhyme was meant to say that our goal was to hit $1.4 million in average volume for our Denver stores in 2004. Guess what? Chipotle didn't reach this target. Why would a regional goal with a catchy rhyme cause hourly employees to want to change their behavior? Well, it wouldn't. And it didn't.

In my case, the thousands of hours I spent with our managers and crew members in our restaurants paid enormous dividends. I not only learned a great deal from them, but my example was followed by our many hundreds of field leaders, who put their effort into ensuring a great customer experience in our stores as well. All the attention was on our restaurant teams, their well-being, and performance. This led to excellent restaurants, extremely happy employees, and industry-leading sales improvements, margins, and profits. And it was a lot more fun!

## TEACH THAT ALL SATISFACTION COMES FROM HELPING OTHERS

If you want to know the key to happiness, empowerment, and well-being, I'll tell you. It is finding a way to help the people around you be at their very best. If you look at all the people in history who have had the most fulfilling lives, again and again, you'll find people who were instrumental in helping others.

Since helping others is what is most fulfilling, any job that gives people the opportunity to do so is a real gift. So as a leader, it is your role to make it clear that success in any role requires helping the whole team succeed.

Of course, there is an incredible added benefit to this. By teaching people, you will also build a culture of top performers, empowered to achieve high standards, which means your organization will thrive as a result.

## BOND THROUGH HARD WORK

At Messner & Reeves, LLC, we had a culture of hard work. As I've described, when I recruited and interviewed new employees, I even took to "trying to scare them away" by telling them we worked extremely hard. We were a tight team, trusting each other, caring for each other, and jumping in to help each other whenever needed. Our new lawyers learned quickly, had a lot of responsibility, and felt important. We were an empowered team, and you could feel it as soon as you walked in the door.

When I first came to Chipotle in 2005, I removed loads of low-performing employees, put a stop to most of the useless retreats and boondoggles, and created a different culture. This culture was based on creating teams of empowered top performers, working to achieve high standards to reach our vision of "changing the way people think about and eat fast food." What is perhaps surprising is that this new culture of working harder, being less wasteful, and focusing on becoming a successful company, was a lot more fun. People bonded, felt important, and had real purpose. Goofing off is fun for a while, but in the long run, making good use of yourself is a lot more fun.

In October of 2015, one of our biggest challenges reinforced the bonding power of hard work. More than fifty of our customers contracted E. coli after eating at Chipotle restaurants. This event was extremely unfortunate, and I took this failure to protect our customers extremely seriously. The event was widely publicized and led to a sharp decline in sales for the first time in our history.

Since news of the illness came in the form of multiple announcements from the CDC over the course of several weeks, it looked like we had an ongoing series of outbreaks of E. coli. This naturally caused widespread concern that our food might be unsafe on an ongoing basis. The reality was that all these illnesses were tied to one incident. Chipotle was in the news for many weeks as a result of these constant news stories, and our sales suffered badly.

Of course, we, as a management team, reacted swiftly to review every part of our food chain to identify the problem and eliminate any possible future problems. We paid for experts to conduct thousands of tests throughout our supply chain and in our restaurants. After doing more than 5,000 tests for pathogens, we were unable to find even a single incident of any pathogen or any foodborne illness in any of our restaurants. Additionally, tests of every single ingredient came up negative for any pathogen. While this sounds like a positive result, it actually exacerbated the problem, because we were unable to identify the ingredient responsible for the illnesses. This made it impossible for Chipotle to assure its customers that it had found the problem and eliminated it, which led to ongoing concerns on behalf of our customers, who were afraid to return to our stores.

In the wake of the food safety crisis, once we took every possible action to make our food safer, I knew that our focus had to remain steadfast on sustaining our excellent operations to win back our customers. I knew this would take time (I estimated three years based on studying other similar companies who had had similar incidents). Due to the impact to our sales and reputation, our stock price fell significantly during this time, which ignited concerns on the part of some of our analysts about the efficacy of our co-CEO structure. This became quite clear when our officer team went on another road show to meet with our largest investors across the country to address any concerns they had with regard to how we were managing the company. During these many meetings, the questions asked by analysts revealed a much higher level of concern and scrutiny concerning the co-CEO structure than we'd ever seen before. Specifically, a number of investors put pressure on Steve to step down as co-CEO and remain chairman of the board. They pointed out that it was not considered a best practice to have a chairman of the board also be a CEO of a public company. For the first time in our history as a public company, these meetings did not feel as warm and friendly.

While this was a very hard time for us, we were determined to use the experience to get better. Our lower sales meant that our profits dropped dramatically. We had to more carefully scrutinize every new hiring decision. Yet, at the same time, we wanted to be sure to do nothing that would undermine our operations. So, we brought our teams together and let them know that with certain exceptions, we were going to freeze all new hires in the corporate office. The company kept right on ticking along and none of our teams reported feeling put out or overworked. Our Restaurateur culture had already created strong teams. It was the perfect foundation and example of how teams could face adversity together and rise above it to prevail. The result was fantastic. Even though many departments had far fewer employees than they had planned for, they drew together and got more work done than ever.

## FOLLOW UP ON ALL REQUESTS, ESPECIALLY FROM JUNIOR EMPLOYEES

When you are in any position of leadership, people constantly ask you questions and share their ideas. These interactions are very important and significant, especially to those who initiate them. It is essential that you follow up and do so consistently.

My personal rule was that the more junior in the organization someone was, the higher I would prioritize getting back to them. There are a number of good reasons I found this practice to be worthwhile.

First, people more junior in the organization do not expect a quick response. They don't expect that they are your priority. When you treat them as your top priority, it is extremely empowering and exciting to them. It just blows them away.

Second, they see that you care, and it gives you huge credibility. They also tell other employees that you care, and you begin to be known as an attentive leader throughout the company.

Third, it sets a very good example for them to follow. If the CEO gets right back to them, they'll be more likely to treat others wanting their time and attention with the same urgency.

Fourth, people who are less senior are more hesitant to give you suggestions, or to ask you for your time. Also, you see such people less often, and they have less of a chance to tell you what is on their minds. When they do, you can assume that it is very important to them and worthy of your quick attention.

Fifth, junior employees tend to be the ones closest to the action, which means that their insights are often more useful.

Sixth, executive level employees feel that they are in a position to remind you to get back to them, whereas entry-level people do not. They'll just think they are not important and will not bother you again. That would be a real shame, send the wrong message, and deprive you of the benefit of their help.

## BE THERE FOR YOUR TEAM

After I graduated law school in May of 1993 and was considering which firm to join as a young associate attorney, I received an offer from the Los Angeles firm of Morris Polich & Purdy. The firm invited me and my girlfriend, Kathy, to their Christmas party, on the top floor of an L.A. skyscraper. At this time, I had several offers from other law firms and really was not sure which one to choose. But Kathy and I figured it was worth at least attending their Christmas party to see what they were all about.

When the elevator door opened on the twenty-eighth floor, Kathy and I were greeted by the most handsome man I could imagine, with the nicest suit, deepest voice, and firmest handshake. "Monty!" his voice boomed. "Yes!" I said, amazed, impressed, and wondering how this impressive gentleman knew my name. "Ted Polich," he declared. Immediately it was clear to me that this was the Polich whose name was on the door, but whom I'd never met before. "And this must be your beautiful girlfriend, Kathy...Hi!" he said. Then as he turned his massive shoulders to address her fully, he continued, "Kathy, Ted Polich, it's a pleasure to meet you!" He then turned back to me and said, "Monty, we are absolutely delighted you've decided to become part of our law firm!"

Kathy and I were blown away. The founder and lead partner of the firm, who we'd never met before, actually *expected* our arrival. He knew our names! My immediate reply to him was, "Thank you so much! I am so honored!" There was no chance I would have said, "Thank you, Mr. Polich, but I still have not made up my mind."

Ted Polich not only knew our names, but he'd found us important enough to greet us as we arrived at his firm. While other firms tried to play coy and treat people as though they were lucky to be there, Ted Polich made it clear that the honor was his, and his team was lucky to have me. I was hooked and landed. I didn't even consider taking one of the other offers that I'd received.

When someone you admire and trust makes a bet on you, when they express their confidence that you are a winner, you will break your back to prove them right. So it was with me. I was on Ted Polich's team, and I was going to prove I belonged there. It took only a few minutes of his time to know a few details about us and be in the right place at the right time. It worked, and I've tried to emulate his example countless times since.

## CONNECT DEEPLY WITH EVERYONE YOU WORK WITH

Sheila Riley, my sixth-grade teacher, was a strict woman who took her job very seriously. She tried to appear intimidating and tough, but couldn't hide her warm, loving heart. One day, when I had the whole class laughing (remember, I was a bit of a clown at the time), she called me out into the hall. I expected her to chew me out. Instead, she said, "Monty, you are an amazing young man. You have so much potential. Of all the kids in the class, I put you on a pedestal. But you are not trying your hardest, and I hate to see you fall short of your potential."

This short meeting had an enormous effect on me. I felt simultaneously very special and ashamed of how I'd been acting in class. From then on, I wanted to be at my best. I wanted to please Mrs. Riley. While I still had moments of clowning around and making others laugh, I reeled it back in every time she'd glance my way. Her glance made me feel special but also responsible. Mrs. Riley's talk was an excellent example of superb leadership. She knew how to connect with me and what to say to bring out the best in me.

You will follow someone if you trust that they are the best person to lead you to a better place than where you are now. You will follow someone if you believe they are capable and desirous of making you better—if they challenge you, teach you, and bring out the best in you. The only way that your team members will trust that you are someone who will bring them to a better place is if they feel that you know them and are committed to them. Such a commitment is best demonstrated by establishing a personal connection.

## THE POWER OF SITTING DOWN

Nothing encourages a team member more than when their leader cares enough to sit down with them, address them one-on-one, and really listen. Once seated, the leader can articulate a compelling and exciting vision, take the time to understand the individual deeply, commit to helping them be at their best, and explain how achieving the vision will enrich the person's life. During a one-on-one, a leader can begin the process of creating encouraging circumstances for their people.

As I began leading Chipotle in 2005, I noticed that field leaders almost always stood (and seldom sat) to talk to their people, usually when the team member was working on a particular task, such as preparing vegetables. In fact, my predecessors had even given this kind of discussion a name. It was called shoulder-to-shoulder training. While this training has a time and place, the problem was that the subject of the discussion would almost always concern the task that was being performed. It was never about the person themselves. What is essential to empowering a person is that the leader commits to focus on the person. Sitting down brings gravity and respect to a conversation. It shows the crew member that they are worthy of our attention. Sitting to talk to an employee shows them that your attention is on them, not the food they are cooking, the dishes they are washing, or the job they are doing.

It is this commitment to focus on the person, as opposed to their work product, that is so critical to creating a culture of empowerment. By caring for the person, a leader cultivates a relationship with the person. Within this relationship, a number of important qualities materialize, including mutual commitment, concern, conscientiousness, loyalty, and devotion. Because this relationship fulfills a number of the person's psychological needs, the person then has the mental bandwidth as well as the desire to give their best attention to the mission outlined by the leader. They are committed, loyal, and passionate about giving of themselves. This leads them to work hard and produce excellent results.

On the contrary, when a person discovers that a leader is more concerned about their work product, the person will not be fulfilled and will need to seek fulfillment elsewhere than from their work. Their passion will be elsewhere and unavailable to devote to the leader's mission. Ironically, a leader's insistence on caring less for the person as an individual and more for how the person prepares vegetables, washes dishes, or organizes their kitchen, will lead them to perform each of these tasks with less care and skill. In this case, the leader can repeat their complaints over and over, and it will not fix the problem. This leads to a paralyzing cycle of constant dissatisfaction. The leader then exhibits their dissatisfaction by complaining more and giving more negative feedback, which only exacerbates the problem. Then the leader feels they haven't the time to undertake the caring behaviors of concerning themselves about their people. At this point, the leader is not a leader at all. They are a manager. A taskmaster. They will never cultivate results they are satisfied with.

People's greatest emotional need is to be seen, understood, loved, and cared for. They gravitate towards people who make them feel that way. Sitting down creates a moment in time dedicated to a person and allows a connection. It makes it clear to them that this moment in time is about them, and that they are important to you. Sitting down also creates space, room for the employee to share openly, without concern, and room for the leader to learn what is going on in the employee's world. For instance, the leader might notice the employee is trying to impress them, and they might ask themselves why this is so. Perhaps it is because the leader subconsciously wants this from their people. If the leader is aware enough to notice this, they can tell the person that it's not important to impress them. All they really want is to see and understand what the employee's real experience is. The leader might notice that the person is shy or nervous to talk to them. The leader might say, "It seems that you're a little nervous. Let me reassure you that I'm sitting with you because I want to truly understand you, your personal experience working here, and what I can do better as your leader. I'm not going to share what you say with others. I just want to learn so that I can be more effective. To the extent that you're willing to share that with me, I'd really appreciate it."

If you're a good, credible, trustworthy person, they'll believe you and will be a bit less nervous, but you need to earn this trust. You might share something personal about yourself to set an example that you trust them. By showing your soft underbelly and openness, an environment of trust will arise. If you notice when you sit with someone that they are rushed or distracted, you can say to them, "Is this not a good time to talk? You seem a little distracted?" If the person is distracted, they will usually let you know the reason why.

When you sit with someone to have effective communication, you have to start by understanding where, psychologically, that person is right now. Are they nervous, scared, rushed, skeptical, irritated? Once you address these possible barriers to good communication, they will be more eager to share their experience, since they'll have seen that you value them enough to notice the truth of their present situation. Then a beautiful unfolding will take place, a true human interaction that will allow you to understand what's going on in their life or situation, whether it be at work, with family, whatever. The more you allow yourself to understand where they're coming from, the more you can start to understand what the solution might be for them to arrive at a better place.

Monty and Gretchen Selfridge, Restaurant Support Officer, interviewing Esmeralda "Esme" Correjudo, moments before her promotion to Restaurateur. Denver, Colorado, 2011.

### EMBRACE FEAR AND CONFLICT HEAD-ON

One very important characteristic that leaders need to develop is courage. It's the ability to push forward in the face of fears, conflict, or discomfort. People are so afraid of conflict, they will tolerate even a miserable status quo in order to avoid the increase in short-term discomfort that even mild conflict might cause them to feel. For this reason, many bosses will tolerate poor performance by their subordinates, because they are afraid to have an uncomfortable conversation with them. Those who are willing and able to address difficult or uncomfortable situations head-on have a huge advantage as leaders.

At Chipotle, I quickly got a reputation as being very direct and to the point. People saw me as the person in the room who wouldn't tolerate nonsense and had very strong opinions. I think all those years as a trial lawyer, dealing with unscrupulous and dishonest lawyers who would take advantage of my every weakness, or even just dealing with the constant conflict that comes with spending all day every day dealing with disputes, must have made me this way.

One of the things I learned when I began to play poker was that the players who were bold and gutsy usually were the winners. Of course, you can't be foolish. But, there is a saying in the poker world: "fortune favors the bold." There is a reason for this. It turns out that the cards you actually hold in your hand are not really what is most important in the game of poker. Instead, it is how you play them. The fact is, at least in the game of Texas hold 'em poker, the vast majority of hands come to an end without a showdown. In other words, the play ends and the money is awarded, because everyone except one player folds their hand. The remaining player wins by default without ever having to show their cards. That means, of course, that the cards that the one remaining player was holding were actually irrelevant!

Often in poker, if you hold a weak hand, but play your cards as though you have a very strong hand and bet heavily, it is likely that you will cause other people to fold hands that are stronger than yours. In order to accomplish this, though, you need to have the courage of your convictions. You need to develop a stomach for taking a risk, based on your beliefs. This process of making a bet and risking losing money solely based on your belief that you are right is a good exercise in learning to confront your fear.

If you learn to develop in yourself the willingness to be bold and assertive to do what you think is right even in uncomfortable or risky situations, you will be a more powerful person and a better leader. You will be more effective in making change. But to do this takes practice. No one is born enjoying uncomfortable feelings or facing their fears. It is a skill that is learned, practiced, and cultivated.

## KEEP IT SIMPLE

There's an apocryphal story about how NASA tried to design a pen that would work in the zero-gravity conditions of space. After spending millions on research, they learned that the Soviets used a pencil. True or not, the story illustrates a worthy point.

When businesses have problems, often there is a simple solution. Yet, as often as not, I see leaders purchasing expensive new tools or new technology in an effort to solve the problem. The trouble is that these tools or technological solutions often do not solve or only partially solve the problem. This is especially true with custom technological solutions, which I find always cost many times what is expected, take many times longer to implement, and consume a lot of resources. Then, once finished, the custom technology is usually unreliable, in need of constant maintenance, and did not solve the problem it was intended to solve anyway.

Shortly after I started in my role as president of Chipotle in 2005, there were a number of people who said that we needed an intranet (not internet, but intranet, which is a restricted private network for use by employees) to better conduct internal company communications at Chipotle. One of our officers insisted that it was absolutely necessary. I asked why email was inadequate, and I was given a number of reasons. In fact, I was made to feel a bit naïve for not immediately recognizing the magical power of this technology that we lacked. After months of requests, late that year, I told the officer who was pleading for this new technology to go ahead and pursue it. Two years later, he'd gotten nowhere on the project, and in another three years, it was long forgotten. Somehow during this time, our results skyrocketed, even without this mandatory technology.

In 2014, a different executive reignited the desire for this apparently crucial communication technology. I reminded him that we'd already been through this, and I argued a bit against it, but his determination was even stronger than the first officer's had been. He was adamant and passionate that if we built this, it would dramatically improve the efficiency of our teams. He went as far as to say that we were negligent not to have it and that we had significant technical debt because we didn't yet possess this system. So, I allowed him to pursue it, and he quickly hired an expensive executive whose only job for a year was to build this intranet. After the year had passed, we were no closer to having this critical and essential system. Yet, our burrito sales were through the roof, and people seemed to be communicating better than ever. Another two years along, we still had no intranet. I retired a year after that, and at that time no one was even trying to build this critical and mandatory technology. Everyone was on to other things, I suppose. I'm quite sure that it remains unbuilt to this day. Yet, somehow, Chipotle lives on.

# CHAPTER 12

# THE ALCHEMY OF VISION, PEOPLE, AND STANDARDS

REMEMBER HOW, AT THE BEGINNING OF THE BOOK, I wrote that the things I teach here are intertwined? Here is where you really see that. As I showed in the previous chapters, empowerment is a foundational principle of great leadership. It's rooted in vulnerability, curiosity, love, and encouragement. There are four other principles of great leadership that interrelate with and build upon empowerment.

They are:

- Share a worthy vision
- Assemble and retain the right people
- Set high standards
- Communicate effectively

In this chapter I'll go into the first three. The fourth, communication, is so important that I discuss it separately and in depth in chapter 14.

## SHARE A WORTHY VISION

I discussed vision in the previous chapter—it is critical. Building a great culture first requires a worthy vision, because great people want to do something meaningful. By vision I simply mean a mental picture of an exciting and worthwhile accomplishment—an understanding of a future situation that will be gratifying, liberating, fulfilling, and exciting. Here are three rules to be sure that your vision is an effective one:

1. **Relatable:** The vision needs to be something exciting that the person can relate to and easily understand.
2. **Realistic:** It also has to be something tangible and finite enough that people can realistically see that they can, by their own efforts, make material progress toward its achievement.
3. **Impactful:** Finally, it has to be something that, once accomplished, will have a materially positive impact on the person's life.

The vision I am talking about needn't be precisely the same as the company's overall vision, but accomplishing it should inure to the company's benefit as well. Often, it is necessary for the leader to illustrate a vision for his team that is more tangible than the overall company's vision. But the company's vision should also be meaningful and worthy of the work of excellent people.

To repeat an earlier example, Chipotle's company vision was: "To change the way people think about and eat fast food." This was a meaningful and important vision, but it was not relatable or realistic or impactful enough, on an individual basis, to motivate our teams. It was hard to see where the work of any one individual could make material progress toward its fulfillment, or how achieving it would directly improve a specific person's life. In other words, it did not fit the three rules I stated above. This is why I created a more relatable vision that fit inside the broader vision. This was the vision of building teams of top performers, empowered to achieve high standards. This vision was relatable, realistic, and impactful. It fit the three rules above.

Finally, the vision must be shared such that it is well understood and aspirational. The team must strongly desire to accomplish it. So, the leader must clearly communicate the vision and make it personal to every person on their team. If the leader doesn't believe in the vision, they won't be able to share it effectively. The best way to share the vision is to have a one-on-one discussion with each team member, as I described in chapter 6.

## ASSEMBLE THE RIGHT PEOPLE AND RETAIN TOP PERFORMERS

Throughout this book, I've referred repeatedly to top performers and how important they are. That, in broad terms, is what I mean by the right people. It's easy enough to agree that we want top performers working for us. But what do they look like? How do you find and retain them?

In chapter 6, I described how it didn't take me long, once I began conducting one-on-one conversations with Chipotle staff at our corporate headquarters, to realize that people were falling into two buckets: those who loved their jobs for what they were able to accomplish for the company and the people around them, and those who loved their jobs for all the things that they didn't have to do.

Clearly, I wanted to attract and retain the first group and repel and remove the second group. In other words, I wanted to build a culture that attracted top performers and repelled low performers. Eventually, I developed this definition of top performer:

**Someone who has the desire and ability to perform excellent work, and through their constant effort to do so, elevates themselves, the people around them, and the organization.**

Do you recall how, on my first day at Chipotle, I told the area managers that "each of us will be rewarded based on our effectiveness at making the people around us better?" That day one idea is baked into this definition since the definition actually requires elevating other people.

Your team needs to know this definition. They need to know that doing excellent work is not enough, that making others better is an essential ingredient to their advancement. In any company or organization that intends to grow, there will be a need for a lot of excellent people to provide a strong foundation for growth. This is why a top performer has to do more than a great job. It is essential that a top performer performs their excellent work in such a way that elevates others. So, while a good worker may produce quality work, all day, every day, a top performer goes further. A top performer's constant effort elevates the people around themselves and the organization as a whole.

As I described earlier, the Chipotle I joined in 2005 was doing a poor job hiring. They were seeking people with fast food experience (in other words, people who'd picked up lousy habits which are hard to unlearn), instead of focusing on hiring people with the right underlying characteristics. When I pointed this out, our leaders quickly came to realize that a change was warranted. They could see that training people with the right characteristics to run great restaurants was better than relying solely on fast food experience. But what specifically were the characteristics we were looking for? What were the most important qualities for an entry-level employee to have that would make them most likely to succeed and quickly move up into management positions? These qualities had to be ones that were easy to identify in even a short interview. But also, these qualities had to be ones that we couldn't train, since we would not want to narrow our search for new employees by anything that could be trained.

Since Chipotle hired tens of thousands of people every year, I was sure that we must be wasting tens of millions of dollars training people who were not able to be successful. It was a shame if this happened even once, since it could be avoided! But I knew it was happening all day, every day, throughout the entire company. For this reason, it felt like an emergency to me. So, I asked our teams to hire only those who had the following thirteen characteristics.

1. Conscientious
2. Respectful
3. Hospitable
4. High Energy
5. Infectiously Enthusiastic
6. Happy
7. Presentable
8. Smart
9. Polite
10. Motivated

11. Ambitious
12. Curious
13. Honest

Again, these were characteristics we sought out during hiring. They were characteristics that would make it more likely that our people, once trained, could be excellent. Since experience was not important to us (we'd rather train people ourselves), we stopped looking for experience at all. One of our recruiting advertisements even said, "No experience preferred!" It was a play on the common "no experience required" placard one often sees in an employment advertisement.

It was essential to hire for these characteristics because they are things that by a very young age, you either have or you don't have. They can't be trained once someone is an adult, at least not without years of psychotherapy!

The characteristics one seeks for various different types of business may differ. But the point is that it is critical to hire for such characteristics that cannot be trained. If certain things cannot be trained, and if they are important to you, you'd better hire folks who already have them.

What was funny, though, is that after I came up with these characteristics, I started to see evidence that our leaders in the restaurants were trying to train people to have them. I'd see posters popping up in the back of restaurants, asking: "Do you have all thirteen characteristics?" I'd see entries in Crew Development Journals, saying, "I'm trying to teach William to be more infectiously enthusiastic and happy." I'd quickly remind the person who wrote such entries that these were characteristics we looked for *in new hires*, but not qualities we tried to train into our existing employees. I'd say, "Don't try to teach people something that can't be taught! Instead, decide whether they can be successful without this characteristic and if so, do the best you can with them." Yet, for as long as I led people, this was an ongoing struggle: trying to teach people to understand that "teaching the unteachable" was a poor use of time. The truth is, there are some things you cannot teach. Trying to teach what can't be taught is a waste of time.

Chipotle's thirteen characteristics may not be the right fit for another type of business, but the point is that a leader needs to be mindful of what type of person will be most successful in a position *before* they begin hiring. Asking, "What qualities would someone have to have in order to be superb in the role I seek to fill?" will encourage putting some thought into what type of person one needs to hire. While experience was not important to us at Chipotle, it is necessary for some roles. You need to speak Spanish and English if your job is going to be translating from Spanish to English. You need to be able to write code if you are going to be a programmer.

Beyond the specific experience that may be essential, it is also critical to hire the right *type* of person. You want to hire a person with the characteristics that will help you build the kind of culture you want in the workplace. These were the characteristics that we hired for, but how were we to retain these people?

The way to retain top performers is to build a culture that appeals to them more than any competing culture. For this reason, a leader must ask about every aspect of their operation. Is it geared to attract and retain top performers?

The things that attract top performers are:

- They want to do something meaningful with their time.
- They want to be challenged by a leader they respect.

- They want their work seen and appreciated.
- They want to be paid based on the merit of their work, not seniority.
- They want to be surrounded by other top performers.
- They want to work hard, do their best, and make a real contribution.
- They want to make others better and celebrate their success.
- They want to constantly develop and improve themselves.

It is worth going through the above list periodically and assessing whether your organization is still doing what's necessary to reward and cherish your top performers. Make sure that careful thought has been given to each and every item on this list and that you have tailored your culture to perfectly fulfill these desires.

Another way to ensure you attract top performers is to make sure that your culture does NOT attract, or pander to, low performers. *After all, the attributes that attract top performers repel low performers, and vice-versa.* So, a good cross-check for a leader to be sure they have the right type of culture is to be sure it doesn't attract low performers. To do this, look at the list that follows and be sure you are not culturally rewarding low performers. Low performers:

- Don't like being challenged.
- Don't want anyone to focus on them or their work product.
- Expect to get paid just for showing up.
- Think that raises and bonuses should be awarded based on seniority.
- Don't like top performers.
- Think hard work is an imposition and not rewarding.

- Prefer an easy day and don't like to be challenged.
- Appreciate it when less is asked of them.
- Don't value the opportunity to contribute more.
- Appreciate being around other low performers who don't rock the boat.

Yet right now, in organizations all over the world, leaders are hanging on to low performers. I have almost never seen an organization, team, or restaurant (other than my Restaurateur restaurants!) that is not harboring a number of low performers, despite these many disadvantages.

Admitting you have low performers on the team is the first step. Next, you need to make sure that you've told them that you consider them a low performer and have provided them with clear and honest feedback in order to give them a chance to improve. If they do not quickly improve, then you need to remove them.

Many leaders cite compassion as their reason for not removing a low performer from the team. This is hogwash! For a leader to retain a low performer is not compassionate. It is selfish, unhelpful, and an act of cowardice. If someone is a low performer, they very likely know it. They feel badly about it, deep inside. Retaining them on the team prevents them from finding the fulfillment they are capable of having if they become engaged in something that is truly fulfilling to them, where they can excel. The real reason leaders keep low performers around is usually because they themselves lack the willpower to have a tough conversation. But having the tough conversation yields so many benefits that it is something you simply cannot afford to avoid.

While I have seen people retain low performers for a long time past when they should have removed them, I have never seen someone act too quickly to remove one. Obviously, if someone has simply not received the necessary training, feedback, or had the appropriate tools, then that is another story. If, however, someone has been given a compelling vision in an effective way, is confident in their ability, is exposed to encouraging circumstances, and is still a low performer, then it is time to remove them. Let them move on to a more fulfilling and successful career. Elsewhere.

How do you know if someone is a low performer? The answer is simple. They are!

Let me explain. You would never wonder if your best employee is a low performer, would you? No. You are eternally grateful for your top performers, who come in every day and give you all they have and produce great results. There are other workers who are not great yet, but who are either new or still learning things they need to know to be effective. For these folks, you aren't wondering if they are low performers. So that means that the only category you may be wondering about, scratching your head about, are low performers!

While I have seen companies benefit from removing low performers hundreds of times, I have yet to see or hear a single time, that "Rats! We should not have fired that person. I wish we had them back!" It just never happens.

## MAKE SURE MEDIOCRE EMPLOYEES KNOW THEY ARE MEDIOCRE

Most leaders, actually nearly all, are not very good at making sure that every single team member knows exactly where they stand. This probably includes you!

Each person needs to know to what degree they are meeting the leader's expectations. It is particularly important that mediocre employees know that you consider their performance to be mediocre. After all, these people are either a potential top performer who has not yet been unleashed, or someone who will never be a great addition to the team. You need to give them an opportunity to become a top performer or to leave and move on to a place where they can have a more rewarding experience.

Time and time again, when I met with low or mediocre performers throughout my time as a CEO, I would quickly tell their supervisor that I found the person to be mediocre.

"Oh, yes. I agree," they would say.

"Well, have you told them that they are a mediocre performer?"

"Oh, yes. They know! I've had a conversation with them about it."

Everyone knew that I was a stickler about people knowing very clearly where they stood with their leaders. I always found it critically important. After all, how likely are you to improve if you already think you are meeting your leader's expectations?

After receiving their supervisor's reassurance that they'd communicated everything clearly, I would follow up with the mediocre performer, just to be sure that they heard the conversation the same way that their supervisor told me it was delivered. I'd sit with the person and have a conversation. After getting to know them a bit, I would pop the question.

"So, how do you feel about your performance here?"

"Oh...good! I think I'm doing pretty well!"

"Do you consider yourself a top performer?" (Everyone at Chipotle knew my definition of top performer.)

"Ahhh...I think so."

"And does your manager agree with you, that you are a top performer?"

"Ahhhh...well, I hope so!"

The bottom line was that most mediocre performers had never received a clear message about their performance, even if their supervisor insisted to me that they had. I'd have a serious chat with the supervisor afterward, letting them know that what they thought was clear was very unclear. This happened thousands of times. Very, very seldom during my follow-up did I find a mediocre performer who actually knew that they were considered as such. I found this a shame because telling someone that they are falling short of your expectations is a huge gift to them. It gives them a chance to get better. To be successful. And, if the message is delivered with love and compassion, such conversations are actually uplifting.

In my CEO roles, I developed a reputation for being extremely clear and direct, yet compassionate. People often told me that they were amazed at how I could deliver a very tough message, yet cause the person hearing it to feel uplifted, excited, and motivated to do better. But there was a reason people felt better after I let them know they were falling short. The truth is that most people know when they are not doing great, and there is a shroud of uneasiness that they live with every day, that they try to ignore. When you come and tell them the truth, you remove the shroud of uneasiness, and they know the fresh, beautiful truth! It is like a fresh wind comes in and blows away the dank, humid, stale air and whisks in the fresh air of hope, truth, and optimism!

It turns out that people are much more comfortable knowing you are not satisfied with their performance, then suspecting it to be so and living in uncertainty. Also, when I told someone they were falling short, I would explain in clear detail what they needed to do to get better, and specifically how they could improve and become a top performer. Then, I would fantasize with them just how wonderful it was going to be for them, how it would bring more satisfaction to their life, including more excitement, fulfillment, and financial success. I would illustrate an exciting vision for their future with enough detail that they could almost taste it. Knowing that I believed in them enough to be totally honest, that I invested time to guide them to a better place, and that they could have a marvelous future, left them feeling clean and invigorated. It was wonderful to watch. So while it was hard for me to deliver tough messages, I became more and more convinced about the incredible value it held for the person and the company. For this reason, I made it a priority to do so quickly and often. I also made it clear to all of my leaders that this was a critical part of their job, and I expected that every single person on their teams would have a clear understanding of exactly what their leader thought of their performance.

## DON'T OVER-EMPHASIZE SENIORITY

As you build a culture that appeals only to top performers and repels low performers, remember that promotions based on seniority are generally favored by low performers. In other words, such promotions are generally a bad idea. Your goal is to establish a meritocracy, where top performers who add huge value to the organization are rewarded. As such, the concept of seniority cannot play an overly significant role. But equally, seniority is not a meaningless concept that can be ignored.

Seniority should not be considered at all for someone who is not and has never been a top performer. In other words, if someone has been in their role a long time, but has never been excellent in it, their time in a position is meaningless, and they should be removed. For top performers, as their time in a position increases, they build up a degree of what I call goodwill that newer

# DON'T HIRE ANYONE WITHOUT ASKING THESE EIGHT QUESTIONS

Hiring new people is fraught with risk. First, hiring someone new is usually not the right call. Second, even if hiring someone is a good idea, no one can do it consistently without making mistakes. You may hire the wrong person who will degrade the culture, do poor work, upset others, give bad service, and upon removal, sue you, or make unfair demands. Since hiring someone is risky, I would exercise extreme caution before doing so. When people ask to hire more workers for their team, I suggest that you **always** ask at least **all** of the following questions:

1. Is everyone on the current team a top performer who is effective and efficient? If not, don't hire a new person. Instead, solve this problem.
2. Is there any simple tool or inexpensive technology that could easily allow the existing team to get more done, such that the additional person would not be necessary? If there is, get it.
3. Is there anything that the team is currently working on that isn't critically important that they could stop doing so that the existing team could get by without another hire? If so, stop doing the not-so-useful activities, so that you needn't hire more people.
4. Is there a team member on another team that has the capacity to take on additional responsibility, such that you could avoid this hire? If so, get help from them.
5. If you must hire someone new, is there a way to find someone strong enough to replace a mediocre performer on the existing team, such that your team needn't grow in size? If so, make the swap.
6. Would it be better to outsource some tasks, such as to alleviate the burden on your team so that you can avoid this hire? If so, do so.
7. Can you use a temporary employee instead of a full-time one, which will allow you to decide later if you really need this as a full-time permanent position? If so, go for it.
8. If it is necessary to hire someone, what specific value or improved result can you count on? Make sure that you have clear, high expectations as to what specific improvement you expect from the new hire.

The reality is that very few times, the answer to all of these questions is "No." So, in my experience, once I asked all these questions, seldom did we make the decision to hire more people.

employees don't have. This goodwill factors in if, for instance, an employee has a period of substantially weaker performance. If an employee has been excellent for fifteen years, it becomes easy to forgive a period of weaker performance, knowing that it is out of character. For an employee who was excellent, but has only been on the job three months, a period of weak performance is a more serious issue and grounds for concern. It may be appropriate to give the employee with seniority the benefit of the doubt, but this may not be appropriate for a short-term employee. Also, in the case of a poor decision, or act of bad judgment, an employee with a long-term great track record may merit more latitude.

The most important consideration in making these decisions is to assess if the employee is a top performer. Do they do great work and make others better? This consideration should trump any consideration of seniority in most cases.

## IF YOU ARE CONSIDERING FIRING SOMEONE, DO IT NOW

No good leader likes to fire people. It is painful, unpleasant, and one of the most distasteful parts of being a leader.

Also, good leaders tend to be top performers. They are the type to see the potential in their people and want to bring out the best in them. They want to see their people thrive, be fulfilled, and soar to success. When a leader sees someone not doing their best, or not doing good work, the leader is saddened. The leader almost certainly starts to give more attention to the person and tries to help them. Good leaders are slow to give up on anyone because it is their passion to be a catalyst for human success. They get their kicks out of seeing people succeed. They always do what they can to ensure their people's success. So, if a good leader has come to the point where they are considering removing someone, it is always the case that it is past time to do so. No good leader would consider firing someone if they were not past due to be fired. I've never seen it happen or heard of it happening.

If you are considering doing it, just do it.

## ELIMINATE COMMITTEES

Committees generally are a waste of time and resources. If you want to get something done, give the responsibility to an individual. If that person wants to bring others' skills and experiences aboard, let that be their call. To give something to a committee to solve is almost always a bad idea.

In a committee, no one person is responsible. Therefore, there is no one who is fully committed to make progress. Also, in committees, politics tend to develop. Some people speak out, which bothers those who don't. Some cower to the perceived dominance of others. The group tends to avoid making decisions, as people instead commit to "look further into that" or agree to "take that issue offline and report back." People who are left out of the committee feel disenfranchised and overlooked, while those who are on the committee feel that they are important simply by virtue of their presence on the committee. Neither perception is true.

Also, committees are cumbersome. They cannot act until someone manages to get all of the members in a room at the same time for a meeting. Since meetings are generally ineffective, unproductive, and inefficient, and since committees typically only act through meetings, they are at an immediate disadvantage. Finally, committees generally fear bold action, because it only takes one committee member to scuttle a good idea or good course of action by their objection to it. In other words, where an individual can take immediate action once they decide it is right, a committee might have a member that opposes such action, causing slow decisions and unwanted compromises.

One reason leaders create committees is to make sure that all interests are represented, and no one is caught off guard by a decision. This is a valid concern. The way to solve this is to be sure that the person you put in charge is responsible to communicate with the various stakeholders who may be affected by the work they are doing. You simply make a list of people who would want to know and make sure they are in the loop. Forming a committee is almost always a bad idea.

## REMOVE LOW PERFORMERS FROM THE TEAM

Retaining low performers does not serve any valid purpose. Specifically:

- They hurt the team.
- They damage the culture of the organization.
- They interfere with others who are trying to do good work.
- They repel top performers.
- They do not produce good results.
- They tend to be dissatisfied and bring down the energy of the whole team.
- They file lawsuits.
- They feel mistreated and try to get others feeling that way too.
- They attract more low performers and repel top performers.
- They take more of the leader's time and energy, which is distracting.
- They expose the organization to risk because of their carelessness and mistakes.
- They harm the leader's credibility.
- They set a poor example for other employees to follow.
- They cause top performers to leave.
- They create a poor culture by spreading negativity.
- They waste company resources.
- They are not fulfilled and happy, since they know they're not performing well.
- They take up a seat that could be filled with a top performer!

Give a project to an individual that you trust and make it clear to them that the company's resources are at their disposal. If they want help from others, they'll ask for it. This empowers top performers, which aids tremendously with their retention.

## AVOID OVERLAPPING JOB RESPONSIBILITIES

Passing one of our Denver area managers in the hall of our corporate office, I once said, "Hi, Pat! Let me ask you a quick question."

"Sure, Monty!"

"If someone in one of your restaurants was poorly trained as to how to properly dice an onion, would you consider that your responsibility?"

"Not really," he said. "I'd say that is more the responsibility of the RTC [regional training coordinator]."

This was completely unacceptable. After all, each RTC had twenty restaurants to oversee, but the average area manager had only six. So how could the RTCs really be certain that all of our employees were well trained? I found the same was true when it came to human resource issues. Our area managers assumed that our group of field HR generalists were the ones responsible for HR issues in their restaurants. The problem was twofold. First, the regional training coordinators and the HRGs were ineffective because they were not experts in restaurant operations, because they had so many restaurants to look after, and nothing was really their direct responsibility. Second, and an even bigger problem, was that their existence made our area managers feel less responsible for restaurant operations and restaurant teams, which are *the two most important parts of the area manager's job*!

People who share a job responsibility with someone else are

less motivated to get it done and more likely to suffer from frustrations that make them more likely to leave the organization.

First, since the responsibility is not totally up to them, each person can slack off and wait for the other person to do it. Second, since more than one person is responsible, it encourages meetings, which are usually inefficient and unproductive. Third, people tend to do their best work when it impacts their own reputation. When their work overlaps with others' work, they know that they will not be credited for its completion, nor blamed for its lack of completion. Fourth, when more than one person is responsible, there is a tendency to compromise between two points of view, which may impact their result. So, it is far better to have separate and distinct job descriptions for everyone.

It seemed obvious to me that each level of management, GM, area manager, and operations director should feel completely responsible for every aspect of the restaurant experience in their stores, right down to chopping onions properly. But when I asked them, I learned that they didn't.

I decided to completely eliminate both the regional training coordinator and the HRG role (and put these employees to better use elsewhere in the company), especially after I found out that these positions were ineffective and did more harm than good. Getting rid of both of these positions and then making it crystal clear to the area managers that they were completely responsible for the performance of their restaurants, saved a lot of money, and it empowered the area managers.

## SET HIGH STANDARDS

Now that you've shared a worthy vision and assembled and retained a team of top performers, it is necessary to articulate the standards that the business seeks to achieve. You need to make sure your people understand not only what standards are expected, but also the reasons why these standards are essential to achieving the vision. Once you do so, make sure that your team is achieving the standards. And, again, you do this by making sure that your team is all top performers and that they are empowered. If the team is empowered, they'll want to achieve the standards.

A common problem I've witnessed is that different people within the organization often have different ideas as to what the standards are. This is not acceptable and needs to be rectified quickly. If people are not extremely clear as to what the standards are and why such standards are important, the team will struggle to achieve them. Leaders need to be sure that the standards are clearly and consistently understood.

When I first started at Chipotle in 2005, our vegetable cut sizes were totally inconsistent in different stores, and everyone seemed to have their own way of prepping vegetables. The trouble was that as managers transferred to different stores, they would carry their own way with them, which resulted in them retraining the crew members when they'd transfer. Meanwhile, the crew members would have seen many different methods of cutting vegetables and became frustrated since the right way to do it changed so often. This lead to us having poor vegetable prep, which led to food that did not taste as good as it could. I solved this by introducing one right way to prepare every single ingredient on our menu. I did this by way of training guides and training videos that were available in every restaurant. It took about a year, but soon enough, everyone knew the right way of doing things, and they got very good at it. As a result, our food quality and taste improved dramatically.

By carefully defining standards, great leaders push the boundaries of what can be achieved. For example, I had a superb tenth grade English teacher, Mr. Burns, who redefined the meaning of getting an "A." He was a tough grader. He boasted to our whole class at the outset of the semester that he might give a single "A" in the class, or perhaps no "A's" at all. I thought he was bluffing. He wasn't. When he handed out my first writing assignment, he gave me a "C." Thinking myself a good writer, I challenged the "C" in a short meeting after class. When I asked him what I could have done better, he told me many things about how to write better, mostly about brevity, avoiding passive language, deleting useless or ineffective words, and so forth. I was pleased and eager to learn these new things, and I started to really try hard in his class. I wanted to achieve *his* version of high standards. I wanted one of *his* "A's!" I think I got a "B" though. Oh, well.

At Chipotle, we wanted a super friendly team that provided great and fast service and delicious food. We did not want to be good for a fast food restaurant. We wanted to be delicious by any standard. We didn't want our service to be good for a fast food restaurant. We wanted our service to be great by any standard. But honestly, it was not hard to articulate what high standards meant to our teams at Chipotle. What was hard was finding a way to get 70,000 people to badly want to meet these high standards. The only way to do that was to empower them!

## TIME DOESN'T SOLVE PROBLEMS

When I consider the traits that helped me become a successful leader, one of them was probably my intolerance of inaction. I grow quickly frustrated if I see a problem with no effort afoot to solve it. Often during visits to a Chipotle restaurant with the field leader, I'd notice something wrong with one of his restaurants and ask him what his plan was to improve the situation. Too often, he'd respond, "We are working on that" or "We're having discussions about that with the GM." But when I'd follow up, what the field leader was really doing, in essence, was waiting for things to get better. This drove me mad.

Nearly all problems in a restaurant can be fixed overnight. Assuming it is a good concept, with good ingredients, what is there that can't be fixed in twenty-four hours? If the restaurant is dirty, you can pull an all-nighter to clean it perfectly before opening time the next day. If it is disorganized, you can completely organize it overnight. If the food prep isn't good, it can be fixed immediately. The only thing that takes longer is replacing a low-performing team and building a culture of empowerment. Even that can be commenced immediately by hiring stronger people and starting to train them. At any rate, there is never a good reason to delay. We can always be solving problems.

I made a visit to an Orlando, Florida Chipotle around 2008. I was with our CFO, Jack and a regional director whom I will call Greg. He was responsible for all of our Florida restaurants. As I walked in, I encountered the team wearing lazy, bored faces, standing over a sloppy and dirty service line. There were dirty dishes all over the chef's table. The walk-in fridge was a disaster. There was literally sour cream smeared on the ceiling! I tried to hold my tongue, to see if Greg would notice how bad it was. The truth is, I was hoping to see his brain beginning to boil. However, as I glanced over at him, he seemed calm. Disturbingly undisturbed. Troublingly untroubled. Upsettingly not upset.

So I asked, in a neutral voice that masked my tremendous disappointment, "What do you think?"

"Could be more organized," he replied, nodding his head with a sort of mock disappointment. To me, this was like saying the

Titanic could've had a better Atlantic crossing. I was astonished by his nonchalance at what I viewed as a horror show.

"Let's just close it down until we can get it right," I told him.

"Well, Monty, I'm thinking there isn't any clear food safety issue, and I'm worried about hurting the morale of the team."

*Good Lord*, I thought to myself. These were possibly the two least valid, least compelling points he could have made. First, the idea that we are OK being open as long as the food is safe was utterly ridiculous. Plus, the idea that the morale of the six people in this store was a more important consideration than the reputation of our company of 70,000 people was just as absurd. I heard my brain say, "Morale? Goodness! This whole team needs to be fired. To hell with morale!" But my outward appearance somehow remained calm.

Finally, I said, "Greg, this place is a disaster. Let's close it down and clean it overnight, replace all the food, and start hiring a better team that cares more about what we are doing!"

I started cleaning the place myself and Jack quickly followed suit. Slowly and hesitantly, the crew of low performers joined in. After we'd scrubbed for an hour or so, with Greg and the rest of the crew, Greg finally said, "Monty and Jack, you guys go to the hotel. You shouldn't have to do this. We'll take it from here."

"That's OK. I'd rather ensure it gets done by morning," I replied as I kept on cleaning. But after Greg begged and pleaded for us to leave so he could work with his team to teach a higher standard, I finally agreed to leave it to them to bring in a new crew to work all night to clean and organize this restaurant.

"OK," I said, "But if you need help or think it won't get done by morning, call us, and we will come and help."

The next morning I asked Greg, "How late did your guys stay cleaning?"

"We stayed until midnight, but I wanted to give the team some rest, so we agreed to come in early in the morning to finish."

My mind quietly exploded. Again, my internal dialogue lit up. "Rest? This team has done nothing but rest, from what I can see!" But once again, on the outside, I remained appropriately calm. As it turned out, we got the store open on time, but just barely. We were cleaning right up to the time we opened.

On the hour-long drive to the airport, I had a long talk with Greg, who was driving. Greg started talking, and it became clear he knew I was extremely disappointed. Finally, he blurted out, "I'm sorry, Monty. I just need you to tell me what to do. I'll do anything to keep my job! I love my job!"

At this point, it was too late. I knew that Greg would have to go, for the good of our teams, our company, and for the benefit of our customers. Greg was a good man, but not a top performer. This was not the right role for him. I'd given him all the time, advice, and resources possible to improve, but it wasn't happening. He wasn't able to create teams of empowered top performers.

"Well, Greg," I said, "I would love to get your ideas as to how to best announce your departure."

When I had many people reporting to me, I would often meet with them to discuss their teams. Was their team strong? How were the people doing? Were there any low performers? What were they doing to make the team stronger? Nearly every time I found that leaders had at least a few people on their team who were in a wait-and-see mode. Some even used those words. "The jury is still out on him," they might say. Or, "She is a work in progress," referring to an employee whom they were unsure would be successful.

But when I'd ask them, "Oh...what are you doing to help her get better?" they'd give me a blank stare.

"Ah...well...I'm expecting to see some improvement by next month. If she doesn't improve, then we're gonna have a tough conversation."

This drove me crazy. I'd say, "How is more time doing a mediocre job going to cause this person to improve?" Another blank stare would follow. Then I'd ask, "What are you doing to make sure she gets better?" Then they'd say a bunch of words to me that were designed to get me off the scent. Words like, "we have a plan" for the employee and that they "were working to make them better" in some way.

Then I'd ask to see the plan, and I would find out that the "plan" was safely tucked away inside the leader's mind. Safe, where it could do no good. The fact was, there was no plan.

There is no excuse for a leader to let any person work a single day at a level that is below what is expected or desired, without some kind of intervention. If the employee is disorganized, then they must immediately be taught organization, and the reasons why it is important to their success. From that time on, the person should be organized. If they aren't, then the leader has to quickly diagnose why not. Does the employee know how to achieve the standard? If no, then they need to be trained again. But if they do understand the standard (which they usually do), then the leader needs to ask whether the employee is empowered, such that they feel motivated to fully devote themselves to the achievement of the standard. If not, then the leader has to create empowerment. If the person knows what to do, and is empowered to do it, and is still failing, then the leader should consider if the person is a low performer. If so, then the person should be removed. But simply waiting for them to spontaneously improve is madness. It is not going to happen.

If things are not right, a leader needs to take action. When you see a problem, don't wait. Make a change. Time won't solve problems, but action will. When you consistently take action, things will get better, not because time has passed, but because the whole team has been working diligently towards great results every single day.

# CHAPTER 13

# DECISIVENESS

OUR FINANCE DIRECTOR ONCE OPENED A MEETING BY saying, "At the close of this meeting, we are going to ask for $50,000 to buy an off-the-shelf IT solution that will allow us to capture $1.5 million a year in tax breaks we are losing now."

She said this because I'd recently made a rule that we should start all meetings with a statement about the goal of the meeting. I found meetings were often ineffective and too long. If we knew what we were trying to achieve, then we'd also know when we'd achieved it, and we could then call an end to the meeting! This was a perfect example where the rule worked marvelously.

"Will this software solution really work?" I asked.

"Yes, we've tested it."

"And you are confident it will lead to the savings you describe?"

"Yes."

"OK. Buy the software. You have your $50,000."

"Really? Thank you!"

"Thank you! Shall we adjourn?

The meeting was scheduled for an hour, but we completed it

in about three minutes. Obviously, not all decisions are this easy. But many are. In this case, I trusted the director's judgment and didn't need to second-guess her conclusion that this technology would save over a million dollars. If it saved even a tenth of that, it was worth it. This was an easy decision. Beyond the obvious time savings, there were other advantages to my approach. It demonstrated to those present that efficiency was important to me. Further, it conveyed to my finance director my confidence, trust, and respect for her judgment when I felt no need to further question her about her decision. This lit her up with pride, and she walked out of the room a bit taller.

If the most important skill of a leader is to build a strong team, the second most important skill is the ability to make many good decisions, quickly. Of course, in some ways, this is a distinction without a difference, since building strong teams requires many good decisions.

When I came aboard in 2005, I felt like a kid in a candy store. There was so much data and there were so many obvious, unmade decisions! I started making decisions right away.

I made the decision that we needed to **hire all of our managers from within,** after seeing data that showed internally developed managers were vastly better performers and four times less likely to quit.

I made the decision that we should **build smaller stores,** when I studied data that demonstrated that our sales were actually higher in the small stores, which felt intimate, cozy, and were easier to clean, easier to manage, cheaper to build, and had lower operating costs. Plus, those stores were easier to find from a real estate standpoint.

I decided to make **throughput** (the speed with which a customer came through the line) our number one operational priority when I saw that: 1) the best teams were the fastest ones (and so throughput was an excellent metric to measure to determine the quality of a team); 2) the only thing customers did not like about the Chipotle experience was standing in line, and we were losing sales when customers walked away from a long line; 3) our average stores had long lines, but had throughput three times slower than our fastest stores, with the same equipment; 4) it cost us nothing to go faster, just better training and an awareness that it was important; and 5) our teams loved the challenge of going faster and were very proud to be measured and rewarded for their ability to speed up.

I decided that we needed a **second make line** in the back of all of our restaurants in order to allow us to make telephone and online orders without interrupting the throughput on our main service line. I knew that in the future we'd have an ever-increasing number of telephone and online orders to contend with.

I made the decision that we should hire people not for their experience (which was bad, fast food experience) but for the **characteristics that would make an excellent** restaurant employee.

While there were thousands of other decisions I made, almost all of them obvious, these were a few of the decisions I made *in the first week on the job* that ended up transforming Chipotle completely. Our same store sales, which were 5 percent year over year when I started, immediately rose to double digits and remained the highest in the industry for a decade. The quality of our employees got much better and our turnover (how many employees quit their jobs) dropped dramatically and stayed low for years. Simultaneously, while our managers were nearly all white men when I started, our promote from within policy soon led women and minorities to represent the majority of our managers, and they were *excellent* managers. Also, we got better crew candidates applying, due to our reputation for being a company that trained hourly employees to be our future managers. We did not have any dead-end jobs like so many other restaurants did. Our new smaller stores caused our new store investment costs, occupancy costs, and operating costs to drop, while sales, margins, and profits shot through the roof, becoming the highest in the industry.

What was amazing to me was that all of these decisions were completely obvious. Yet no one had made any of these in the ten years the company had been operating before I arrived. Leaders tend to struggle, even with obvious decisions. While some decisions are difficult and require extensive analysis, most decisions a leader has to make on a daily basis are quite obvious. There are very few close calls. Yet even the obvious decisions seem to lead most leaders to scratch their heads, wring their hands, study, and request more data to be sure that a decision is the correct one. Generally, this is a waste of time and bad for the organization.

Perhaps it's my background as a trial lawyer that led to my penchant for quick decisions. Since I billed by the hour, I wanted to make sure that I did not waste a lot of time pondering. After all, the actual process of making a decision happens in the blink of an eye. It is nearly instant. It's all the data gathering and chatting about the data that takes time. Back in my lawyering days, I had to fill out time cards with descriptions of the time I spent on various tasks. A typical entry might have read, "Confer with client about motion to dismiss Plaintiff's complaint: draft motion to dismiss. Prepare for filing and service of same." Or, perhaps, "Attend pre-trial conference. Draft letter to client regarding same." But, never in all my years of practice do I remember writing, "Think about whether or not to file motion to dismiss. Decide whether to write motion to dismiss. Ponder the best course of action to best represent client's interests." Of course, the reason I never wrote that is because no one wants to pay us to ponder, think, and then decide. They want us to know what to do and get down to the business of doing it!

## MAKE DECISIONS QUICKLY

While I was still a lawyer for Chipotle, I'd show up at company meetings ready to contribute. As I walked in, there'd often be someone in the room who'd make a comment like, "Uh-oh! We are on the clock now! We'd better get to work!" This happened all the time, and it was meant in a friendly way. The obvious insinuation was that I, as a man who was billing my time by the hour, was expensive, and everyone had better hurry and get through the part of the meeting that I attended, so as not to spend too much money. The irony was that if you looked at the salaries, restricted stock awards, options, and benefits of the fourteen people in the room when I came in, these folks cost the company more per hour than I did! Just because they didn't keep track of their hours or bill Chipotle for their time didn't negate the reality that their time was very expensive! They didn't think of it that way. Only when I came in did the clock start ticking from their point of view.

I never lost my habit of seeing every person in every room as being on the clock. I was extremely careful to ensure that they spent time in a way that added value to our business. This was an enormous departure from how they'd thought about it before I arrived and some of them didn't like it. They loved sitting around chatting and debating things that were obvious and calling long meetings, with expensive catered lunches, that had no real purpose. In the Chipotle I walked into in 2005, the very fact that you were in a meeting was assumed to mean that you were working hard. But as I attended many of these meetings, I quickly learned that most were either unnecessary (like trying to make a decision that was completely obvious) or much too long. Worse yet, everyone I knew at Chipotle who'd worked in another large company told me that the places they'd worked for before were much worse than Chipotle. From these experiences and from the many companies I've been involved with since, I've concluded that most companies are extremely wasteful and inefficient.

Decisions take almost no time. What takes time is reviewing data, considering what information is at our disposal, and what conclusions we can draw from it. Chipotle had loads of people collecting and analyzing data. It was wonderful! They prepared beautiful charts, graphs, spreadsheets, and so forth. When I reviewed them, obvious conclusions leapt right off of the page!

But again, I found people very slow to make decisions, even when they were obvious. There were several reasons for this. First, there was no pressure to make decisions. People were paid no matter what they did or did not do.

Second, making decisions was viewed as risky. What if they made a mistake? They felt that they could look bad if they made a decision, but felt safe being indecisive.

Third, the business was doing fine, so why upset the applecart by changing things?

Fourth, by making a decision, they'd end the meeting, and the meeting was sort of fun. These were cultural issues and I worked hard to make it clear to people that we rewarded decisions, and that we were not punitive about mistakes.

Most of the time, it is clear what to do next. Yet astonishingly often, we find ourselves discussing, debating, chitchatting, or bullshitting about what to do next, instead of actually doing it.

Maybe this is why the Nike slogan *Just Do It* is so popular. It is often a good piece of advice.

We see this so often in relationships. Our friend who is in a bad relationship talks for years about how their boyfriend isn't what they wish he was, that he is insensitive, mean, impatient, uncaring, not helpful enough, unreliable, and so on. But what does all this talk really do? The truth is there must be something about the relationship our friend is attracted to since they're choosing to stay in it. If there wasn't, perhaps our friend would actually get out of the relationship.

When we find ourselves complaining, we should always ask ourselves, "What are we trying to accomplish by complaining?" Are we pretending to be a victim, who cannot change our personal situation? Do we feel a bit better being a victim for some reason? Do we think that by complaining, providence will intervene to solve our problem? These outcomes are unlikely. I know I have often found myself complaining. But I've yet to see complaining solve anything at all.

Likewise, in a business setting, we often hear complaints or lengthy debates about what we should do. But if we are honest, the answer is usually obvious. But watch closely, and you will see that long after the answer is obvious, the discussion continues. One reason for this is that sometimes there is discomfort with actually doing the thing that needs to be done. The most obvious example of this occurs when we need to remove a low performer. We tend to discuss it, consider it, and debate it for weeks, months, or even years, to avoid the discomfort of getting it done.

People love to be social. They want to bond with each other and feel closer. One way they do this is to talk on and on about things that merit no further discussion. This is OK, to the extent that it's human nature. But it is wise to keep an eye on it because such discussions can greatly delay progress. One smart way to allow the bonding but avoid delays for the company is to simply make the decision, and then go out and celebrate it. Get the decision in place, so the company can move forward, and then go out and party with your workmates. Then at least it's done and the bonding can commence without the need to pretend that there's further need to discuss the issue. It sounds like I'm kidding. But I'm serious. People need some time to goof off and celebrate. It's going to happen. So you may as well call bullshitting and chitchatting out for what it is, rather than pretend it's work.

Anytime you find yourself in a long talk or group discussion about an action that needs to be taken, ask yourself if the real purpose of this discussion is to make a better decision, or is the real purpose of this discussion to make us more comfortable by putting off the action needed? More often than you know, the reason the discussion is taking place is the latter. Usually, decisions are obvious. When they are, make them, take action, and move to the next one. Decisive leaders, leaders who are biased towards action, are better leaders.

Making decisions quickly is an excellent policy, since the correct decision is usually obvious, and your business needs the better results that such a decision will bring about. The sooner, the better!

## FOLLOW YOUR GUT

There's another reason to make decisions swiftly. While it is counterintuitive, the truth is that you'll make better decisions when you make them quickly. Intuition is powerful!

There is a saying in poker circles: "Think long, think wrong." The concept is, when facing a decision to bet, raise, check, or fold, one's initial intuition about what to do is usually the correct decision. When you slow down and start to really think about it, all sorts of other mental tools, none of them as powerful as intuition, come to bear on your decision. For instance, let's say the guy in front of you makes a huge bet which your intuition tells you is a bluff. Obviously, if he is bluffing, you should call the bet! But you may think:

"Damn, it would be expensive to call this bet, and we are almost done for the night. I am about even money on the night, even though an hour ago, I was down $1,000. I'd hate that feeling of being broke again. Also, I hate the feeling of losing. Besides, he may have a good hand this time, even though I feel he is bluffing and even though he was bluffing a lot earlier. Now that I've been thinking about it so long, I will look stupid if I call the bet and I'm wrong. But if I just fold, they'll assume I made a good decision, instead of knowing for sure I made a bad decision if I am wrong."

But all of the deeper thinking in the preceding paragraph is actually *unhelpful* to making the right decision! The more careful and more reasoned thinking in the above paragraph is wrong! You are here to play poker, and bluffing is a reality of the game. Your intuition is that he is bluffing. Yes, you could be wrong and lose another $800.00. But your intuition told you it is a bluff, so you have to call! If you're not willing to back your intuition with action, you shouldn't be playing poker.

Our mind, biologically, is set up to make quick decisions. Humans, along with all other animals, are prewired with powerful instincts. When we look at animals in the wild, they decide things so quickly that it is hard to detect any decision process, brainstorming, or analysis. What we see instead is just action.

They know what to do. Their actions stem from hundreds of thousands of years of genetic intelligence passed down in their genes. This hardwiring comes from a long line of distant relatives who made decisions that allowed them to survive. The animals that made great decisions quickly lived to have offspring and the offspring that made great decisions quickly had more offspring. You are that offspring! We often forget that we are animals. We are imbued with millions of years of evolutionary intelligence and that intelligence is available to us as instinct or intuition. This intuition is extremely intelligent and powerful.

A major reason for many of our discussions in life is to avoid making decisions, rather than to assist us in making better ones. But one thing is certain: the cost of not making decisions quickly is a huge waste of resources and time. It paralyzes the healthy functioning of a business.

Businesses tend to be very risk-averse. The people who run them don't want to stick their neck out. In most organizations, a good path towards job security is to keep your head down, do what you're told, and not make waves. The more mediocre and low performers the organization has, the more prevalent this tendency. The result is a mediocre organization that will struggle. People will call meetings to talk a lot about things that everyone already knows. They'll sit around and agree with each other over lunch and coffee and at expensive retreats. Meanwhile, innovation and creativity suffer. People who make quick decisions and hatch new ideas tend to threaten the group. New ideas are seen as an implicit criticism of the way things are being done now—the status quo. It leads to a stale, ineffective, and stagnant culture. It also chokes innovation, leading to a dubious future.

The subconscious is a wiser and more powerful force than the conscious mind. The reason for this is complex, but millions of years of evolution are prewired into our subconscious. Yet most business decisions continue to be made by studying and analyzing, which are functions of the weaker conscious mind. It is much more effective to make decisions quickly, employing the wisdom of the subconscious mind, as soon as we have a sample of evidence sufficient for the subconscious mind to know what's right. This is true even if the evidence is insufficient to allow a complete analysis by the conscious mind. Therefore, leaders who make more quick decisions will, as long as they are not reckless or ambiguous, be more effective.

Making many decisions quickly is refreshing, invigorating, and healthy for an organization. It is the stuff that fuels growth, innovation, excitement, and progress. It is far better to make hundreds of obvious decisions quickly and make a mistake or two than to only make a few decisions and no mistakes. Of course, every now and then, there is a really hard decision. For that one, go ahead and take your time. Even call a meeting if you'd like! But don't do it too often.

# CHAPTER 14

# COMMUNICATION

WE ALL KNOW THAT COMMUNICATION LIES AT THE HEART of excellent leadership. I've saved it until now because it is such a critical tool for effective leadership. What you've learned in the rest of this book will not be as powerful if you cannot communicate well.

Right after leaving Chipotle, I became a pilot. I spend a lot of time flying now, and I really have a passion for it. Pilots take communication very seriously. Clear communication can be a life or death matter, so it's not left to chance. For example, a pilot needs to read back every single instruction they get from air traffic control, verbatim, and then recite their tail number (the number that identifies their specific plane) to be sure the pilot heard the message correctly, and that the message was intended for that specific airplane. You'd be shocked how often this procedure catches mistakes which, if not corrected, would lead to a lack of control of the airplanes above us. While most business communications are not life or death like those governing airplanes, they are still very important. They often involve the allocation of huge amounts of financial and human resources. Since getting communication right doesn't happen by accident, it is important to be intentional about it.

People like very clear communicators, because they feel uncomfortable living in uncertainty. For this reason, I've found that the leaders who are clear in their communication most often are the leaders who have the respect of their teams, are trusted, and are most loyally followed. Conversely, leaders who communicate unclearly are often disliked, not trusted, and viewed negatively.

My twenty years in a CEO role taught me that most people, including leaders, are poor communicators. Consequently, I spent much of my time teaching others to communicate more effectively. It was a pleasure to teach people this critical skill because when I did, I often saw enormous rewards. I saw good decisions being made more quickly. I saw people become more efficient: they wasted less time and more quickly focused on what was important. Overall, better communication is a lubricant that causes the whole organization to run better: to have more horse-power while burning less fuel.

A person's ability to communicate is impacted by many different traits—confidence, ability to be vulnerable, fluency, connection to their audience, comfort in the subject area, level of desire to be understood, and others. Additionally, there are many different methods by which people communicate. Gaining an awareness of and paying attention to these methods will help us improve this critical skill, which affects nearly every aspect of our lives. Like any skill, our ability to do it well will improve dramatically with practice.

I am personally very frustrated by poor communication, and I see it daily. I see poorly written materials, brochures, instructions, recipes, advertisements, contracts, letters, mission statements, and speeches everywhere I look. There is no excuse for it. It causes people and organizations to spend energy going nowhere, or in the wrong direction. It confuses people and then they're not efficient and effective. It frustrates customers, resulting in poor service and lost sales. Overall, I see so little good communication that I have concluded it is largely a lost art. I even notice popular speeches and TED talks that are replete with poor communication.

## UNDERSTAND COMMUNICATION BROADLY

When we use the word *communication*, most of us think about speaking. But speaking and even words themselves are only a small fraction of what makes up communication. It is important to constantly bear in mind that communication includes all the methods by which people or animals share information.

Talking is certainly the most familiar form of communication. It is also the one we practice the most. Ironically, it is not the most powerful or reliable method in many cases. If it is our goal to really understand what someone is communicating, the words they say are only a small and often unreliable fraction of the information being shared. There are many other methods by which information is conveyed, both verbal and nonverbal.

On the verbal side, there are the words, the cadence with which they are spoken, pace, volume, the space between words, pauses, silence, laughter, tone of voice, and choice of words. Nonverbal communication methods include touch, absence or presence of eye contact, gestures, body language, spatial proximity, silence, ignoring behaviors, a person's presence or absence, their posture, facial expressions, the actions they take, and even pheromones. The sum total of all these methods conveys a message that is often, if not usually, at least partially inconsistent with the words that someone says. Part of this is because language is an inexact way to make a point. Words are inherently limiting. This is obvious to anyone who tries unsuccessfully to describe a very funny moment, or an incredible sunset. But another part of this is that we have learned to fake our words: to say things for reasons other than to convey the truth.

Most of us are not nearly as skilled in faking the other forms of communication, which is why they are more reliable. For example, most people do not practice making hand gestures or using body language, or changing the cadence of their speech. So, since they are not intended, if we learn to read these involuntary gestures, we will get a much more honest grasp of what is really being communicated.

Poker again offers lessons here. Playing this game well requires one to learn to glean when someone has a strong hand or a weak hand, and when they want you to call, or want you to fold. Since lying is perfectly acceptable in poker, it is clear that you must not rely on someone's words to figure out their hand. This is such a broad and important topic to professional poker players that there are whole books written about the *tells* by which you can read what sort of hand your opponent is holding and make profitable decisions as to how to play your cards. These same books often offer advice as to how to prevent your opponents from being able to read your hand.

With so many possible nonverbal types of communication, it is almost impossible for people to avoid communicating, even if they try! Imagine you have a job interview at 10:00 a.m. To your horror, traffic delays your arrival and you find yourself pushing the elevator button to get up to your appointment at 10:15 a.m.

Is it accurate to say that you have not begun the interview? Are you not yet communicating? You bet you are! You have communicated that this job is not important enough to you to be on time, and you have communicated to your interviewer that you do not value their time as much as your convenience in not showing up early to avoid the possibility of making them wait! You have likely completed a portion of the interview that is more important than any words you say during the interview, if it still takes place at all.

Let me give another example. Imagine if your spouse or best friend enters your home after you've not seen them in a while. You are very busy concentrating on a difficult task, and you don't wish to communicate with them at the moment. How can you avoid it? If you don't say a word, it is nearly certain that they will think you strange, or even interpret your failure to acknowledge their presence as hostile or dismissive. You don't wish to be dismissive, it's just that you're really focused on your project. Yet your very silence, your failure to speak, is communicating something, even if not intentionally. Avoiding talking to, or looking at them at all, is likely to trigger negative reactions. In short, it would probably save time and angst to just say, "So glad you are home! I'm in the middle of something, but I will be with you shortly."

Here's another way to understand nonverbal communication. Try sitting with a friend and looking at each other without speaking. You are likely to communicate more by sitting silently looking at each other than you would if you used words. With words, you could engage in small talk that carried little underlying meaning: "Wow, what a hot day!" But if you do not speak, and you're looking into another's eyes, all sorts of communication begins to take place! In fact, so much takes place that it feels quite intimate. The odds are good that one or both of you will laugh, look away, or smirk, as a way to diminish the vulnerability and intimacy that is taking place. You will likely defend against the depth of the intimacy that develops, precisely because too much is being communicated for you to remain comfortable.

Communication is nearly always taking place, even when we do not intend it. Since we tend to be more careful with our words than we are with our other nonverbal methods of communication, the words we say tend to be less powerful (less honest and less accurate) than other forms of communication we use. This happens whether we intend such other forms to be communicative or not. If we truly want to convey a clear meaning, and we want people to believe us, it is critical that the nonverbal and verbal aspects of our communication are consistent. This is true because all of us have, instinctively, managed to learn to sniff out inconsistencies in communication to determine whether people are being honest or dishonest, friendly or threatening.

Imagine a loved one saying they love you, but saying it as if it were a question, "I love you?" You'd be confused. You would not take it as a loving comment. You'd probably ask them to repeat what they said, in order to resolve the inconsistency. Or, imagine a car dealer telling you that he is offering his best price on a new car, while shaking his head sideways, as if saying no. You would probably not feel he was being honest. If you'd like, you can even try an experiment all by yourself to help you see how these consistencies are built into our brain's wiring. Try to say the words, "Yes. That is definitely true! It's 100 percent accurate!" while moving your head sideways as if to say no! Doesn't it feel sort of silly? Even difficult to do?

To understand others, we need to de-emphasize our focus on their words and increase our focus on the other verbal and nonverbal cues.

# MONEY TALKS

All of a leader's actions communicate, but especially how you handle compensation. Compensation is a lightning rod, and everyone pays attention to it. They're watching like hawks! Since you have their attention (whether you want it or not), you need to use this opportunity to communicate what you are looking for from your team.

Pay is, perhaps unfortunately, a significant factor that people use to measure their worth in the eyes of their leader. Employees should believe that the leader will pay people who make a greater contribution more than those who make a lesser contribution. That's why part of the leader's job is to be sure that all employees know what performance the leader is looking for and what metrics compensation decisions will be based on. If the leader isn't crystal clear about how they're going to make these determinations, the team will come up with their own reasons. And trust me, they'll come up with reasons you won't like or agree with. If you leave this one to chance, it will bite you every time. It is essential to get ahead of it.

Getting this right will help a leader send a clear message to the team and help clarify expectations. The leader should make compensation decisions that are consistent with the culture they're trying to build. Since you're building a culture of top performers, empowered to achieve high standards, you must design the compensation program to favor those who most powerfully create or support such a culture. In a growth company, for example, you will want to reward those who perform excellent work and have the most powerful impact making others better. This made perfect sense at Chipotle, since making others better was part of our definition of a top performer.

One common trap that leaders fall into is being overly concerned about pay disparities between different people in the company. I've seen it countless times. A leader wants to pay a superstar more, but is concerned about what the others will think if they find out. The answer is, as long as the disparity is correctly aligned with the leader's clearly communicated strategy, and thus well-deserved by the employee receiving the greater compensation, the leader needn't be concerned what others think of it. If anything, the leader should relish the opportunity to have a discussion with the concerned employee about a disparity in pay, since it is a chance to more deeply communicate the behaviors and actions that the leader is seeking to reward through pay decisions. Pay decisions speak loudly. Make sure to get them right.

When we created the Restaurateur program at Chipotle, Restaurateurs were entitled to a bonus of $10,000 for each crew member they developed into a general manager role. Area managers were the ones to whom Restaurateurs and GMs reported, and they began to complain that Restaurateurs would have the ability, if they developed a lot of GMs, to earn more money than the area managers, who had historically always earned more.

When I heard these complaints, I publicly reminded our area managers that this was intentional. Any Restaurateur who developed a lot of GMs was very valuable to the company, indeed more valuable than an area manager, since we badly needed talented GMs for our restaurants. I also told the area managers that any of them, if they wished, could become a GM and try to achieve Restaurateur status so that they too could avail themselves of this bonus opportunity. The truth was (and I made this plain), I valued Restaurateurs more highly in terms of their contribution to Chipotle since they had the ability to develop teams of empowered top performers. This was extremely valuable to our growing company. I wanted it clear that this position, Restaurateur, was elite. It was critical, prestigious, and well-compensated. Anyone who didn't like that was free to try to become one, knowing that becoming one took greater dedication and skill than being an area manager.

Only a few area managers took me up on the offer to jump back into a restaurant and try to become a Restaurateur. The rest got back to work with a better understanding of what was valued at Chipotle—building excellent teams who could deliver a great experience to our guests. It was a huge win.

## DEEP COMMUNICATION

In the previous chapters, I wrote about the need to connect with people, to be vulnerable, to show love, to seek truth. These are foundational concepts to my idea of leadership, and they influence everything I do. They lie at the heart of what I call deep communication, which I've mentioned previously. Let me explain it fully here.

If you ask someone, "How are you doing?" they might say "Pretty good" in a tone that makes it clear that they are not doing very well at all. In such a case, you have two choices. You can say "great" and move on with your day. Or, you can choose to ignore their words and focus instead on what they are communicating, and ask, "What is the matter?"

If you choose the second option, you have instantly built some credibility with them, because you were willing to ignore their deceptive words and take the harder, more time-consuming step of seeing what was actually true (that they are not well). Acknowledging that they are not well, and asking them for more information, makes it clear that you want to help them. Obviously, it is easier to just say, "Great," and move on with your day. But going deeper shows that you care. That you are listening not just with your ears, but with your eyes and heart. This wakes people up! It catches them off guard, in a good way. You are with them, present, curious, nonjudgmental, and caring enough to want to know their reality. That causes them to feel safe and allows a deeper vulnerability to arise in them. They feel at liberty to allow a deeper, less guarded communication with you. In other words, they open up. They share their heart, because you shared yours. This creates space, which allows room for love, trust, and understanding. In this space, deep, truthful, and liberating communication can exist. We've now transcended the usual egoic, deceptive, and illusory nonsense that often passes for a conversation. We are relating in a deep and intimate way. What follows is a flow of emotion, love, compassion, truth, and understanding. This is what I consider deep communication.

Put another way, really listening requires curiosity. You want to know the truth. This requires you to be present, open, and relaxed. To use all of your senses. You may have to allow a few moments of silence, even if it is uncomfortable. You need to open your heart to allow something to unfold, without trying to direct how it unfolds. You give focus and attention to the person and create space for their truth, without judgment. Allowing truth without judgment allows someone to feel safe being their most genuine self. You need to bring love and acceptance to the moment. The reason for this is that as soon as you put up a defense to the vulnerability of real listening, whether by laughing, turning away, guiding the conversation elsewhere, or any other method, you are choosing to abridge your interaction with someone. You are distancing yourself from their truth, and therefore, from them.

Deep connections like these have served me incredibly well in both of my CEO roles, at Messner & Reeves, LLC and at Chipotle, and they will serve you well also. By genuinely communicating and listening, you will gain a deeper understanding of how your employees feel, what motivates them, and what drives them to commit their time and their passion towards the success of your organization. They will share their most genuine feelings with you, and you can use this information to make much better business decisions.

With practice and attention, everyone can improve these skills. As you develop the ability to create this space with others, you will be more powerfully able to help them become the best versions of themselves.

## CAUSES OF POOR COMMUNICATION

Why is there so much poor communication in the world? I've identified four big reasons.

### TRYING TO SOUND SMART

People often try to make simple things seem more complex because they think it makes them sound smart. This is usually an effort to increase their sense of importance or justify their salary or position. At Chipotle, I taught our teams the silliness of useless words. I explained the importance of selecting words designed to increase understanding.

For instance, restaurant industry executives, afraid they'll be judged unimpressive, since it's a simple business, often use jargon to make what they are saying more complex so that they might sound smarter. For instance, on an earning's call, an industry executive might say:

> "We've not been immune from the headwinds most other restaurants have experienced because of the El Niño winter and resulting marginal rising costs in our market basket, which negatively impact our COGS and restaurants' level margins. For this reason, we are analyzing the degree to which there might be resistance if we go to the menu board in order to assure margin preservation, or whether it is more prudent to avoid any possible loss of foot traffic by accepting a temporary decline in restaurant operating margins associated with the likely uptick in cash outflow for our commodity purchases."

A leader committed to better communication might say exactly the same thing as follows:

"Food costs are rising because of bad weather, so we will either raise prices or accept lower margins so we don't lose customers."

Of course, the latter statement says the same thing, in a way that anyone can understand.

Another example:

"We have seen the lunch daypart contributing a larger share of our overall growing transactions and sales, and in particular have seen that the poultry protein selection has driven an outsized portion of product mix. In fact, it has become 65 percent of our entrée selection by customers leading to increasing margin due to more favorable prices on poultry from our larger growers."

...would be better said:

"Lunch sales are increasing and margins are higher, particularly because 65 percent of our sales are chicken, which costs us less."

## FEAR OF CONFLICT

A lot of bad communication also stems from people being afraid that being clear will expose them in some negative way to others. They know that if they are clear, others may not like what they say, disagree with them, or judge them. To avoid this, they use words that are general, indirect, or empty.

For instance, if a salesman at a furniture store suggests a certain sofa to a customer that the customer doesn't like, the customer might use many words and intentionally communicate unclearly, to avoid saying, "I don't like that couch." For instance, they might say, "Oh yes...that one is sort of cute, isn't it? I sort of like that fabric, but I'm not sure I like it as much as the blue one. What do you think? I wonder if the way the arm curves would go very well with my side table which has really straight sides. I'm not really sure. Should we look at the blue one again? I don't know...hmmm..." This is a waste of everyone's time, and it is done to avoid discomfort with the salesman.

People are also afraid of appearing unprepared, unwise, or incorrect. They'll often avoid words that could highlight such weaknesses. It reminds me of the famous saying, "Better to keep quiet and risk someone thinking you don't know what you are talking about than to open your mouth and remove all doubt!"

If you communicate clearly, you are at serious risk of being understood! Have you ever mumbled someone's name when you were not sure how to pronounce it, rather than say it loudly and make it clear that you don't know? In the same way, people communicate poorly to avoid saying something definite. Politicians often use this style of speaking to avoid saying anything that might subject them to criticism.

A politician is quite safe saying:

"We must consider all the factors at play here! We must do what is in the best interest of the American people while moving forward with the kind of integrity that made this country great! We must remember at all times the great sacrifices made by our grandparents and their grandparents and take the kind of actions that will honor their memory!"

It would be hard for such comments to draw criticism. But it is less safe for the politician to say something clear and definite, such as:

"I believe in a woman's right to choose!"

In the latter case, they've really put themselves out there. There will be people who strongly disagree and even people who do not like them. This is why politicians often favor long speeches that don't have much substance.

It's not just politicians. The same motivation to avoid saying words that open us up to criticism is prevalent with all kinds of people in all kinds of situations.

This tendency to avoid conflict is extremely prevalent among leaders, who often want to be popular and well-liked. This desire to be liked is often more powerful than the desire to give clear direction, make crisp decisions, and powerfully focus their team on what is needed for the organization to succeed. It stems largely from fear of conflict. This same fear is what causes leaders to beat around the bush when giving necessary critical feedback to their team members. When I would notice they were failing to give critical feedback to a low performer, they would often say, "I'm really afraid of hurting their feelings or bringing them down and making them feel less motivated." But this excuse is not honestly what was holding them back. What they really feared was their own feelings. They feared being on the receiving end of a negative reaction by the person receiving their critical feedback. It was NOT because they were afraid of hurting the person's feelings. It was because they themselves were afraid of the person being mad at them, thinking them to be unfair, or having a lower opinion of them as a leader. For this reason, most leaders are *not* clear with their critical feedback. They avoid being clear by saying too many words, usually burying any criticism in a bath of words so dilutive that the recipient doesn't get the benefit of the criticism at all.

# DON'T TRY TO BE LIKED: DO WHAT IS RIGHT

I recently made an investment in a small company founded and run by a man named Jonathan. In addition to being intelligent, Jonathan is also highly emotional, sometimes troubled, and often unfocused. In short order, I found myself chairman of the board. Chairman is a very significant position because it is the chairman's job to select the management team. In other words, the chairman is responsible for picking the CEO.

I initially declined the invitation. But Jonathan started to really push me to become chairman. I told him to be cautious because if I were to accept that role, I would be obligated to do what was in the best interest of the company, even if that meant removing him as the CEO. He persisted, and I accepted.

Soon, I started to notice that Jonathan was mismanaging funds. The company could not attract any additional investment dollars. We were in crisis; days from bankruptcy. I sat down with Jonathan and had a tough conversation. At one point, he asked me, "Do you think I can be an effective CEO here?"

"No," I said. "I really don't think you can. All the things that are most important for a CEO to do are things you really don't like to deal with."

While he initially accepted my opinion calmly and maturely, at the next day's board meeting, he exploded. He was filled with venom and anger. At the beginning of the meeting, he pointed his finger at me and told the others, "That guy thinks I can't be the CEO anymore!" The rest of the board sat low in their seats, hoping to disappear and avoid the discomfort in the room. As we discussed this, eventually others quietly offered to him that "maybe Monty is right." For two weeks, Jonathan kept calling board members, furious and telling them he'd never step down. This time was very hard for me, and I know it was hard for Jonathan.

Two weeks later, at another board meeting, he apologized and resigned as CEO. "I know this is the right thing for me and the company," he said, tears flowing from his eyes. And he thanked me for making the right decision, even though it was hard. It was clear that he spoke directly from his heart. I felt tears in my eyes as well, as I accepted his apology and my heart went out to him.

Jonathan remains a shareholder of the company, and it is going very well now. He seems happy. He tells me he has enormous respect for me. I feel the same way about him. I consider him a friend. But I knew that in doing the right thing, I risked that relationship. I was not sure he'd ever agree with me and if he didn't, I was sure he'd never forgive me. On top of his very powerful personality and presence, it was very scary and difficult to tell him he was not the right leader for the company. I took the risk, and it was the right thing to do.

I tell this story to illustrate how doing what's right, rather than seeking to be liked and approved of in the moment, is the right way. It's critical to develop this very rare ability. To ensure you continue to "take the harder right, rather than the easier wrong," it helps to focus not on the road immediately ahead, but on the longer-term destination. When you see a fork in the road, one side may be smooth pavement and the other might be rocky and filled with mud and potholes—a much more difficult drive. However, if the easy road leads to mediocrity and the rocky one to excellence, then you need to turn onto the rocky one. It will be a rough ride, but you can manage it, and take your team to a place where they realize their vision, feel proud, and are most fulfilled.

The vast majority of people, when faced with a decision between having an uncomfortable conversation that is likely to help a team member, or having a more comfortable, vague, and ambiguous conversation that is very unlikely to help a team member, will choose the latter.

This is due to the same impulse that causes overweight people to choose a bowl of ice cream instead of exercise. The inherent human desire to avoid short-term pain (of going without ice cream) and having short-term pleasure (of eating ice cream), is stronger than the desire to avoid long-term pain (of being unhealthy) and secure long-term pleasure (of being fit). Managers usually will avoid tough conversations, even though doing so harms the crew member by depriving them of an opportunity to improve and ensuring their failure in the job. They're just too uncomfortable taking the risk of feeling the pain of a possible negative reaction or being seen as the cause of disappointment.

This happens incessantly, and it plagues all organizations. The fix is to discuss this with managers and make it clear that it is the manager's job to make certain that everyone who works for them knows, in very clear terms, what the manager thinks about their performance. Managers need to be taught that to do otherwise is uncaring, cowardly, and amounts to poor leadership. Having the tough talk is actually an act of caring, love, and grace. It is an act of placing one's self in a vulnerable position in an effort to make someone else better and help ensure their success.

It takes practice, discipline, and hard work to learn to communicate well. But it also takes focus, effort, and guts. Most people would prefer to avoid this hard work and simultaneously avoid the risk of confrontation that may happen when they communicate in a way that is clear and understandable. But once someone gets better at communicating and sees the incredible benefits which arise from it, they will usually remain good at it. The rewards are truly compelling. Good communicators make better leaders, better friends, better spouses, and can bring more positive change to our world.

## NEGLECTING TO DEVELOP SKILLS TO LISTEN AND COMMUNICATE

How does someone develop better skills at communicating and listening? Practice and hard work.

First, a leader must commit that they are going to insist on good communication from themselves and the others in their organization. Second, the leader needs to ask someone in a close relationship with them, who is willing to challenge them, to review and critique their written and spoken communication. Third, the leader needs to make good communication a central part of the culture by announcing to the whole organization the importance of it. The leader's announcement should first explain that good communication means:

- Selecting words that convey information as clearly as possible, in a way that everyone can understand (avoiding industry jargon).
- Being direct and using as few words as possible to accurately convey meaning.
- Ensuring meetings have a clear agenda, are as short as possible, and are staffed by only those whose help is needed to make the decision. (An exception is town hall meetings that may be appropriate to convey information to large groups at the same time.)
- Informing all employees about the vision, direction, and important decisions of the company.
- Insisting that all writings be carefully reviewed for accuracy, brevity, and clarity before they are sent.

The leader should then explain this new commitment to good communication, while explaining how poor communication is:

- Eroding the company's efficiency.
- Damaging the company's credibility.
- Preventing people from focusing on what's most important to the success of the organization.

Then, the leader must lead by example. Speeches and presentations must be excellent, crisp, and helpful. Aimless ramblings need to be avoided. When leaders witness poor or ineffective communication, they need to compassionately but swiftly put a stop to it, recognizing that precious time and resources are being wasted.

When I wrote emails to the field, I knew that thousands of people read them. If there was a typo, I was demonstrating to thousands of people that sloppiness was acceptable. Any extra words would demonstrate that I didn't care about brevity, or wasting thousands of people's time. Allowing a meeting which did not solve a problem or advance an initiative was an example of me permitting corporate waste. I needed to be zealous in order to shift a whole culture to improve.

This may seem strict and a bit tough. However, leaders are expected to exercise discipline in how they run their organizations. They will be appreciated for it, as long as people know that their leaders care about them, want the best for them and the organization, and do not ask from others what they are unwilling to do themselves.

## BECOMING IMMUNE TO POOR COMMUNICATION

Poor communication can be so prevalent that it goes unnoticed. Over time, people have become accustomed to saying things that have little or no meaning. We have come to accept that empty, repetitive, or even incorrect statements are the norm. This is true in families, companies, and government. Expectations are very low, and these low expectations are consistently met.

As parents, leaders, and as a society, we can and should commit to communicate better. We can be clear. We can use words accurately. We can say what we mean. We can be brief.

We can keep things simple. If we choose to be more disciplined in this way, we will accomplish more in our lives and in our organizations. To accomplish this takes commitment, hard work, and constant correction. Bad habits take time to break.

While deep communication takes hard work, the rewards are far-reaching. By learning to use words well, and by learning to listen beyond the limitation of words, one begins to forge a deeper connection with others. This is satisfying and liberating. It allows us to know ourselves and others in a much deeper and more interesting way. These deeper connections become so important that you want more of them. You begin to lose your tolerance for small talk and other forms of less effective communication. You'll thirst for a real connection, and when it is absent, you may even feel lonely.

Good communication is absolutely critical to your success as a leader. Yet as essential as it is, good communication is very rare. Every leader benefits by making it a daily focus—constantly improving their own, as well as their team's communication skills.

Part of making it a daily focus means assuming you're not communicating clearly enough, or often enough. If you study this subject, you will find countless examples of inadequate or insufficient communication, but you'll never find a single leader communicating too much, or too clearly. In my career, when I started communicating more and more, even at times to the point that I felt like I might be overdoing it, the results were stellar! Employees lit up, felt in the know, and were more empowered than ever.

I wrote earlier about how people tend to think they've communicated clearly, even when they haven't. While most people think they're the exception to this rule, I have met very few leaders who are clear enough with their people about expectations and about their evaluation of people's performance.

One powerful method to ensure your people have received your message clearly is to simply ask them questions. Ask them how they would evaluate their own performance. Ask them what they believe you think about their work and compare that with what you actually think. If they say anything that isn't completely accurate, use that as an opportunity to clear up any misunderstanding. In short, always communicate as clearly as you can and then make sure the recipient of your message has received the meaning you intended. It's like a radio transmission. First, you make sure the transmitter is working well and sending a strong, clear signal, and then you verify that the receiver is working.

# CHAPTER 15

# PASSING THE REINS

THE E. COLI CRISIS IN 2015 HAD BEEN A BIG ONE FOR CHI-potle. Our sales and reputation had both been hit hard. Our stock price had been beaten down. These events ignited concerns on the part of some of our analysts about the efficacy of our co-CEO structure. This became quite clear when our officer team met with our largest investors across the country. Two institutional shareholders revealed in late 2016 that they were going to make a request at the next annual shareholder meeting that Steve be removed as chairman of the board.

Activist investor Bill Ackman's fund, Pershing Capital, revealed they were purchasing 10 percent of Chipotle's stock. That's a big piece of a public company for one shareholder to own. A large purchase like that can often be a signal that the buyer wants to force the company into a merger, a breakup, or some other drastic action. We met with Bill, whom I found to be a very smart and shrewd investor. He made it clear that while he may have suggestions that he would like us to listen to, he strongly supported our existing management team. I was satisfied he did not intend some kind of hostile action toward management, but Steve and some of the other leaders were not.

For several months, my fellow officers and board of directors were gripped by fear and anxiety. Because of this, Steve started to reengage in the business, attending meetings again and spending more time at the corporate office. People who reported to me began to complain that Steve was distracting them, disempowering them, and giving them inconsistent instructions that left them baffled about how to proceed with their work. While they bemoaned Steve's reinjection of himself into the daily running of the business, I tried to reassure them that Steve only wanted what was best. Yet many people told me that Steve was working to improve his reputation while trying to cast doubt on my leadership.

At the end of 2016, I took a five-day trip to Fiji over Thanksgiving, during which I had an opportunity to step back, look out at the sea, and contemplate my incredible journey at Chipotle. I felt an uprising of immense gratitude for having had the opportunity to work alongside such a wonderful team of people. To build a company and culture that harnessed hundreds of thousands of people to work as one towards developing empowered teams, worthy and capable of changing food culture and in our own important way, the world.

In all, I estimate that I worked alongside over a million people during my time at Chipotle, and the accomplishments of this outstanding team were simply monumental.

We built a culture that hired people with no experience and then, in a job category many don't think highly of (fast food), we trained and empowered them so profoundly that their job satisfaction scores were the highest the survey companies had ever seen—so much so that they demanded meetings with me to find out what our secret sauce was. We built a training system (complete with online videos, training manuals, practice guides, and reference materials) so outstanding that our employees were able to earn a living while also earning college credit as they progressed from crew positions to managing a multimillion dollar a year business. We promoted our managers from within, and in 2015 alone, we promoted over 10,000 managers from crew positions. Many of our crew, who started at scarcely over the minimum wage, went on to earn senior leadership positions, overseeing hundreds of restaurants, thousands of people, and earning millions of dollars.

We built thousands of restaurants, allowing us to serve around half of a billion customers annually. We accomplished the seemingly impossible feat of serving high-quality ingredients at a very low price, yet consistently maintained the best margins, restaurant level returns, and highest profits in the industry. Our year-over-year sales increases led the industry for two decades. Our investors enjoyed outrageous returns, as our share price went up by over 3,400 percent. Industry surveys consistently found our food to be the most desirable, healthiest, and the best value of any restaurant chain.

For twenty years, Steve and I had been extremely close friends. We shared every detail of our personal lives and, of course, everything about Chipotle. We shared thousands of incredible victories—taking the company public, achieving the best financial performance in the industry, watching our own stock holdings go from $1 dollar a share to $750 a share, and creating an unparalleled people culture and restaurant experience that everyone seemed to love. We worked together so closely that I felt I almost had two families! One with my wife and kids and the other with Steve and Chipotle. Overall, it was absolutely thrilling. It was a roller coaster ride of excitement and a seemingly nonstop ride of success and celebration.

All the while, we accomplished milestones that most others wouldn't even dream of. We had eliminated all trans fats from our food by 2004. We eliminated all genetically modified ingredients (GMOs) from our menu in 2015. We supported and encouraged better farming and agricultural suppliers by insisting on better standards for animal welfare, environmental stewardship, and produce farming, and rewarded these better systems and farmers by investing billions of dollars buying their better ingredients.

## CLARITY

But of all these accomplishments that swam in my mind during those five days in Fiji, what warmed my heart the most was my relationship with thousands of our crew members. Their dedication to creating an incredible culture. Their hugs, their tears of joy, their pride, their love and compassion for each other. Their undying belief and support of me and my vision and dream: the dream of creating a culture of enlightened leadership that would effectively teach tens of thousands of people that the best life is a life of giving to others. A life dedicated to making others better. A life of service, care, and compassion. A life where each of us leaves a legacy of love.

As I watched waves fan up over the beach and recede again seaward, I realized that I also felt a lot of pain in my heart. I realized that despite hundreds of thousands of crew members completely understanding and living in accordance with this powerful and incredible culture, politics had started to tarnish my experience in the corporate office. The illnesses suffered by our customers in the E. coli event had led to more scrutiny of our food safety efforts, which was expected. We answered that scrutiny expertly. But the same scrutiny seemed to bring out a different side of my co-CEO than I'd ever seen before. Where we'd always worked constructively, it started to feel adversarial. Many of the leaders who reported to me told me about things Steve was saying and doing that I found distasteful and unconstructive.

Overall, being a co-CEO is tricky. For me, it amounted to all the work and responsibility of being a CEO, with diminished acknowledgment and credit for all that I accomplished, plus the friction of dealing with competing emotional needs. For a long time, all of this was OK. It was worth it. The vast majority of the time, I felt fulfilled with my relationship with Steve and with my position. I am very grateful to have worked alongside such talented and interesting people. Besides, being a leader isn't supposed to be easy or smooth sailing. You need to give constantly of yourself and put the interests of others ahead of your own.

I understood times were hard for Steve since a number of investors were challenging him and calling for him to step down. At any rate and no matter what the cause, I didn't feel I could be as effective as I needed to be anymore. With surprising clarity, I knew what I should do.

A few days later, just after Thanksgiving 2016, Steve and I interviewed a potential new board member in a Washington, D.C. conference room. After the candidate left, I asked Steve if he planned to stay on as CEO. He told me he felt he just couldn't leave.

I responded that I thought it best that I retire.

"It seems so unfair that you should be the one to leave," he said.

"I guess it is a bit unfair," I answered. "But that's OK. Sometimes life isn't fair. And really, I am OK with that."

"The only reason I feel capable of taking over as CEO is from watching you do it for the last twelve years!"

"Thank you so much for saying that, Steve. It really means an awful lot!"

His comment had been so strangely and refreshingly honest. It reminded me instantly why I had come to love him so much, despite the many struggles and challenges we'd been through over the years, all of which one would expect from two people working so closely together for such a long time.

While he was always a complex person and often very difficult, he still had this incredible ability to snap back to moments of astounding self-awareness, which always were very refreshing to me. It made it easy to forgive him and move on. On this occasion, despite the immensity of my decision, I did just that. I had such enormous loyalty to Steve. Most of those closest to me have told me for many years that I had too much loyalty to him. Steve had founded the company, and he had brought me on. I wanted to respect and honor him for that and for our deep friendship. I didn't want to cause a board level fight, or try to engage in any action that would encourage him to step aside. There was already enough pressure on him from other sources to do just that, and he had opted to hold firm. I wanted to respect that choice to let him leave on his terms.

After some brief discussion, Steve asked me, "But what does this mean for our friendship?"

It was a good question, since Steve and I had by that time shared such a close and intense relationship for so long, that I knew we both would have thought it a tragedy to lose it.

"This doesn't have to hurt our friendship at all," I said. And I meant it.

"Good," he said. "I would never want anything to come between us."

We then hugged each other goodbye and Steve said, "I love you, Monty."

"I love you too," I replied.

A few days after I left, we had a phone conversation during which Steve asked if he could make a certain representation to the *New York Times*, which was scheduled to interview him the next day. "When they ask why you left, is it OK if I tell them that we both agreed that it would be best for Chipotle that I be the sole CEO?"

The question upset me, because I found it very unfair. I had just left this job I loved out of loyalty to Steve, because I knew if I stayed we would end up in an adversarial position that would damage our friendship. Now he wanted me to allow him to say something so untrue!

"No, Steve!" I answered. "That is not acceptable to me at all. To be clear, I am leaving because I know you want to stay, and I cannot be at my best with you there. I believe that the best thing for Chipotle would be for you to step down and let me proceed as sole CEO, as we have been discussing for over ten years."

Steve and I had discussed him stepping down for years and years. Literally from before I even came aboard and every year since! But it had become clear to me that he never would. That he just couldn't.

"Wow," he said. "I really thought you would give that to me."

I was confused. I guess he meant that he thought I would give him a public endorsement. At any rate, I was not OK with it.

"You can tell the *New York Times* that we spoke, and the result is that I am retiring, and you are staying on," I said. "The reality is that people will read that to mean the same thing as you are asking my permission to say anyway," I reassured him.

That is what happened, and that is the way many people read it.

As far as I can recall, that was the last time we spoke. So strange. He has not called me. I have not called him. I am not sure why. It is almost like our relationship was so intensely bound up in Chipotle that neither of us are sure what it is without Chipotle. However, I feel the same warmth and love for him in my heart that I have always felt.

As soon as I sent notice that I was retiring, my mailbox, email inbox, and phone exploded with thousands of letters, emails, and texts. The letters I received were filled with words of respect, love, praise, and admiration so touching that for months I was in tears, as I worked week after week to answer every single message. This outpouring of gratitude was so profound that I could hardly believe it. People told me that I had changed their lives, their marriages, the way they raised their children, and some said that I had given them a whole new lease on life. They all spoke about the culture at Chipotle, the Restaurateur program, and they told me it had been the most powerful teaching of their lifetime.

I have been so humbled by these messages, so honored, that I can scarcely discuss them without falling to tears.

# CHAPTER 16

# NEXT

AFTER RETIRING FROM CHIPOTLE, I TOOK MY MOTHER back to her birth town of Breslau, Germany, which, due to borders shifting after World War II, is now called Wroclaw, Poland. My mother had not returned to her birthplace in seventy-two years, since she was four, and she had many emotions associated with this visit.

Before returning home, we visited friends of my mother's named Jorge (pronounced "Yurg") and Wendy, in Berlin, Germany. Wendy and Jorge had been married for around fifty years and were, in some ways, an unlikely couple. He was a retired doctor and the son and grandson of Nazi soldiers and officers; she was a Jewish woman from Southern California. Jorge was seventy-nine years old, in excellent physical shape, and strikingly handsome. Wendy was a few years younger but had severely advanced Parkinson's disease. She was confined to a bed or a wheelchair, and her body was emaciated, badly bent and shook from the ravages of this cruel disease.

As I met them, I hugged them, as is my custom with nearly

everyone I meet. It was easy to hug Jorge but very awkward to bend down and hug Wendy since she was in her wheelchair, had trouble coordinating her movements and was bony and thin. I was concerned I might hurt her or make her uncomfortable.

We spoke for some time, and I noticed I felt distant from Wendy. Her situation was so foreign to my own, and I wasn't sure what to say. She looked terribly uncomfortable in her wheelchair. Her feet were turned sharply inward from the ravages of her illness, and she wore down slippers to keep them warm. She was clearly super intelligent and mentally sound, but her arm movements, mostly involuntary, distracted me because I did not understand her condition.

Instead of sitting there thinking these thoughts, I went ahead and asked her all the questions that were in my mind, questions I suspect few others would risk. "How do you feel? Is it uncomfortable to have this disease? I have never met someone with Parkinson's before."

Wendy turned her head toward me sharply, as if offended, her short, gray hair shaking with the sudden alertness of her movement. Her eyes looked deeply into mine, and I waited curiously for her answer. For a moment, a seemingly long and silent moment, she said nothing, and I was apprehensive that my inquiry had offended her. But I just looked patiently and lovingly into her eyes, let myself feel my anxiety and allowed my heart to be vulnerable to receive her answer.

"It hurts!" she barked. Then her voice softened. "It's really hard."

"Does your medication provide some relief? Is there anything you can do to make it better?"

"That's one thing that's so hard," she continued. "If I take just the right amount of medication, it can feel better for a time, but if I take too much, it only makes it worse. And the amount seems to change all the time, which is frustrating."

"How long have you had it? How did you find out?"

She looked at Jorge. "When was it? Thirty years ago?"

"I knew she had it before she did," said her husband. "But we were both in denial for a while."

A wonderful lightness suddenly fell over the room like a gentle wave and the conversation that followed blossomed. We spoke all about the disease. We spoke about their marriage, their children, and some incredibly difficult times involving his Nazi heritage and her Jewish background. We talked about his parents' refusal to accept her and their difficulty with that. We spoke about his pain from having almost no relationship with his father, who withdrew into a deep depression after the war and after being chastised for the atrocities that he had condoned as part of the Nazi regime.

The couple then asked me about my career and about what I had planned to do next. I spoke a little about how I had become a pilot and was working on some business deals, but that I remained unsure about what my next big move would be.

I asked Wendy and Jorge how often they were able to get outside for a walk together, since I had noticed on my way up to their second-story apartment that there was no obvious handicapped access. It looked like a very challenging building, even treacherous for a person in a wheelchair, with a number of steps, thin passageways just to get to more stairs, and no elevator. Even within the apartment itself, it looked nearly impossible to get the wheelchair to the kitchen. There were numerous changes in levels and very narrow halls. So while it was a beautiful apartment, I saw it as a bit of a prison for Wendy and as an incredibly difficult situation for Jorge.

"Well, it is getting really tough to get Wendy downstairs, because we need three different wheelchairs. We need one to get her out into the hall, another tiny one to get her down the stairs, and then at the bottom a different one to navigate the steps at the front of the building."

"Why don't you guys move to a building with handicapped access?"

"Well, we have lived here for ten years now," he continued, "and the real estate market here in Berlin is tough. There are not many places for sale and very few that would suit our needs."

"You'd only need to find one," I gently challenged. I don't recall where the rest of this conversation went, but I remember feeling that I'd said enough to plant a seed. I really wanted them to be able to get Wendy in and out easily, as I saw that as the key to them both feeling a life of freedom.

As the time to go drew near and my mother and I began to say goodbye, Wendy, in a voice so abrupt and loud as to nearly sound rude, barked at me, *"I know what you need to do!"* It was clear that Wendy had been thinking about my retirement and what the next move was for me in my new life.

"What is that?" I asked, waiting eagerly to hear what idea she had that was so important that it had moved her to nearly shout at me.

Then, with glassy, tear-filled eyes, filled with rectitude and determination, as though she had solved the greatest mystery in my life, she said, *"You need to ask questions!"*

I responded only by looking into her eyes for many moments. I felt a tear well up in my eye and start to roll down my cheek as it dawned on me the significance of her statement. I realized that for Wendy, my questions had been a powerful force of change in the room with her and her husband, causing them to come alive and reconsider old ways of thinking. I knew without asking that she meant her words in the broadest, most profound way. She meant that I needed to get out in the world and ask questions, to put my curiosity and intellect to work solving problems in this world.

Two weeks later, my mom called and told me, with tears in her voice, about a conversation that she had just had with Jorge and Wendy. They had called her and said that our visit to their apartment had been the most powerful visit that they had in twenty years and that they were asking fresh new questions about their relationship and their lives.

These were people who had both been involved in intensive spiritual work for over twenty years. In fact, that is how my mom met them. She had been their spiritual teacher. Yet somehow, my questions about their history, their relationship, World War II, and other topics were a catalyst that challenged them to explore their relationship even more deeply. I had asked questions with only a motive to understand these beautiful people better, and something about that desire for me to know them rekindled their own desire to know themselves.

## WHAT WENDY TAUGHT ME

This story reminded me of how powerful questions have been in my life. I had known that this was true at Chipotle and in my career. But the moment when Wendy insisted that I needed to ask questions, and she said so meaning that *this is what I needed to do with the rest of my life*, was profound to me. It caused me to realize how I had developed something special in my ability to ask questions. I had developed a way of asking really direct, pointed questions, but somehow without offending. I could even evoke gratitude in the person on the receiving end of my many inquiries. So I wondered what it was about the way I was asking that made it different.

As I have described throughout this book, the answer begins with curiosity. I am deeply curious about things that I don't understand, and my questions stem from my effort to learn. I also am very direct. I ask exactly the thing that I want to know about, in a way that leaves no room for misunderstanding. Finally, I ask questions with a deep respect for the person. In a sense, I ask them as a small child would ask them, with deference, respect, and innocence. The person to whom I direct the question is in the dominant position, and I am in the subordinate position. I am in the vulnerable position of being the one who wants to know, and they are the ones with the answer. This role reversal is critical. It is the opposite of the lawyer who is cross-examining and asking the question in order to pin down or defeat the witness. Since they are in the dominant position, my questions are not threatening. For this reason, the person on the receiving end of my question is disarmed. They don't feel defensive. Rather, they see that they're in a position to be of help, and they want to help.

This has been the source of much of my power and success as a leader.

In my experience, people really want to answer questions. They want to be the source of clarification. They want to help get the truth out. They even like being on the spot, as long as the context and environment are such that it's safe to answer, and they'll not be hurt or negatively judged for having answered. By asking questions with genuine curiosity, care, love, and a deep desire to really understand, people answer, and they answer honestly.

I used questions at Dairy Queen and the Boulder Senior Citizen's Center to quickly and deeply understand patrons, learn about the path they had chosen in life and how their actions had shaped where they were today.

I used questions as a trial lawyer to obtain unlikely confessions that allowed me to win cases.

I used questions as the new president and then as co-CEO of Chipotle to quickly get a deep understanding of what was really going on in the company, such that I was able to bring new and unique solutions, which strengthened the whole organization.

I used questions to guide my friends and loved ones to make better life decisions.

I used questions at every stage of my life to learn extraordinary lessons from people. Maybe most importantly, I used questions to develop the deepest and most satisfying relationships in my life.

Taking Wendy's advice, Monty's now filming a docuseries in which he asks questions to elicit the wisdom from people from all walks of life. Here shown with Iniskim Hungry Wolf of the Blood Tribe on the Blackfoot Nation, Alberta, Canada, 2019.

I firmly believe that the greatest legacy any of us can leave is to have made others in some way better. This is what makes us more fulfilled at work and, more importantly, in life. The most powerful way to do that is with love, vulnerability, curiosity, and an open heart. Giving to others and helping them is the most rewarding experience of all. Not only for the personal joy it gives us, but the example we set for those watching. But setting an example is not easy work. In fact, it's difficult and takes effort. It takes looking inward first, dealing with and confronting what is in the way of being your truest, most authentic and loving self.

Remember, the decision to follow a leader is voluntary. You cannot force people to follow you. They might do what you say, but that does not make you a leader. There is also no academic degree, list of accomplishments, or impressive resume that will cause people to follow you, either. To be effective as a leader, you need to illustrate for people a bright path. A better future. A place where they can be and feel their very best. Then, they need to see that you care for them, that you see them, value them, and understand them. Because you care for them, you will lead them to a better place.

The challenges facing our society and our world are immense. To solve them, you are desperately needed. The people, animals, and environment around you need you to be at your very best. Becoming your best means cultivating your vulnerability, coming to know, understand, and accept your fear, anxieties, and weaknesses, and learning that you no longer need to defend yourself, since reality needs no defense. By doing this and then sharing yourself with others, you will make the authentic human being inside you more available. You will brim with the kind of compassion, love, understanding, and acceptance that will make your existence more authentic and meaningful, and you will begin to empower the people around you to blossom and grow as well.

By sharing your vision and by using your curiosity to discover and empower, you can lead those around you to grow and develop into leaders as well. The greatest legacy you can leave is to have made others in some way better. You have unique skills and attributes that will allow you to do that in a way that no one else can. Your own legacy of love. I wish you the very best on your journey of leadership.

**loveisfree.com**

# ABOUT THE
# AUTHOR

**MONTY MORAN** is a curious guy who found that asking questions and listening carefully to the answers took him a long way. He is best known for his co-CEO role at Chipotle Mexican Grill, where he built a culture that took a Denver-based burrito company to Fortune 500 status. He worked at Chipotle for twelve years, beginning as president and COO, a role he inhabited while helping take the company public in 2006. He was quickly promoted to co-CEO, a position he held until 2017. While at Chipotle, Monty successfully led the company and its 70,000 employees to spectacular business results, while helping grow the company from eight restaurants to more than 2,100 locations.

Prior to joining Chipotle, he was head of litigation and then managing partner and CEO at the Denver law firm of Messner & Reeves, LLC, where he worked for ten years.

Monty grew up in Boulder, Colorado and holds a Bachelor of

Arts degree from the University of Colorado and a Juris Doctor degree, cum laude, from Pepperdine University School of Law. Since his retirement in 2017, Monty has founded Old Tale Productions, LLC and earned his pilot's license and instrument rating so that he may fly throughout the United States to pursue his interest in better understanding and serving the people in this country. During this time, he has also served as a director and chairman of several corporate boards, including the real estate company, TRELORA. He also is an advisor to many entrepreneurs and businesses.

Monty is married with three children and lives, plays, and works in Boulder.

CPSIA information can be obtained
at www.ICGtesting.com
Printed in the USA
BVHW030752191020
591317BV00009B/32/J